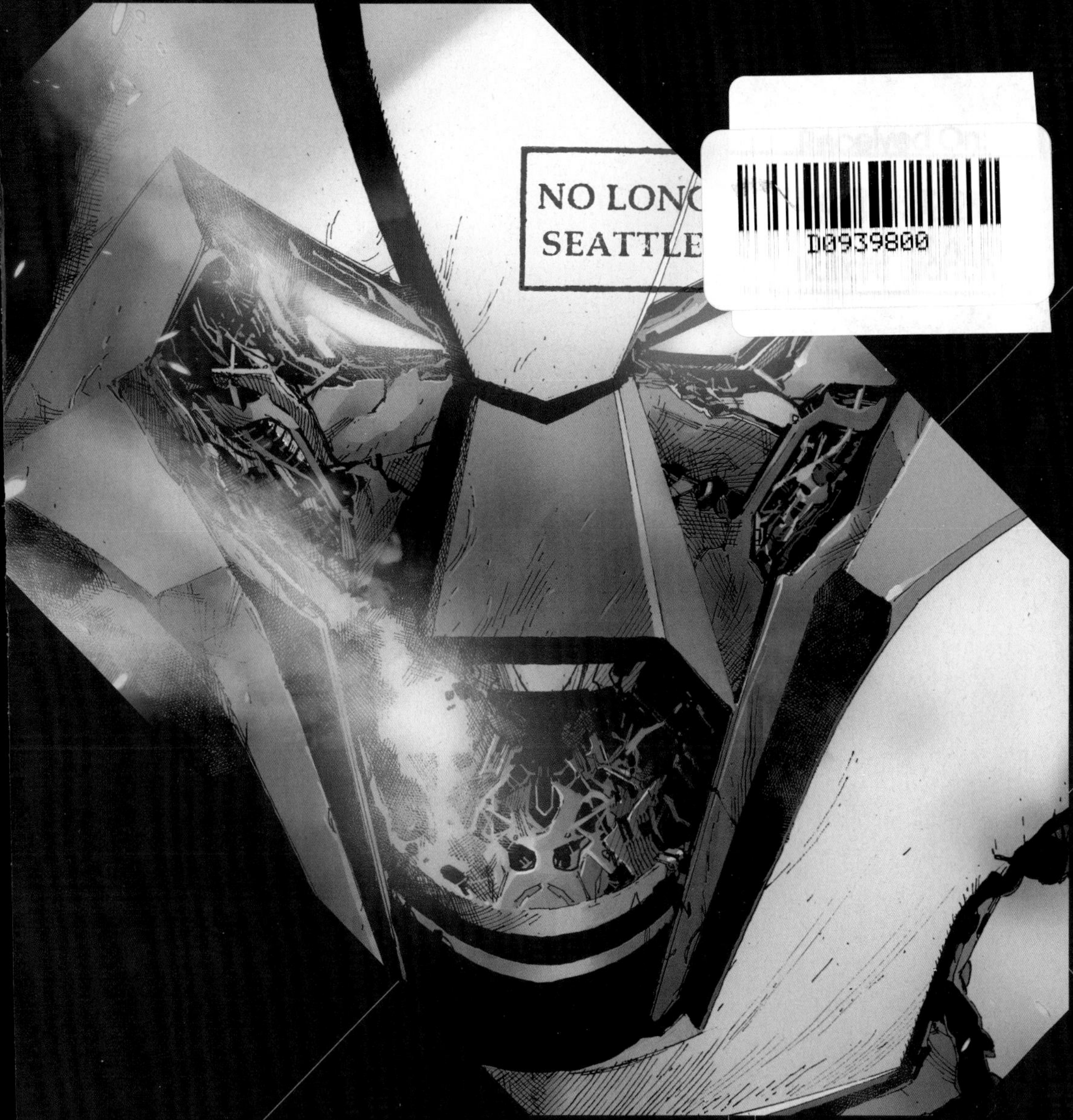

REIGN OF X VOL. 8. Contains material originally published in magazine form as CABLE (2020) #10, CHILDREN OF THE ATOM (2021) #3, EXCALIBUR (2019) #20, X-MEN (2019) #20 and HELLIONS (2020) #9-10. First printing 2021. ISBN 978-1-302-93371-5. Published by MARVEL WORLDWIDE, INC., a subsidiary of MARVEL ENTERTAINMENT, LLC. OFFICE OF PUBLICATION: 1290 Avenue of the Americas, New York, NY 10104. © 2021 MARVEL No similarity between any of the names, characters, persons, and/or institutions in this book with those of any living or dead person or institution is intended, and any such similarity which may exist is purely coincidental. **Printed in the Canada.** KEVIN FEIGE, Chief Creative Officer; DAN BUCKLEY, President, Marvel Entertainment; JOE QUESADA, EVP & Creative Director; DAVID BOGART, Associate Publisher & SVP of Talent Affairs; TOM BREVOORT, VP, Executive Editor; NICK LOWE, Executive Editor, VP of Content, Digital Publishing; DAVID GABRIEL, VP of Print & Digital Publishing; JEFF YOUNGQUIST, VP of Production & Special Projects; ALEX MORALES, Director of Publishing Operations; DAN EDINGTON, Managing Editor; RICKEY PURDIN, Director of Talent Relations; JENNIFER GRÜNWALD, Senior Editor, Special Projects; SUSAN CRESPI, Production Manager; STAN LEE, Chairman Emeritus. For information regarding advertising in Marvel Comics or on Marvel.com, please contact Vit DeBellis, Custom Solutions & Integrated Advertising Manager, at vdebellis@marvel.com. For Marvel subscription inquiries, please call 888-511-5480. **Manufactured between 11/5/2021 and 12/7/2021 by SOLISCO PRINTERS, SCOTT, QC, CANADA.**

10 9 8 7 6 5 4 3 2 1

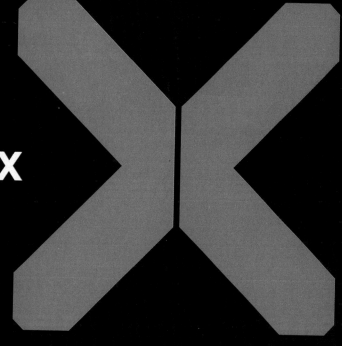

REIGN OF X

Volume
8

X-Men created by Stan Lee & Jack Kirby

Writers:	**Gerry Duggan, Vita Ayala, Tini Howard, Jonathan Hickman & Zeb Wells**
Artists:	**Phil Noto, Paco Medina, Marcus To, Francesco Mobili & Stephen Segovia**
Color Artists:	**Phil Noto, David Curiel, Erick Arciniega & Sunny Gho**
Letterers:	**VC's Joe Sabino, Travis Lanham, Ariana Maher & Clayton Cowles**
Cover Art:	**Phil Noto; R.B. Silva & Jesus Aburtov; Mahmud Asrar & Matthew Wilson; Leinil Francis Yu & Sunny Gho; and Stephen Segovia & Romulo Fajardo Jr.**
Head of X:	**Jonathan Hickman**
Design:	**Tom Muller**
Assistant Editors:	**Chris Robinson, Shannon Andrews Ballesteros & Lauren Amaro**
Associate Editor:	**Annalise Bissa**
Editors:	**Jordan D. White & Mark Basso**
Collection Cover Art:	**Leinil Francis Yu & Sunny Gho**
Collection Editor:	**Jennifer Grünwald**
Assistant Editor:	**Daniel Kirchhoffer**
Assistant Managing Editor:	**Maia Loy**
Assistant Managing Editor:	**Lisa Montalbano**
VP Production & Special Projects:	**Jeff Youngquist**
SVP Print, Sales & Marketing:	**David Gabriel**
Editor in Chief:	**C.B. Cebulski**

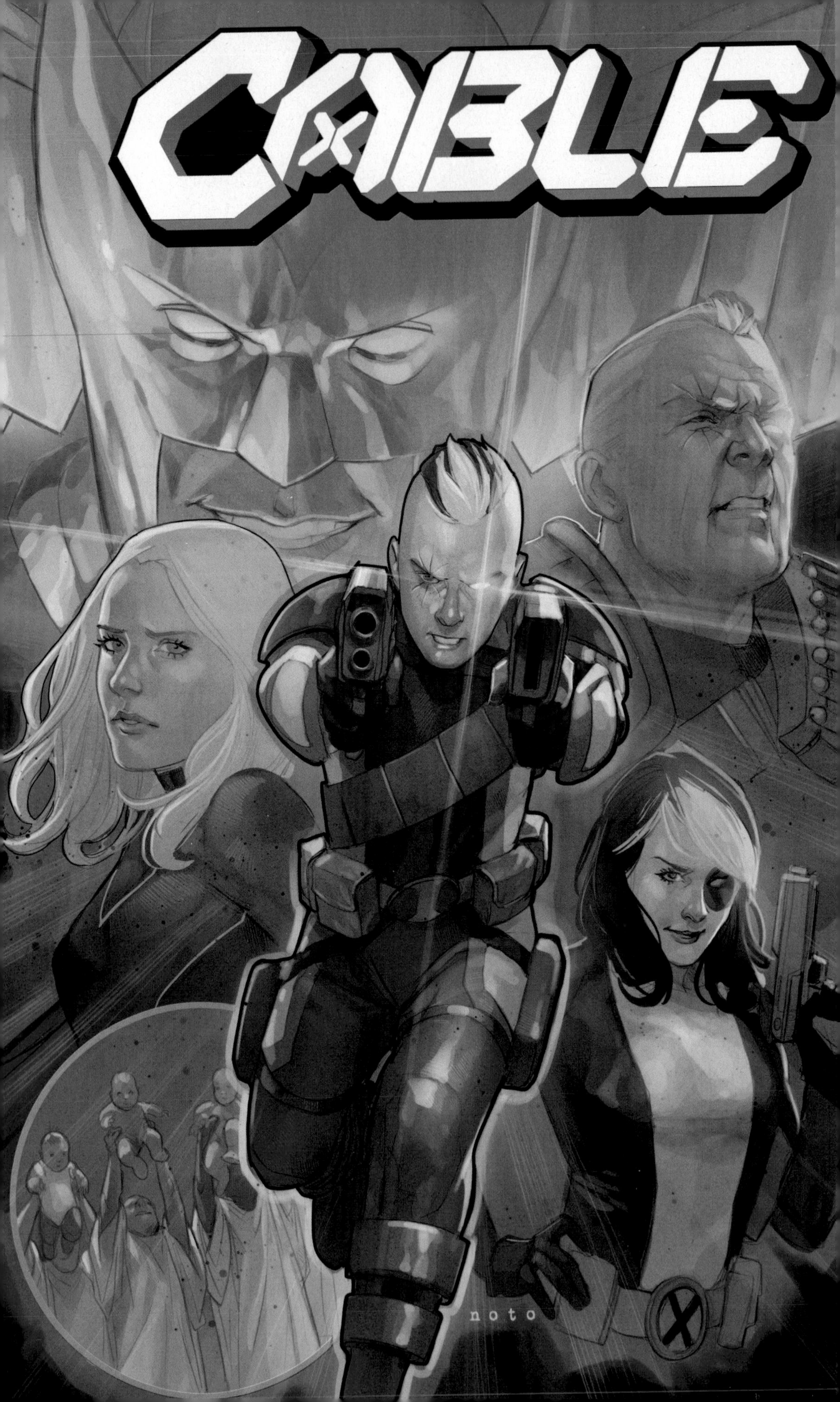

CABLE
noto

[ca__[0.10]
[ble_[0.10]

More important than how you
kill Cable is *when* you kill Cable.

-- ANCIENT STRYFE PROVERB
FROM THE FUTURE

[ca__[0.XX]
[ble_[0.XX]

[ca__[0.10].....]
[ble_[0.10].....]

[Cable_alpha.]

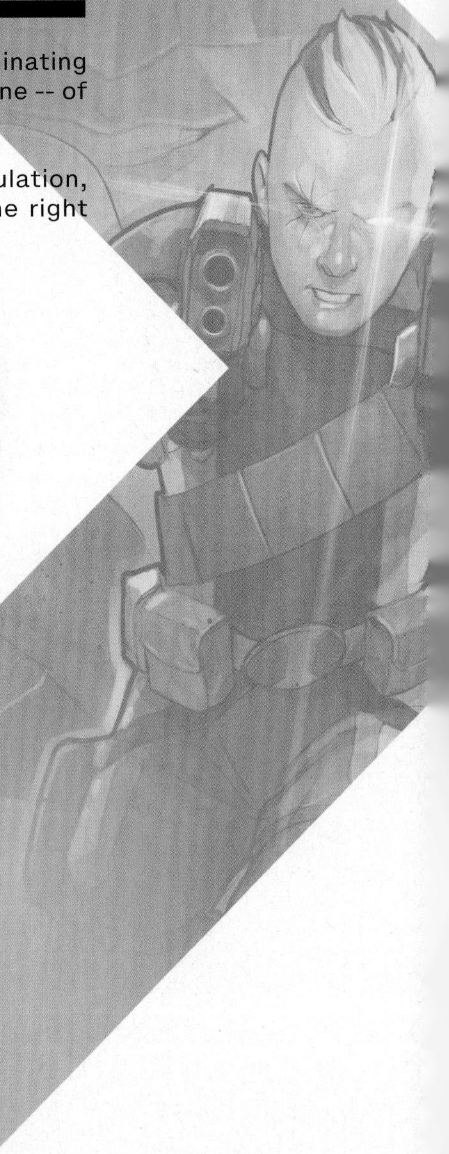

YOUTH IS WASTED ON THE YOUNG

CABLE's life has been nonstop chaos lately, culminating in the revelation that Stryfe, the enemy -- and clone -- of his older self, is alive and well.

And with every new complication, trial and tribulation, he's becoming more convinced that he's not the right guy for the job...

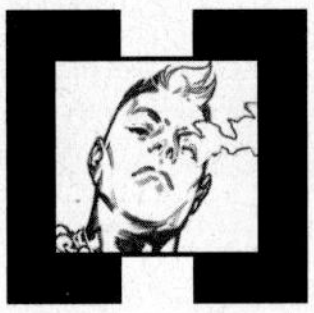

Cable

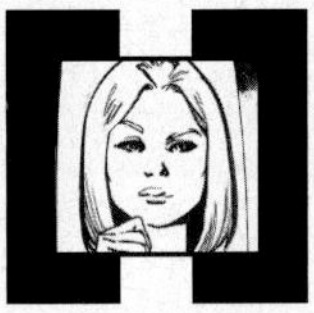

Emma Frost

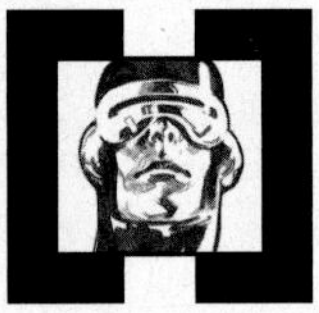

Cyclops

[00_Reign]
[00___ofX]

CABLE
[X_10]

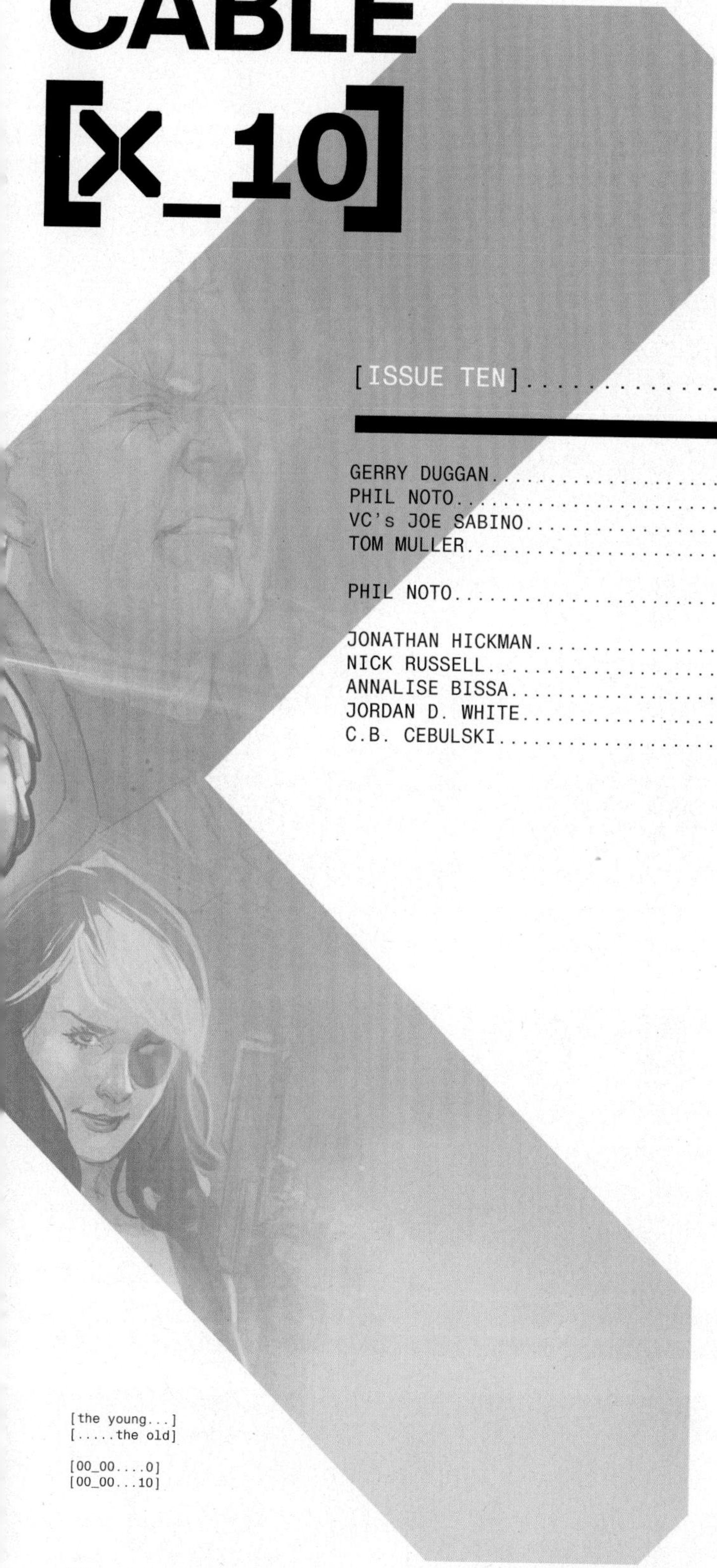

[ISSUE TEN]........................DEPRESSION

GERRY DUGGAN....................................[WRITER]
PHIL NOTO.......................................[ARTIST]
VC's JOE SABINO.................................[LETTERER]
TOM MULLER......................................[DESIGN]

PHIL NOTO.................................[COVER ARTIST]

JONATHAN HICKMAN.............................[HEAD OF X]
NICK RUSSELL................................[PRODUCTION]
ANNALISE BISSA........................[ASSOCIATE EDITOR]
JORDAN D. WHITE.................................[EDITOR]
C.B. CEBULSKI..........................[EDITOR IN CHIEF]

[the young...]
[.....the old]

[00_00....0]
[00_00...10]

[XX___past]
[00_______]

[00_______]

[future_XX]

I have to be war ready.

And I know now that means being ready to fight...

...and to make the hard decisions.

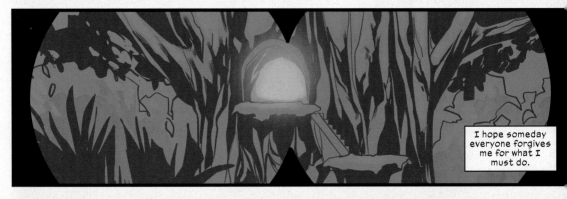

I hope someday everyone forgives me for what I must do.

Tsk. Nathan, there are less painful paths to exile...

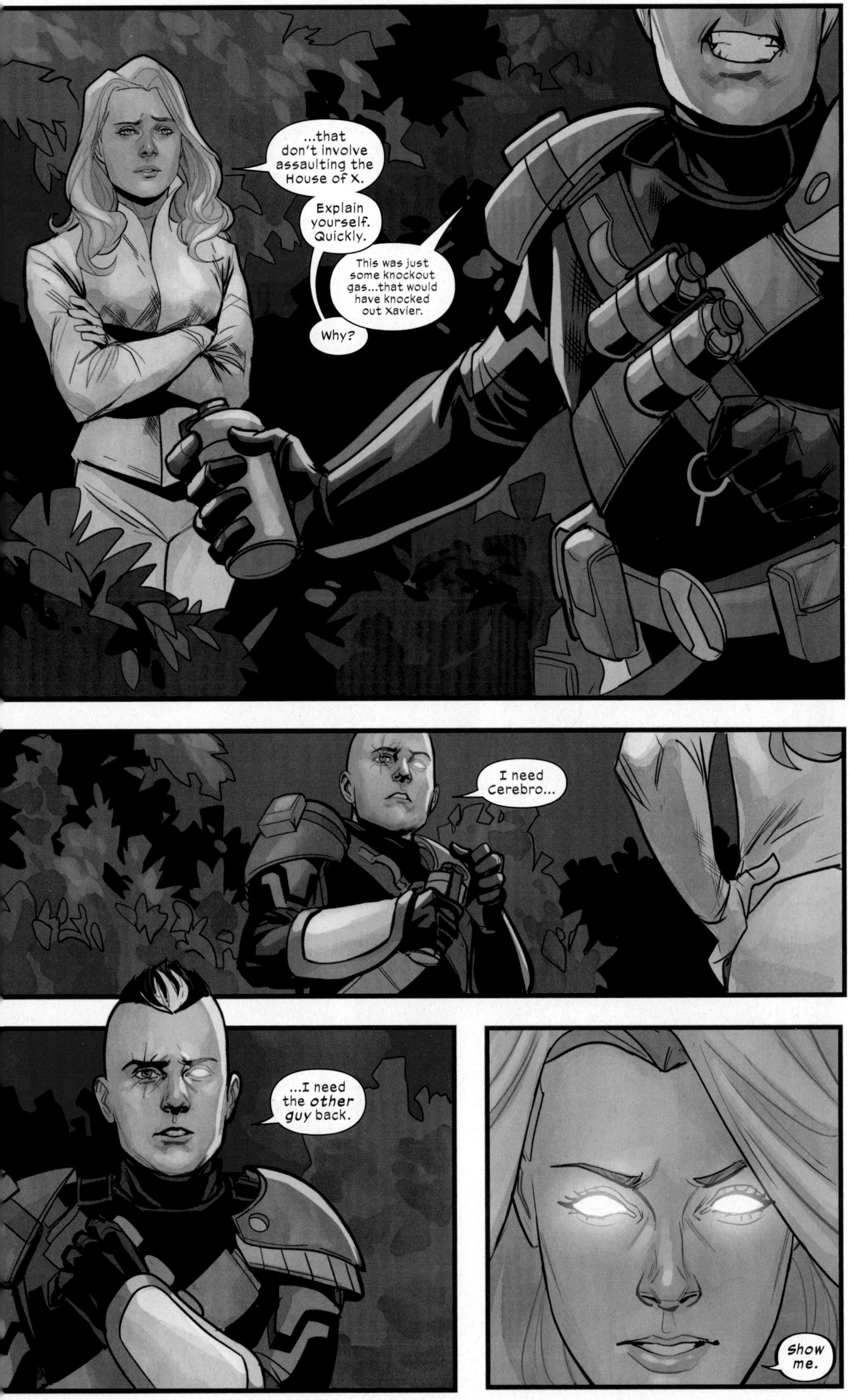
...that don't involve assaulting the House of X.
Explain yourself. Quickly.
This was just some knockout gas...that would have knocked out Xavier.
Why?
I need Cerebro...
...I need the *other guy* back.
Show me.

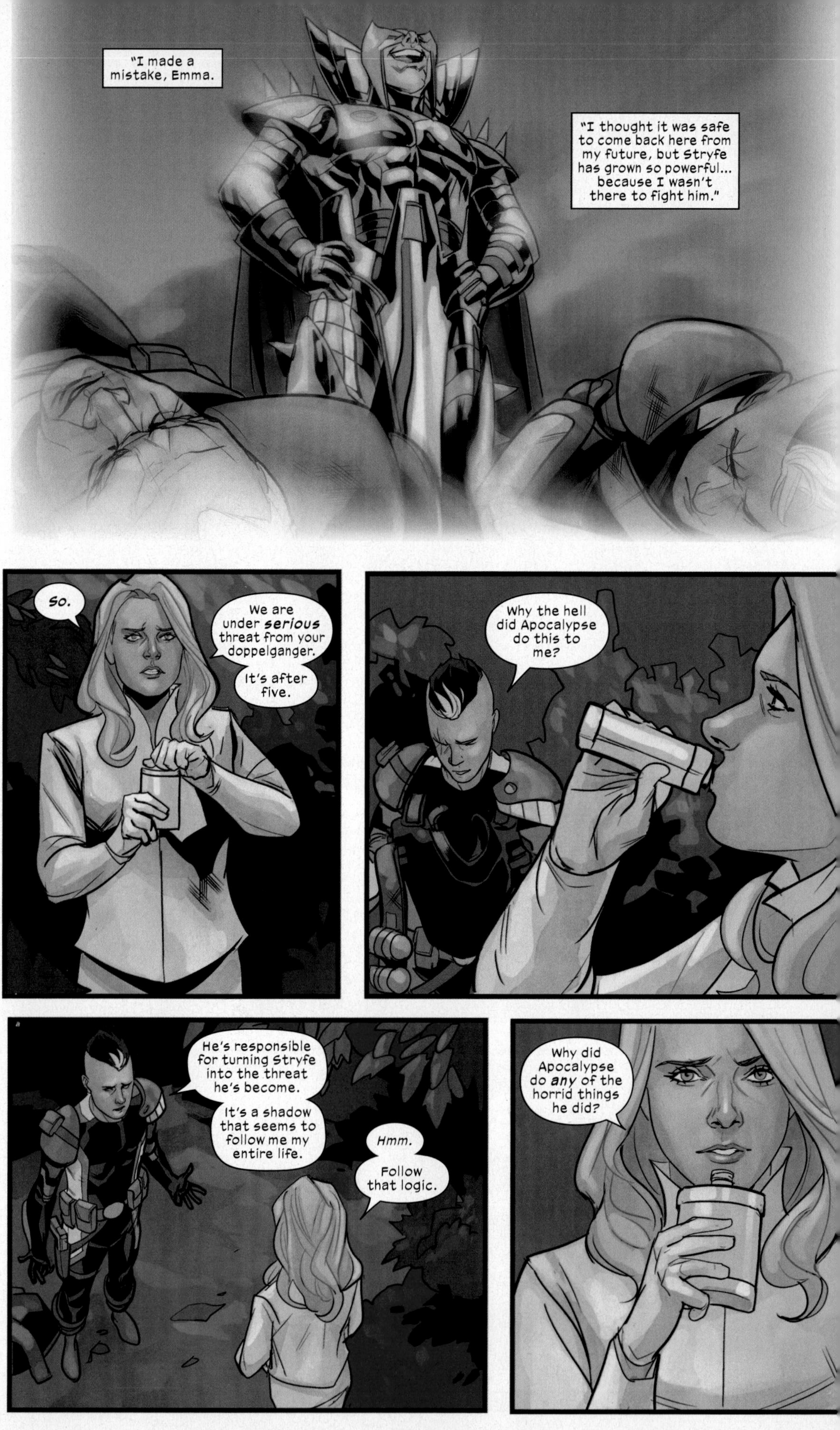
"I made a mistake, Emma.
"I thought it was safe to come back here from my future, but Stryfe has grown so powerful... because I wasn't there to fight him."
So.
We are under *serious* threat from your doppelganger.
It's after five.
Why the hell did Apocalypse do this to me?
He's responsible for turning Stryfe into the threat he's become.
It's a shadow that seems to follow me my entire life.
Hmm.
Follow that logic.
Why did Apocalypse do *any* of the horrid things he did?

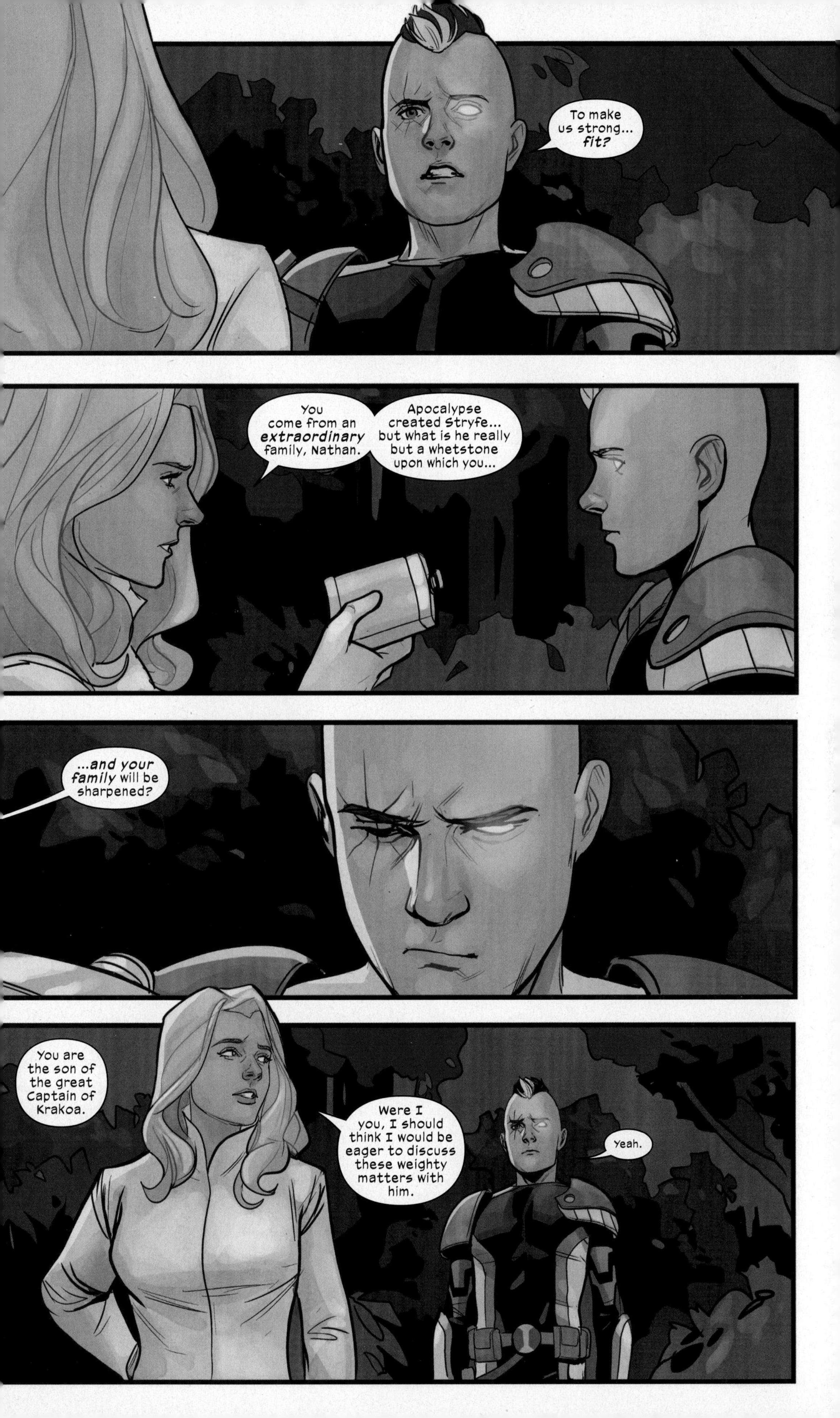
To make us strong... fit?
You come from an extraordinary family, Nathan.
Apocalypse created Stryfe... but what is he really but a whetstone upon which you...
...and your family will be sharpened?
You are the son of the great Captain of Krakoa.
Were I you, I should think I would be eager to discuss these weighty matters with him.
Yeah.

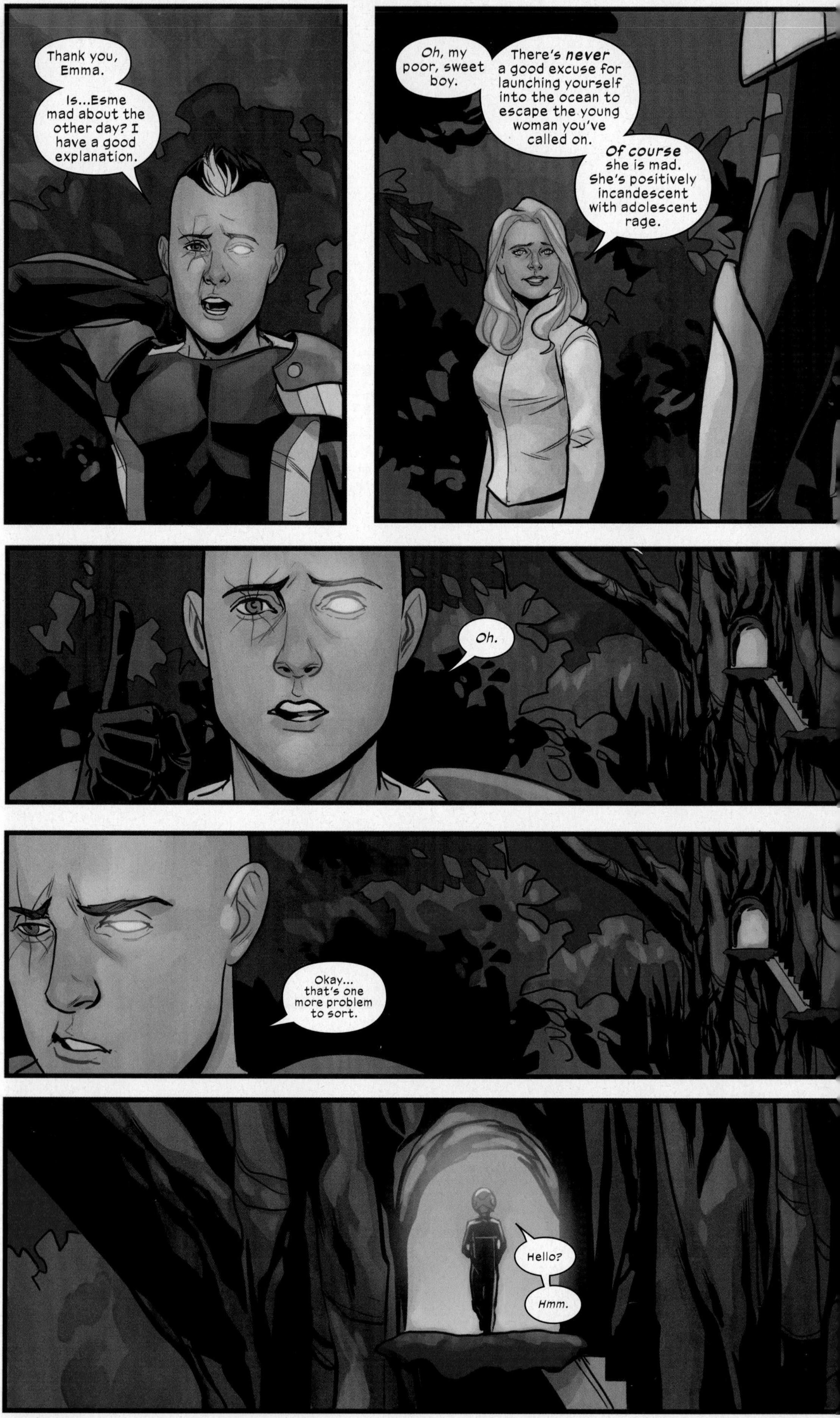
Thank you, Emma.
Is...Esme mad about the other day? I have a good explanation.
Oh, my poor, sweet boy.
There's never a good excuse for launching yourself into the ocean to escape the young woman you've called on.
Of course she is mad. She's positively incandescent with adolescent rage.
Oh.
Okay... that's one more problem to sort.
Hello?
Hmm.

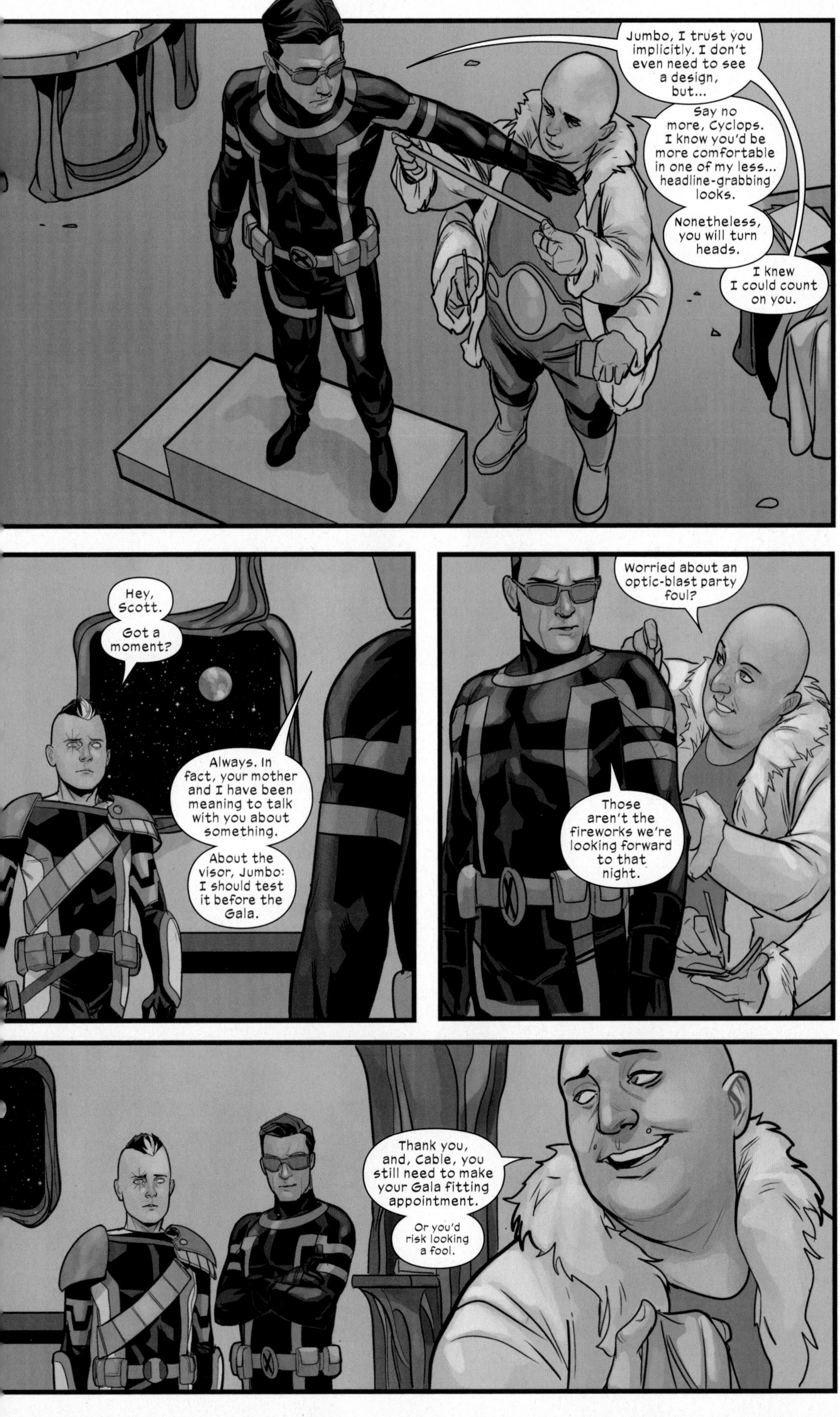
Jumbo, I trust you implicitly. I don't even need to see a design, but...
Say no more, Cyclops. I know you'd be more comfortable in one of my less... headline-grabbing looks.
Nonetheless, you will turn heads.
I knew I could count on you.
Hey, Scott.
Got a moment?
Always. In fact, your mother and I have been meaning to talk with you about something.
About the visor, Jumbo: I should test it before the Gala.
Worried about an optic-blast party foul?
Those aren't the fireworks we're looking forward to that night.
Thank you, and, Cable, you still need to make your Gala fitting appointment.
Or you'd risk looking a fool.

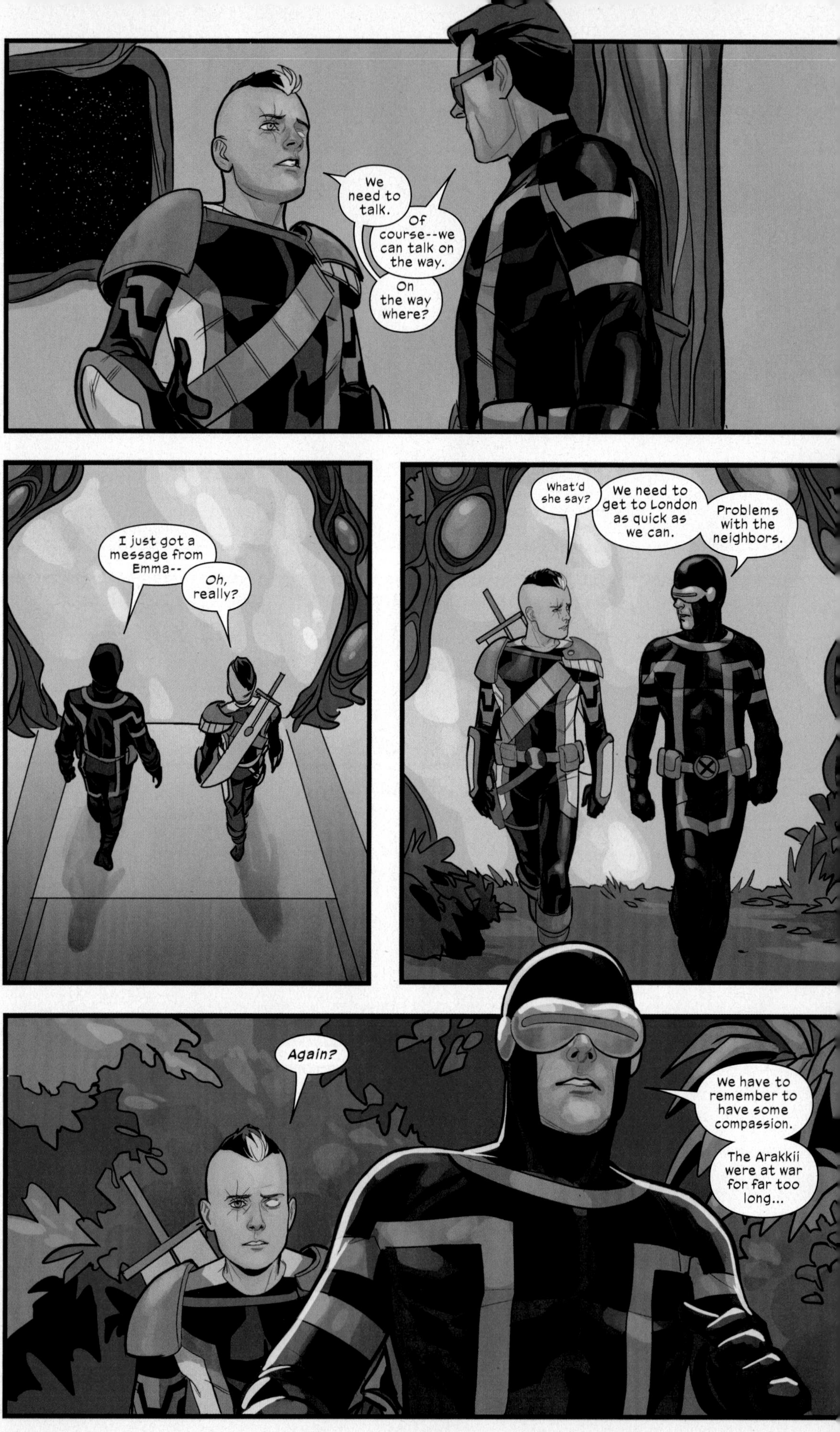
We need to talk.
Of course--we can talk on the way.
On the way where?
I just got a message from Emma--
Oh, really?
What'd she say?
We need to get to London as quick as we can.
Problems with the neighbors.
Again?
We have to remember to have some compassion.
The Arakkii were at war for far too long...

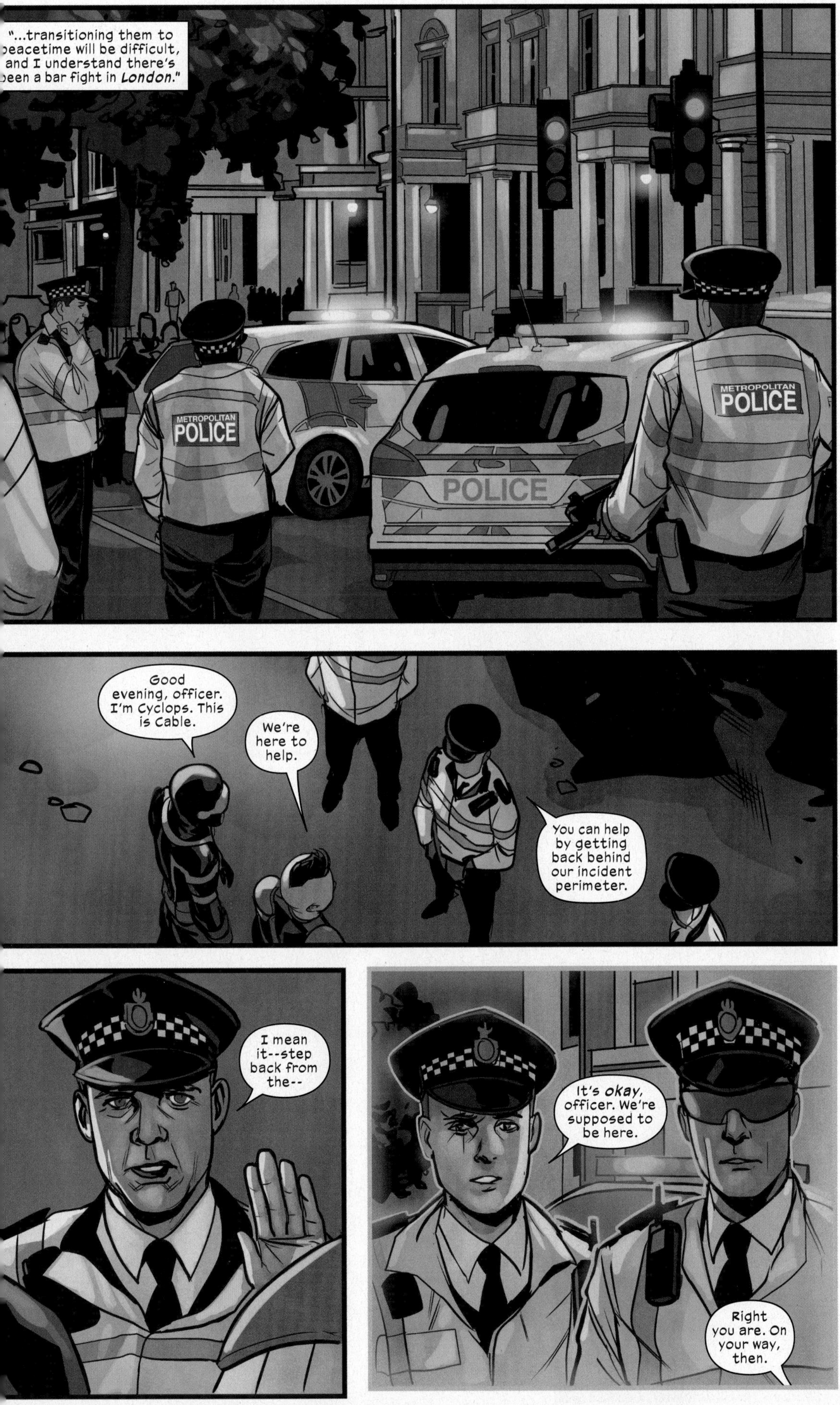
"...transitioning them to peacetime will be difficult, and I understand there's been a bar fight in London."
METROPOLITAN POLICE
POLICE
METROPOLITAN POLICE
Good evening, officer. I'm Cyclops. This is Cable.
We're here to help.
You can help by getting back behind our incident perimeter.
I mean it--step back from the--
It's okay, officer. We're supposed to be here.
Right you are. On your way, then.

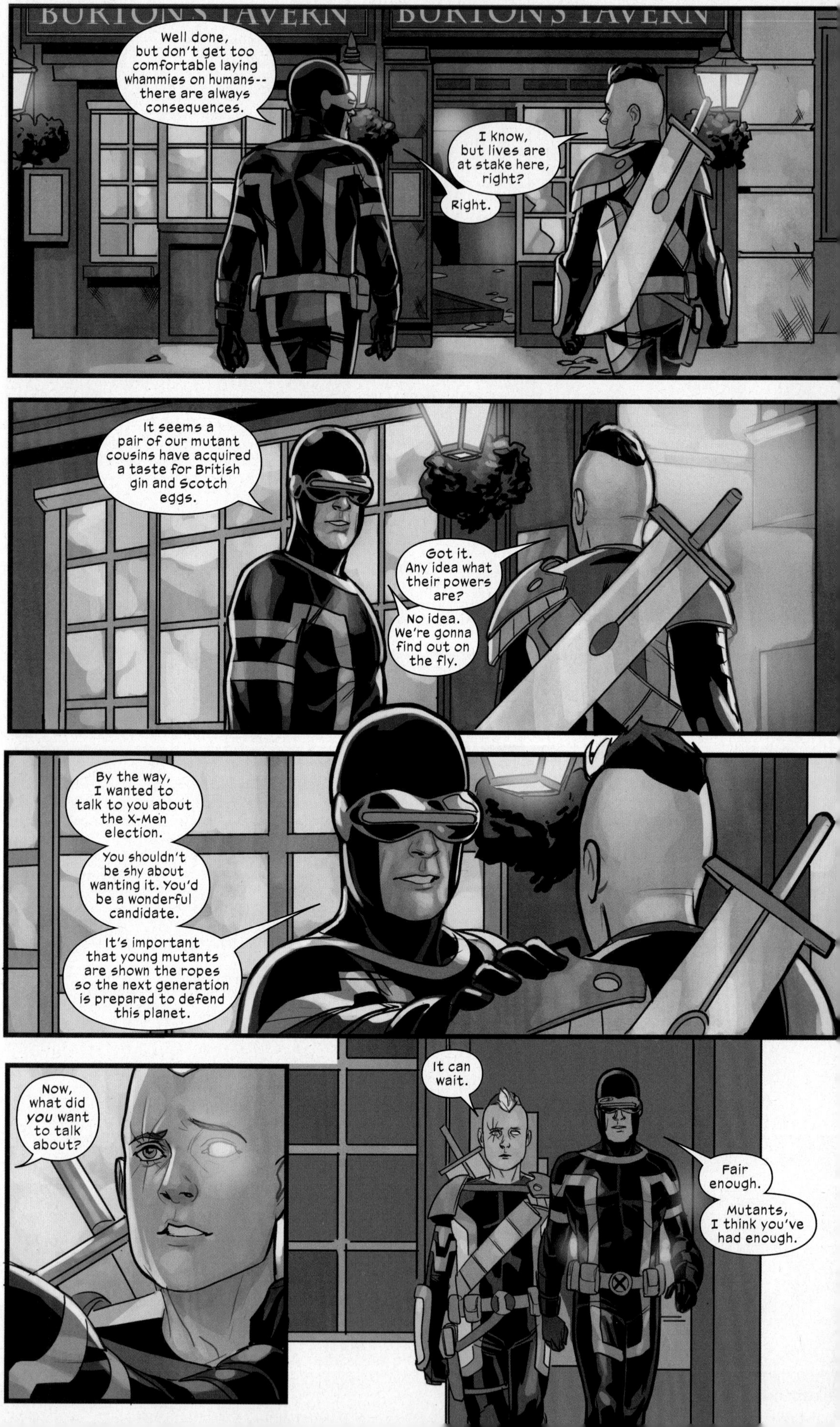
BURTON'S TAVERN
BURTON'S TAVERN
Well done, but don't get too comfortable laying whammies on humans-- there are always consequences.
I know, but lives are at stake here, right?
Right.
It seems a pair of our mutant cousins have acquired a taste for British gin and Scotch eggs.
Got it. Any idea what their powers are?
No idea. We're gonna find out on the fly.
By the way, I wanted to talk to you about the X-Men election.
You shouldn't be shy about wanting it. You'd be a wonderful candidate.
It's important that young mutants are shown the ropes so the next generation is prepared to defend this planet.
Now, what did *you* want to talk about?
It can wait.
Fair enough.
Mutants, I think you've had enough.

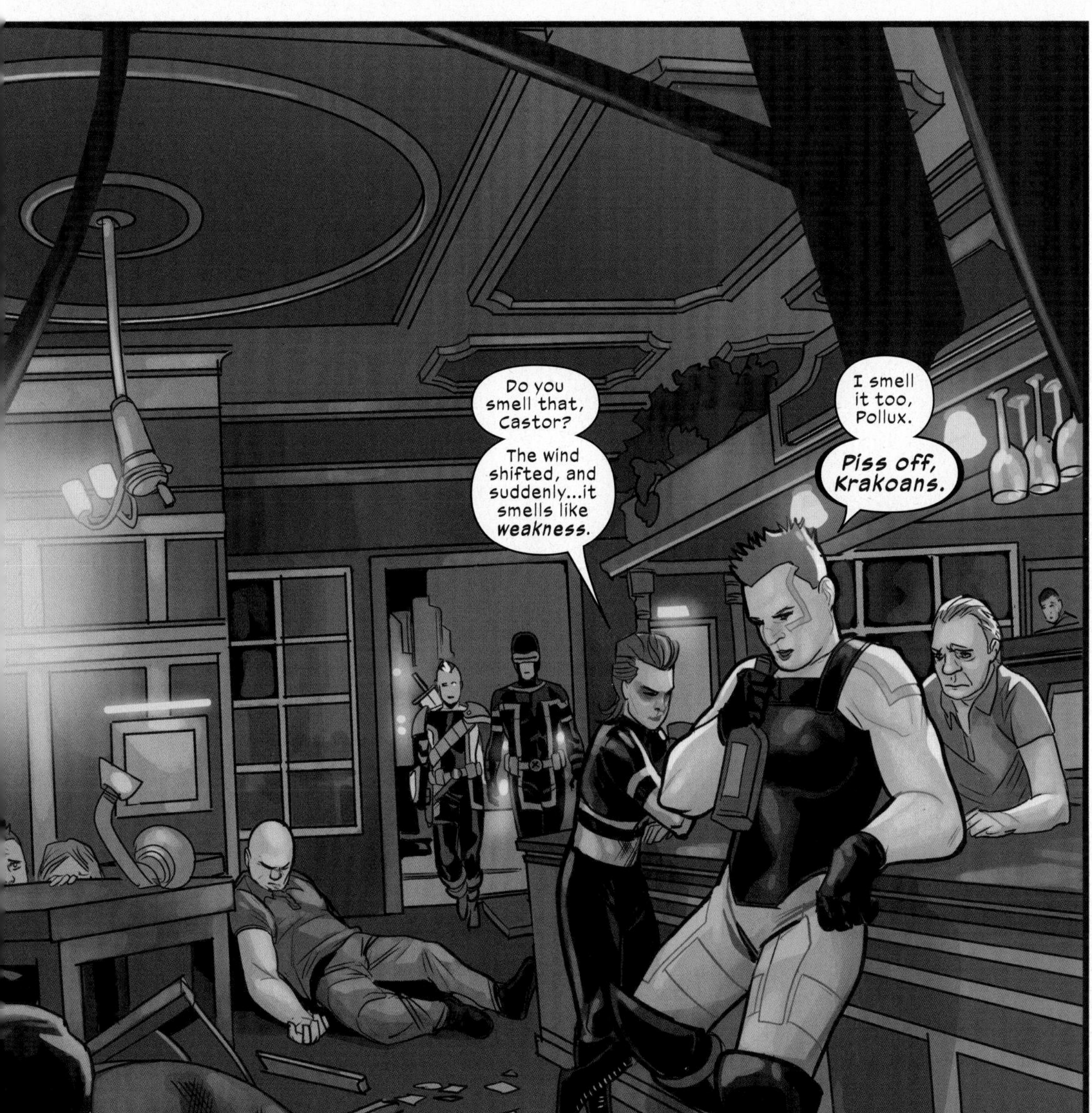
Do you smell that, Castor?
The wind shifted, and suddenly...it smells like weakness.
I smell it too, Pollux.
Piss off, Krakoans.

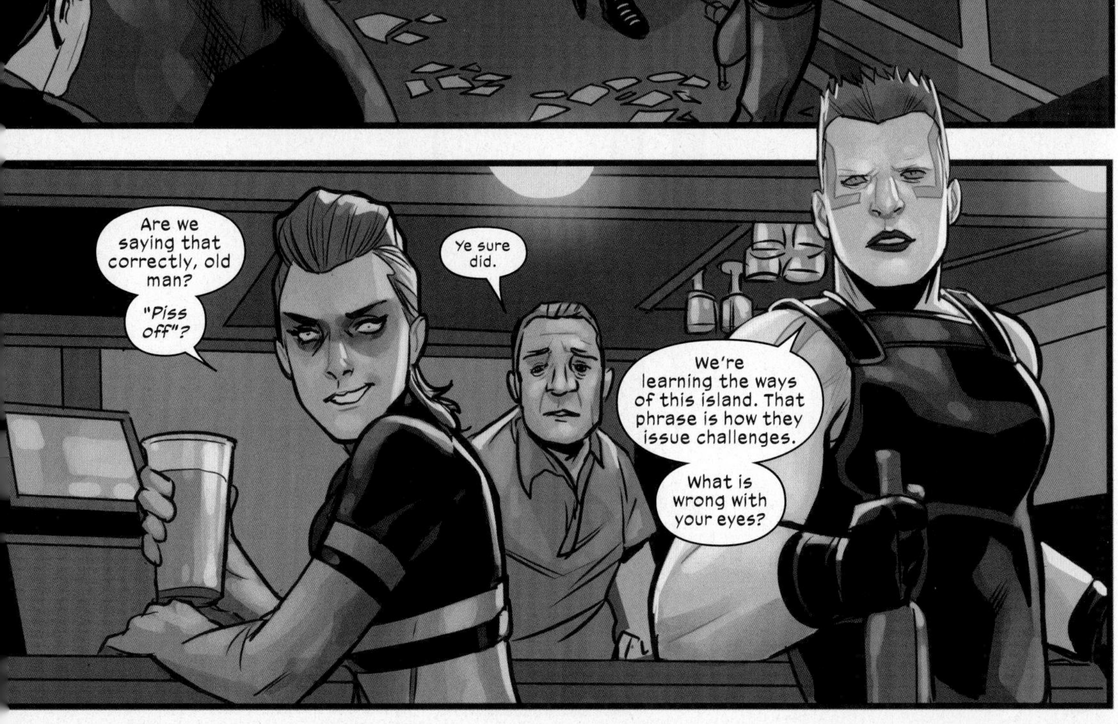
Are we saying that correctly, old man?
"Piss off"?
Ye sure did.
We're learning the ways of this island. That phrase is how they issue challenges.
What is wrong with your eyes?

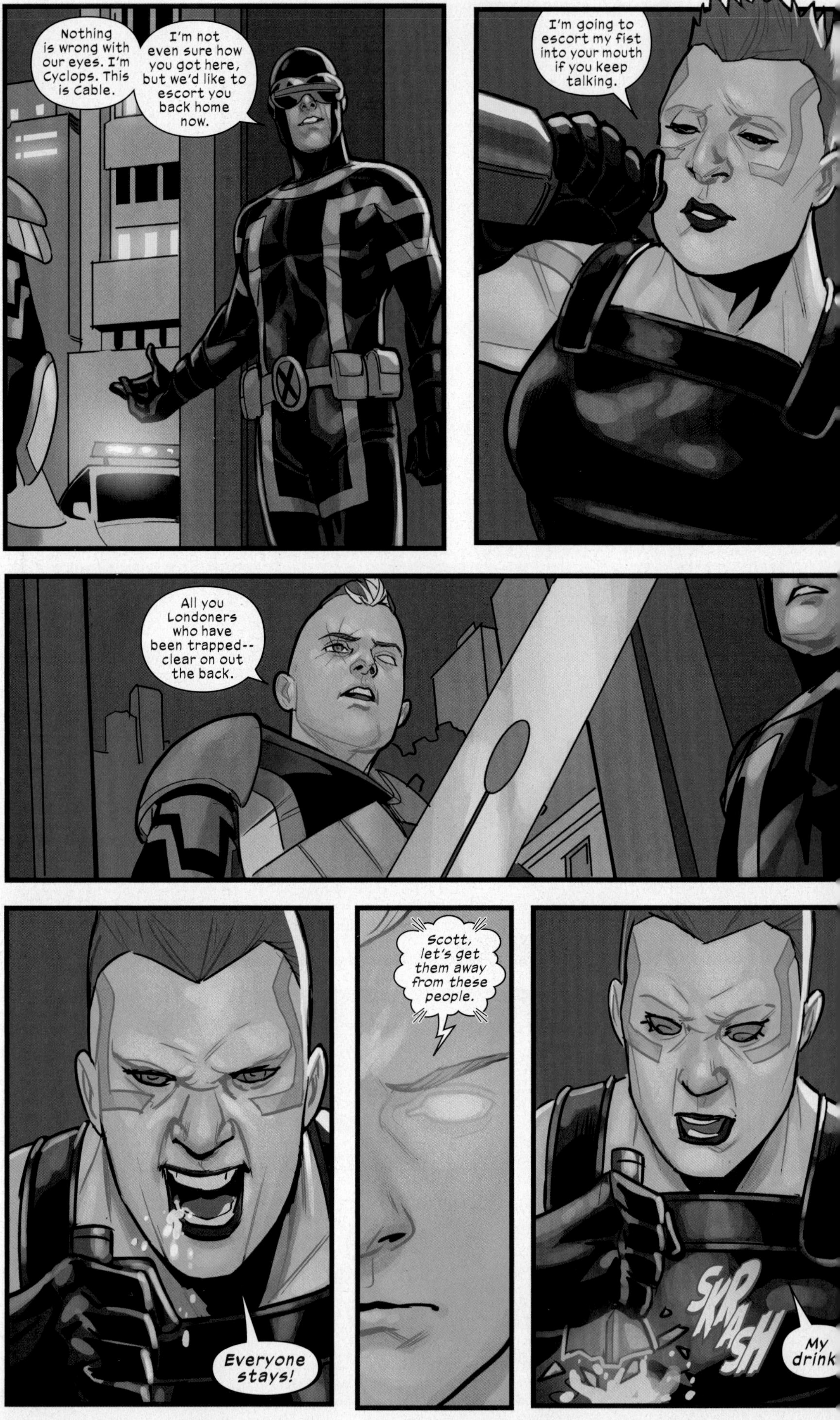
Nothing is wrong with our eyes. I'm Cyclops. This is Cable.
I'm not even sure how you got here, but we'd like to escort you back home now.
I'm going to escort my fist into your mouth if you keep talking.
All you Londoners who have been trapped--clear on out the back.
Everyone stays!
Scott, let's get them away from these people.
SKRASH
My drink

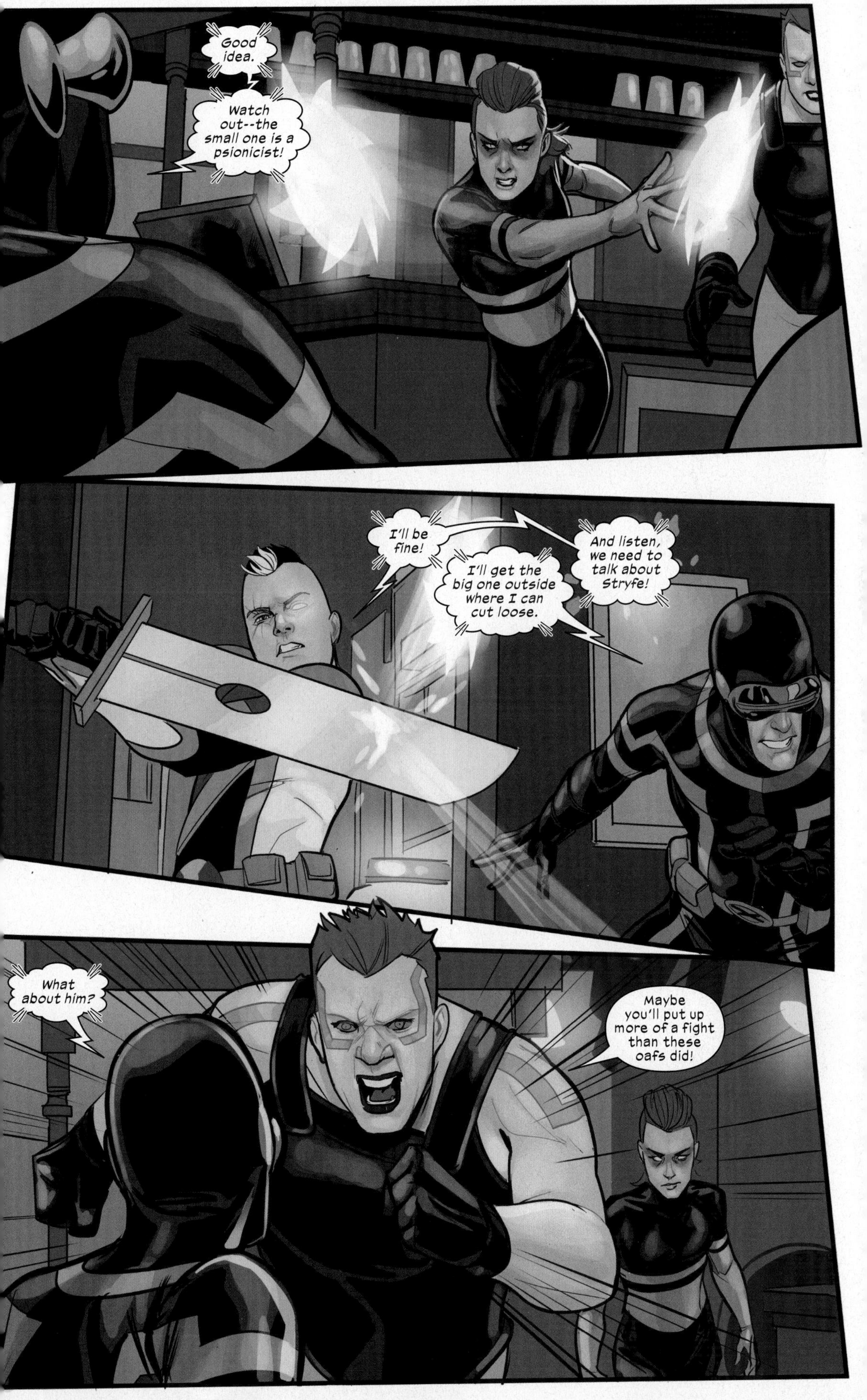
Good idea.
Watch out--the small one is a psionicist!
I'll be fine!
I'll get the big one outside where I can cut loose.
And listen, we need to talk about Stryfe!
What about him?
Maybe you'll put up more of a fight than these oafs did!

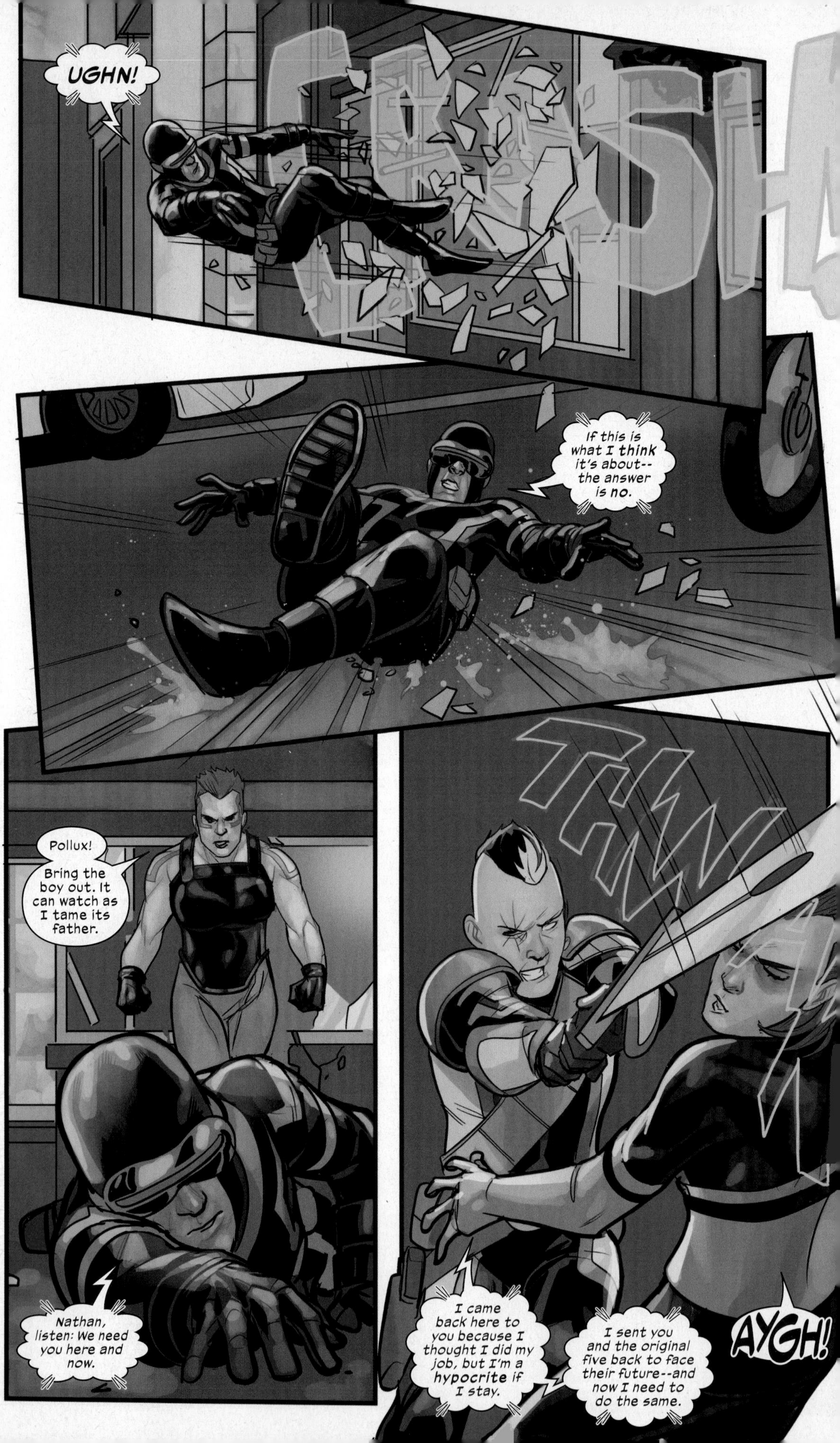
UGHN!
CRASH
If this is what I think it's about-- the answer is no.
Pollux!
Bring the boy out. It can watch as I tame its father.
Nathan, listen: We need you here and now.
I came back here to you because I thought I did my job, but I'm a hypocrite if I stay.
I sent you and the original five back to face their future--and now I need to do the same.
AYGH!

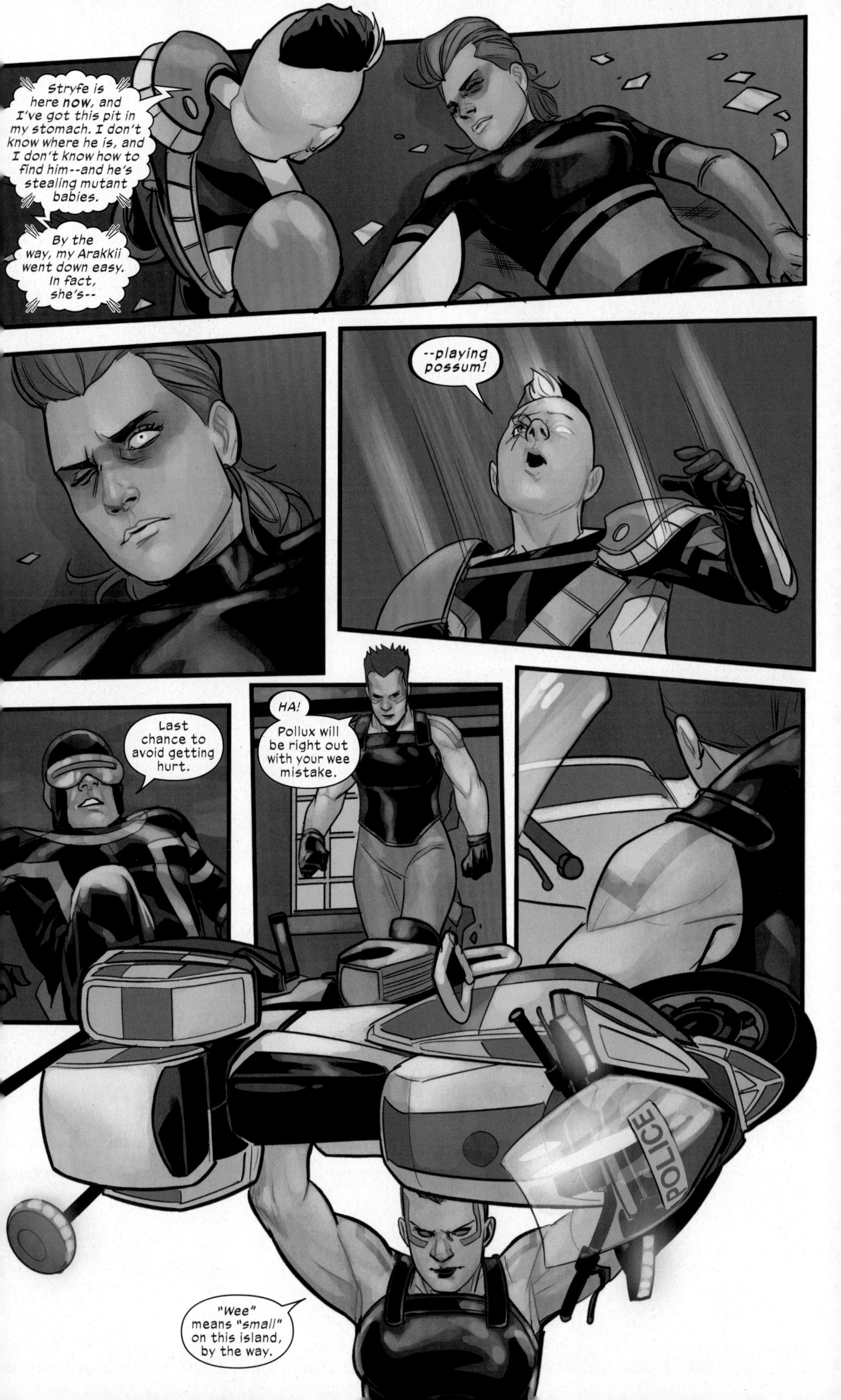

Stryfe is here now, and I've got this pit in my stomach. I don't know where he is, and I don't know how to find him--and he's stealing mutant babies.
By the way, my Arakkii went down easy. In fact, she's--
--playing possum!
Last chance to avoid getting hurt.
HA!
Pollux will be right out with your wee mistake.
POLICE
"Wee" means "small" on this island, by the way.

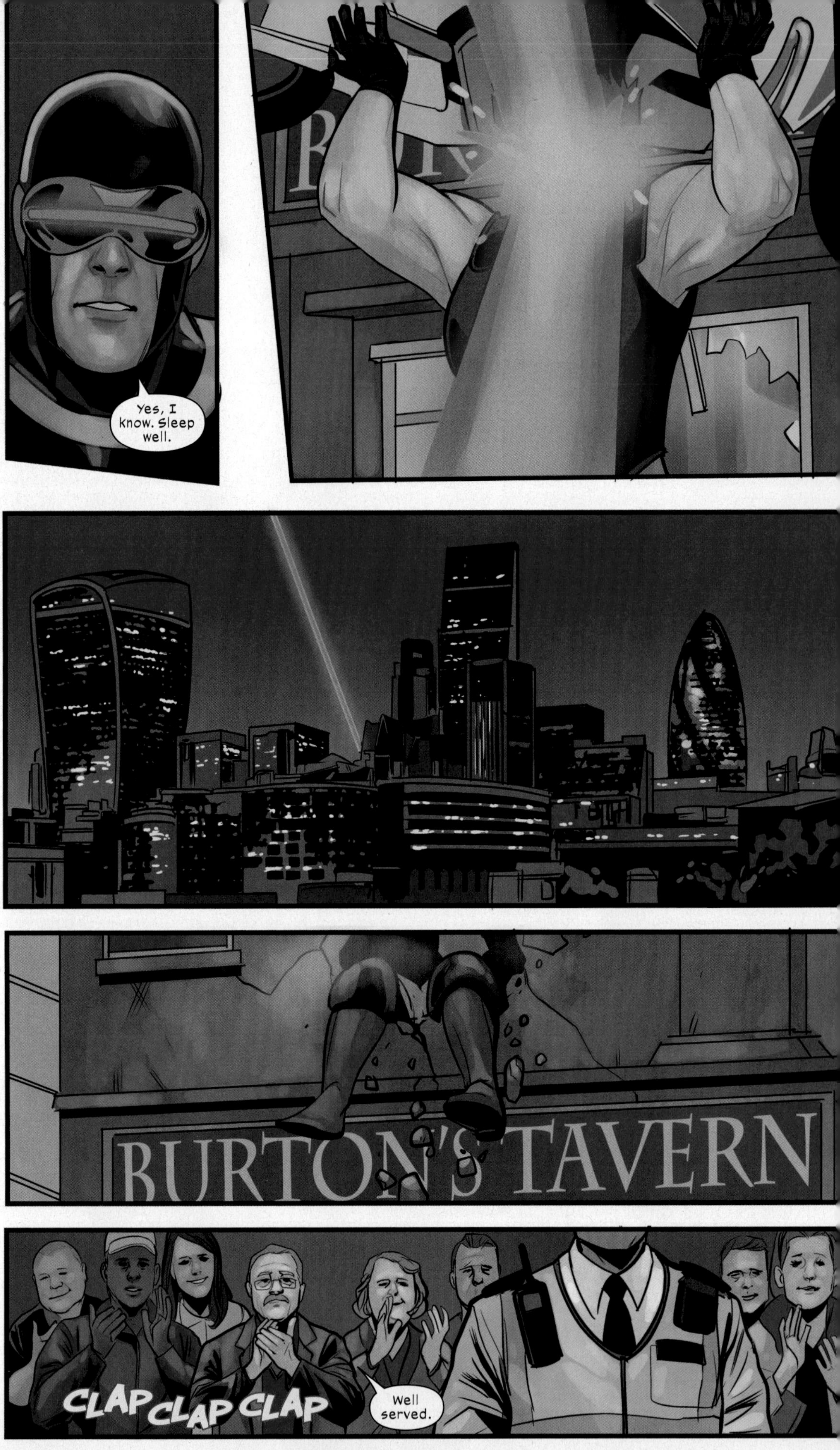
Yes, I know. Sleep well.
BURTON'S TAVERN
CLAP CLAP CLAP
Well served.

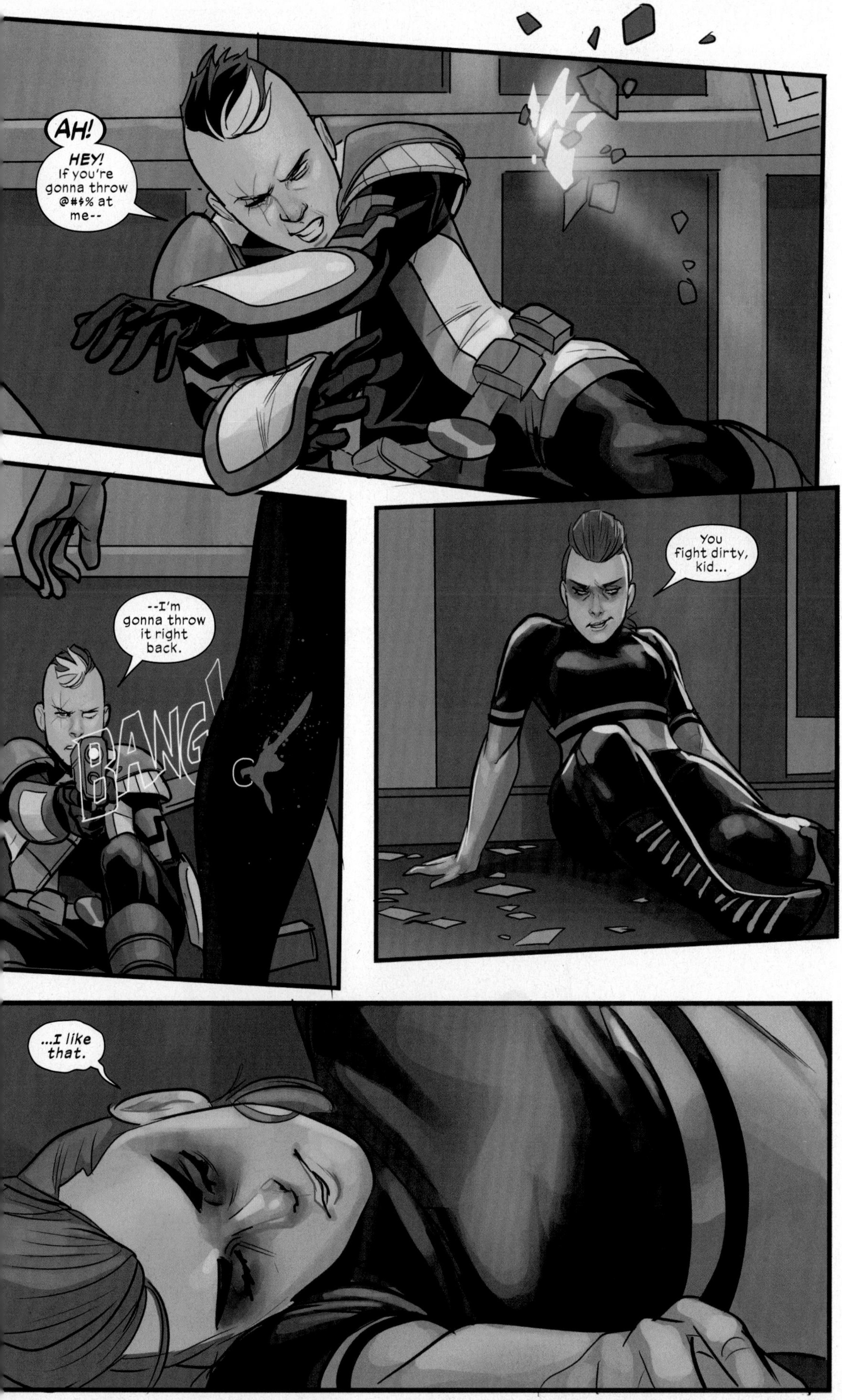
AH!
HEY! If you're gonna throw @#$% at me--
--I'm gonna throw it right back.
BANG!
You fight dirty, kid...
...I like that.

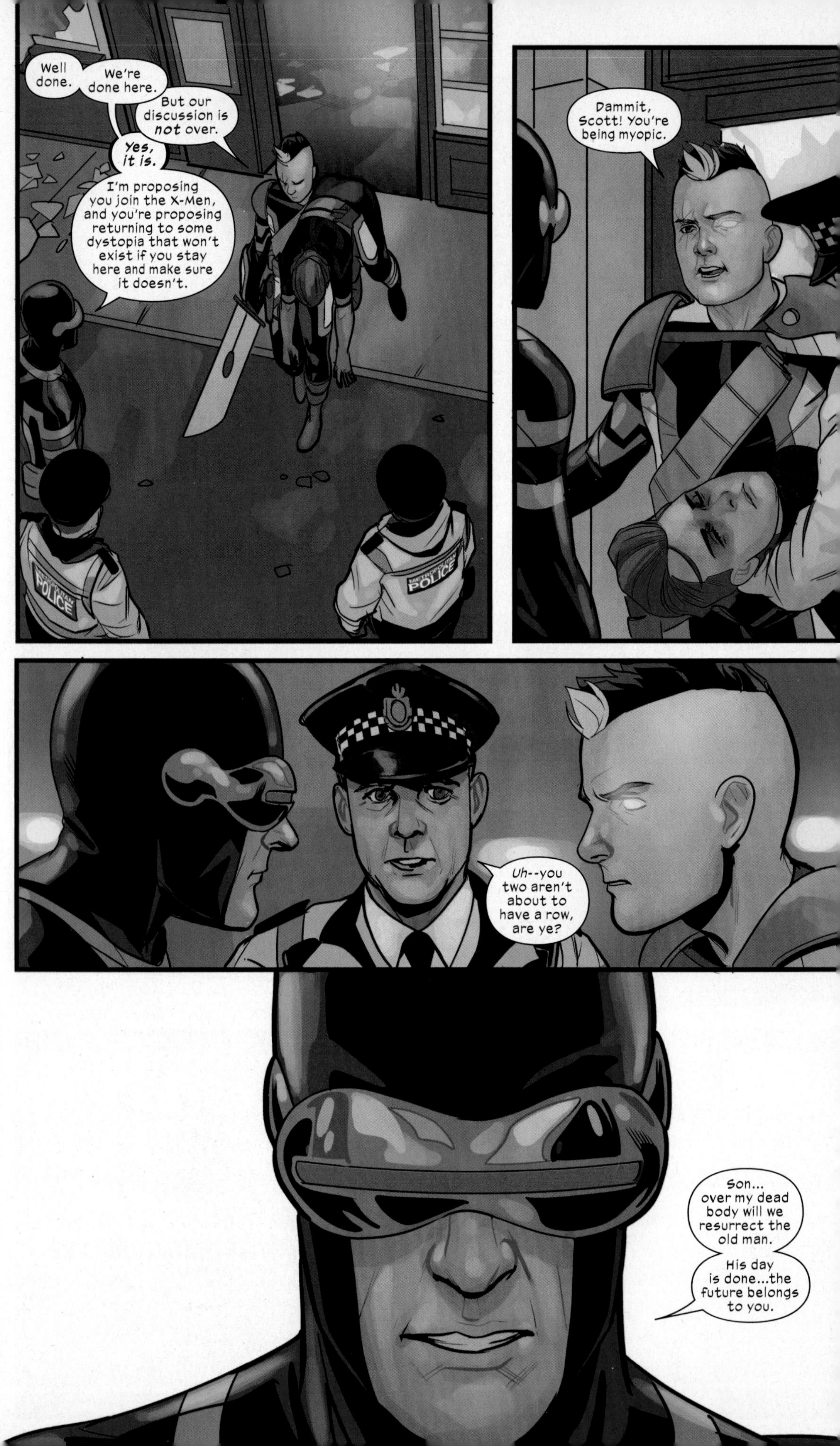
Well done.
We're done here.
But our discussion is *not* over.
Yes, it is.
I'm proposing you join the X-Men, and you're proposing returning to some dystopia that won't exist if you stay here and make sure it doesn't.
Dammit, Scott! You're being myopic.
METROPOLITAN POLICE
METROPOLITAN POLICE
Uh--you two aren't about to have a row, are ye?
Son... over my dead body will we resurrect the old man.
His day is done...the future belongs to you.

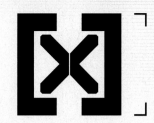

When Cable was slain by his younger self just before the Dawn of Krakoa, it initiated the old man's Casket Protocols.

The most immediate concern Cable had over his eventual death was to secure his remains. This was accomplished on his behalf by Deadpool.

This action was accompanied by a change in defensive posture. Cable's safe houses shredded data and removed safeties from all traps.

Cable's Graymalkin Station remained cloaked in high Earth orbit. The station had been reconstituted in secrecy from the spoils of technology seized during the second Great Armor Wars of the 3030s.

It was highly likely that Stryfe had compromised Cable's first artificial intelligence, the Professor, at some point, and Cable never fully trusted it again. He turned to his home-brewed A.I. Belle to run point on the sleeping station. Belle's initial determination that Stryfe was responsible for killing Cable in the department store was revealed to be false after seeing the exploits of "Kid Cable" A.K. (AFTER KRAKOA) in the media.

Belle gained additional situational knowledge of the mutant baby kidnappings after Cable and Esme Cuckoo inserted themselves into the Philadelphia police department investigation. Belle skimmed info from the servers and concluded before Cable did that an attack was underway by Stryfe.

The assumption that Stryfe was attacking backward through time and seeking to replace Kid Cable with a clone of himself was proven true when Cable and Domino found and destroyed the clone pods hidden in Tokyo, Japan.

The middle-aged Stryfe clones inserted into the pro-mutant human cult "the Order of X" and the one safeguarding the Tokyo clone pod were killed by Cable. It's unknown if any sleeper Stryfe clones are still embedded in human society.

Five mutant babies remain missing, and it's not clear if there is a larger plan for them or if they were simply bait for Cable.

The first Hellfire Gala of the Krakoan Age is days away, and Cable has not discovered any of his safe houses or Graymalkin Station.

Belle watches, waits, observes and remains on guard.

Another time. Another place.

Wake up, old man. The boss wants a chat.

Oh, I've been awake the whole time.

I'm guessing you filth don't have any possums in this @#@$&%#$...

...If you did, you might have done a better job of pacifying me-- and searching my robot hound...

...you might've have found the Light of Galador...

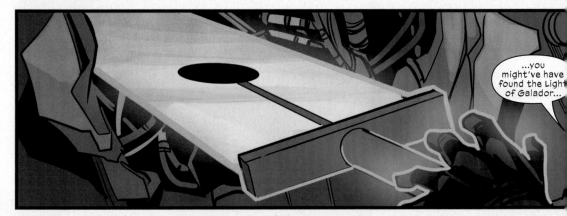

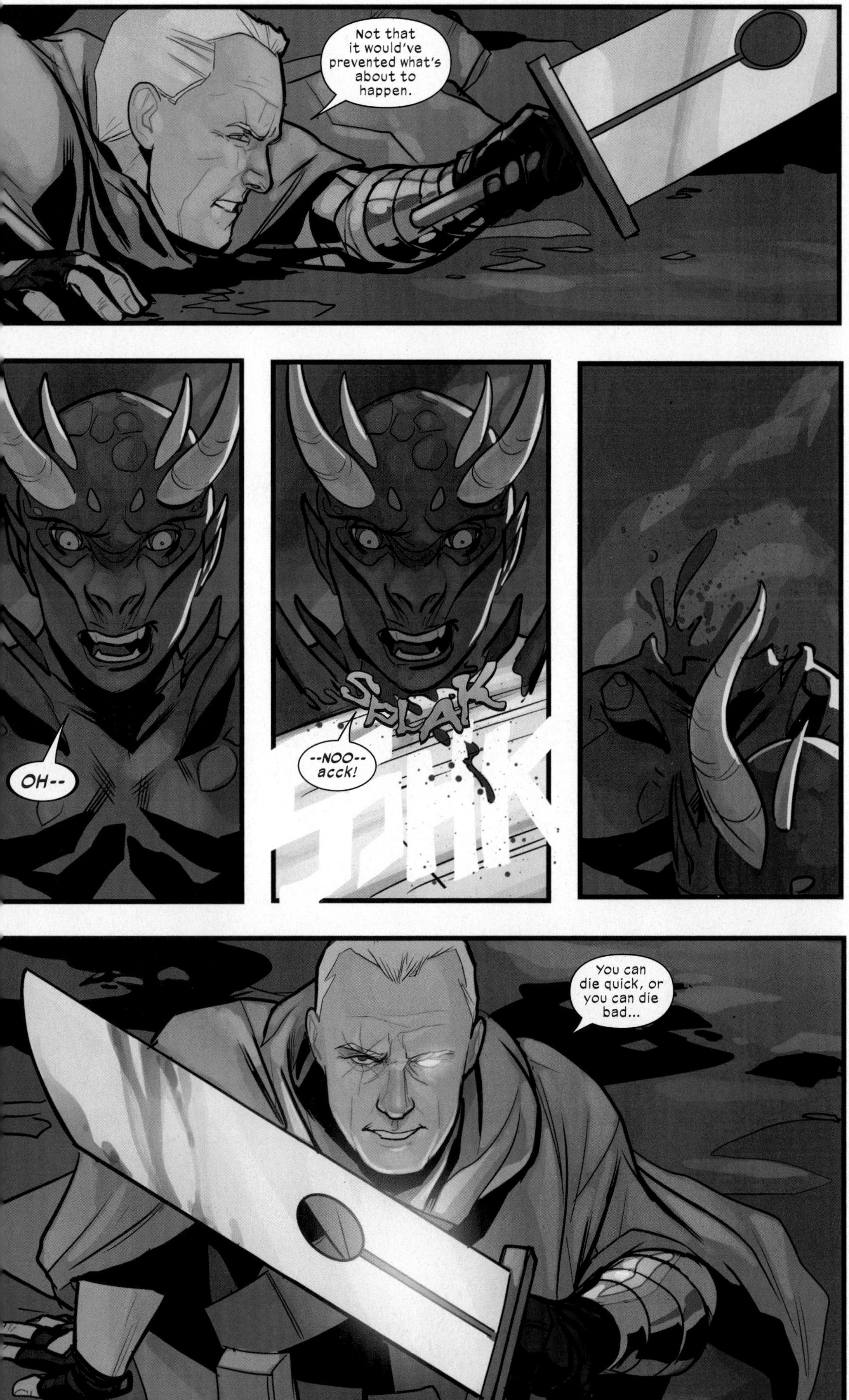
Not that it would've prevented what's about to happen.
OH--
SPLAK
SHK
--NOO-- acck!
You can die quick, or you can die bad...

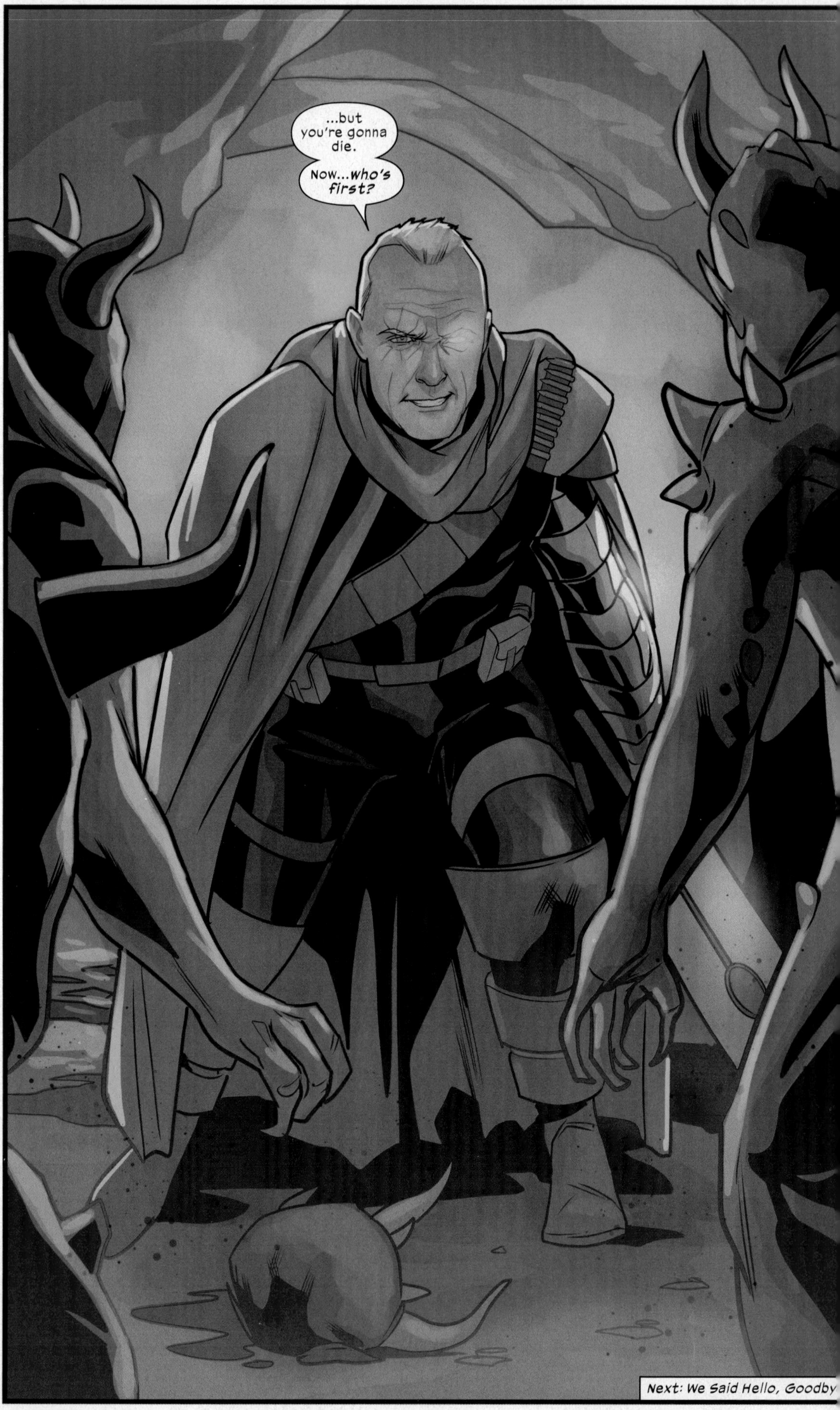
...but you're gonna die.
Now...*who's first?*
Next: We Said Hello, Goodby

[reign_of_x]

[kra_]
[koa_]

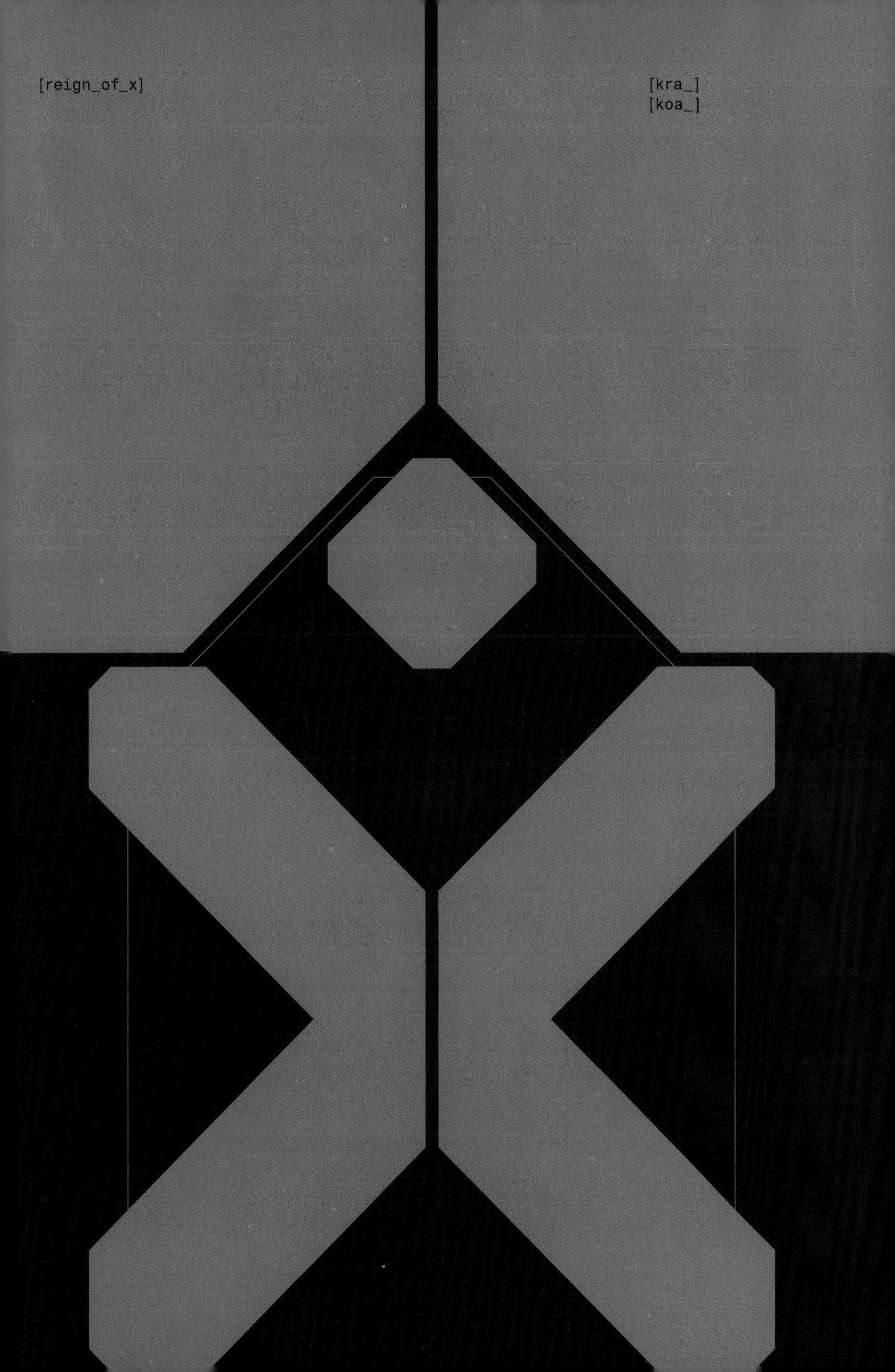

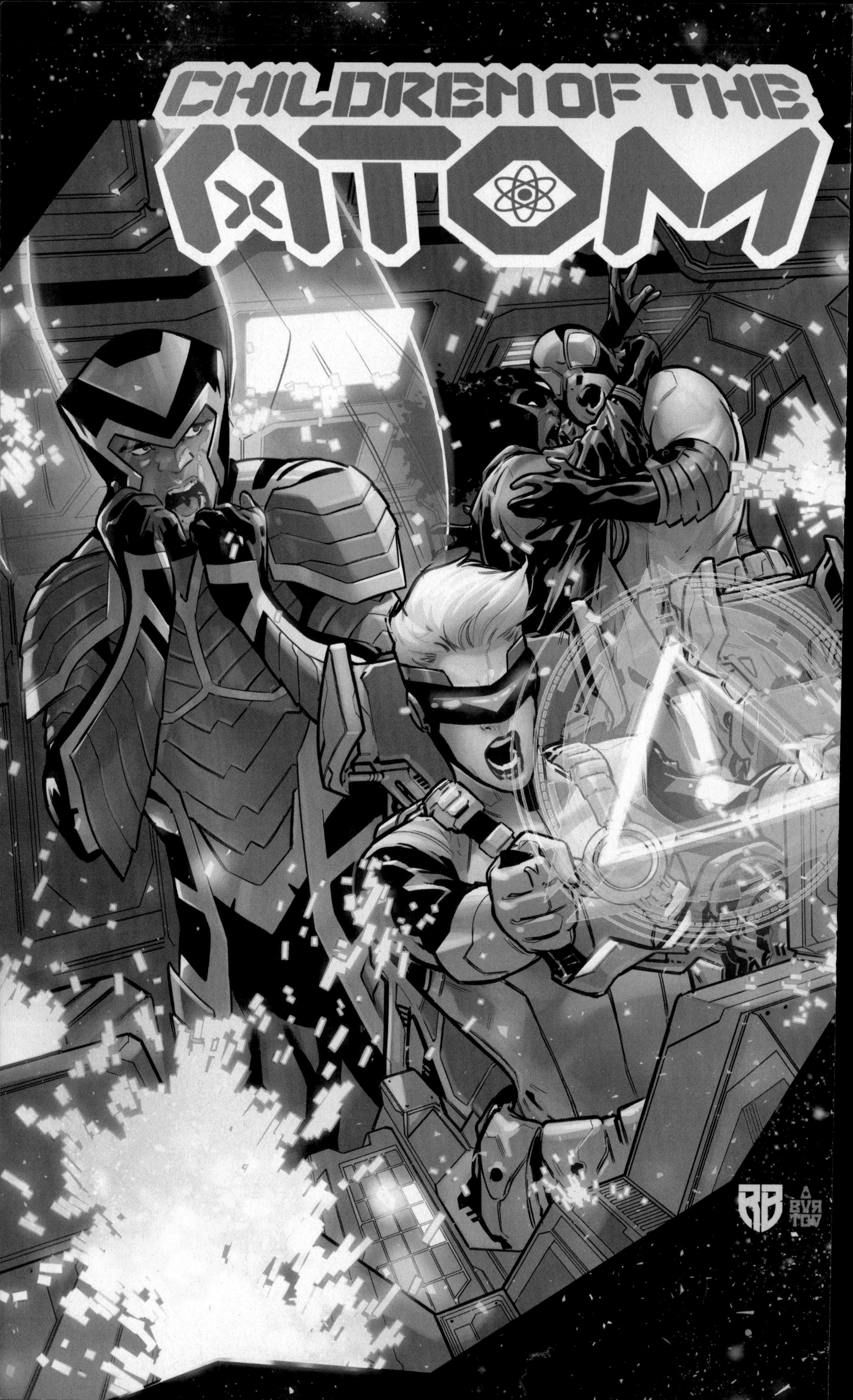
CHILDREN OF THE
ATOM

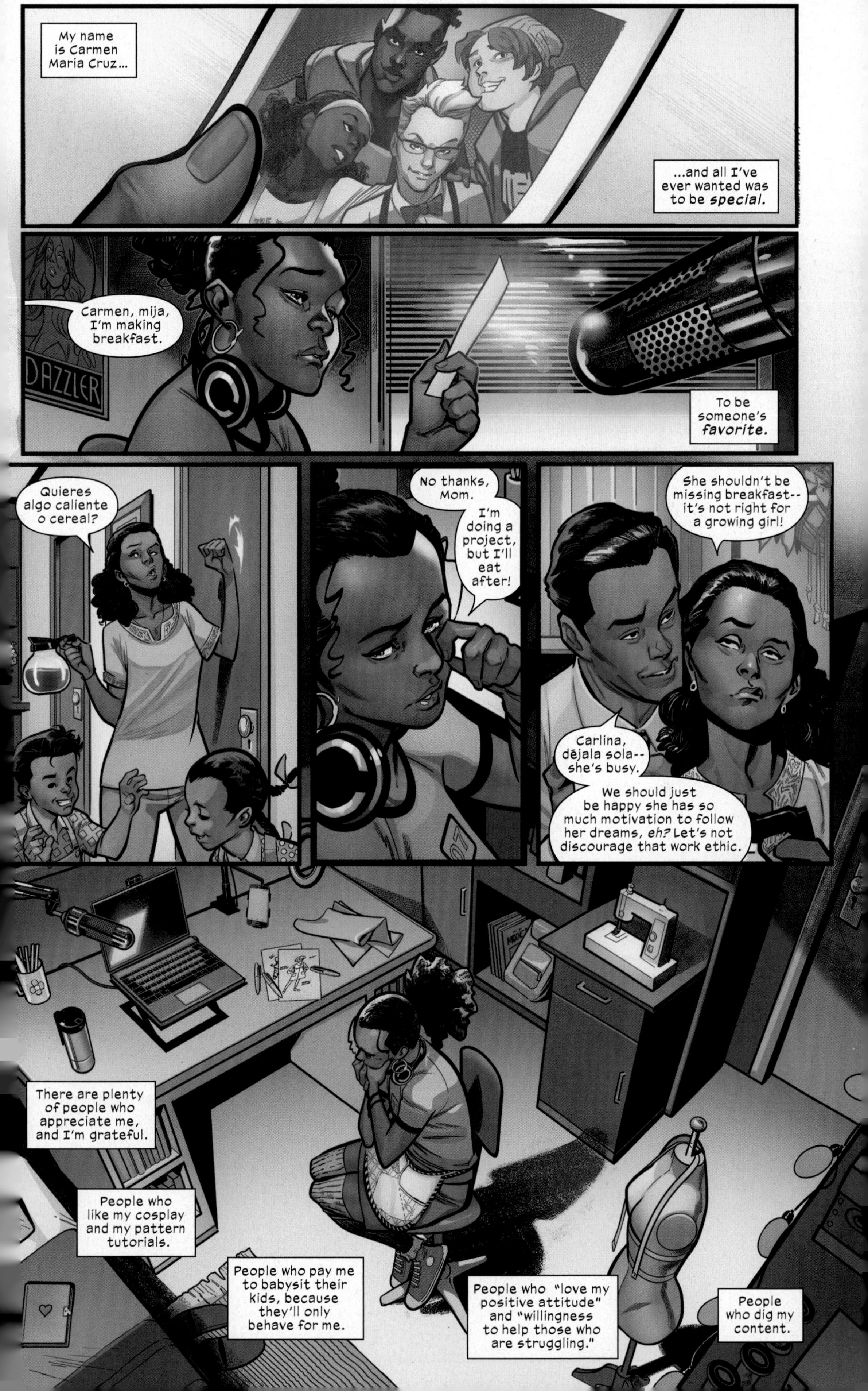

My name is Carmen Maria Cruz...
...and all I've ever wanted was to be *special.*
Carmen, mija, I'm making breakfast.
To be someone's *favorite.*
Quieres algo caliente o cereal?
No thanks, Mom.
I'm doing a project, but I'll eat after!
She shouldn't be missing breakfast--it's not right for a growing girl!
Carlina, déjala sola--she's busy.
We should just be happy she has so much motivation to follow her dreams, *eh?* Let's not discourage that work ethic.
DAZZLER
There are plenty of people who appreciate me, and I'm grateful.
People who like my cosplay and my pattern tutorials.
People who pay me to babysit their kids, because they'll only behave for me.
People who "love my positive attitude" and "willingness to help those who are struggling."
People who dig my content.

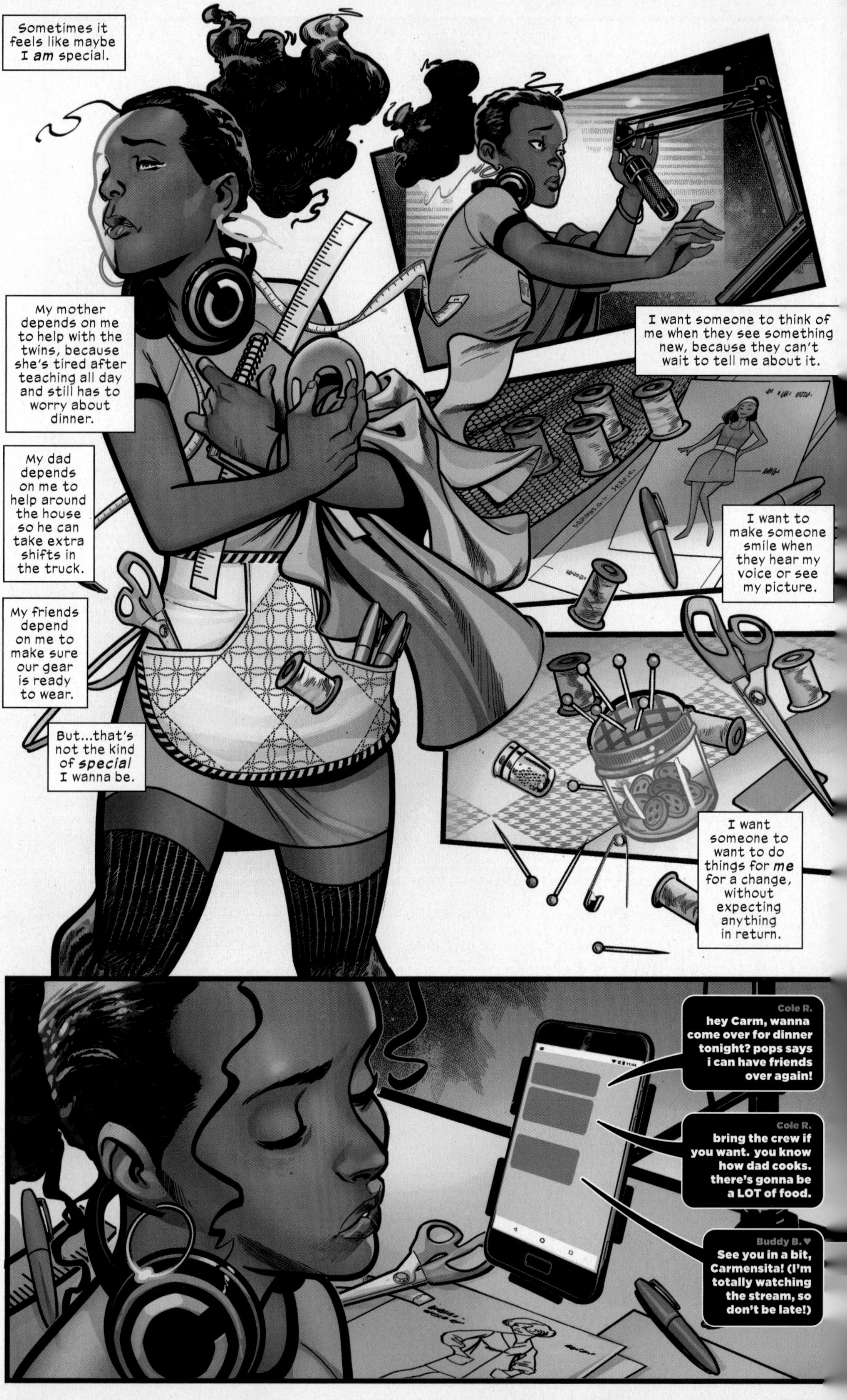
Sometimes it feels like maybe I *am* special.
My mother depends on me to help with the twins, because she's tired after teaching all day and still has to worry about dinner.
My dad depends on me to help around the house so he can take extra shifts in the truck.
My friends depend on me to make sure our gear is ready to wear.
But...that's not the kind of *special* I wanna be.
I want someone to think of me when they see something new, because they can't wait to tell me about it.
I want to make someone smile when they hear my voice or see my picture.
I want someone to want to do things for *me* for a change, without expecting anything in return.
Cole R.
hey Carm, wanna come over for dinner tonight? pops says i can have friends over again!
Cole R.
bring the crew if you want. you know how dad cooks. there's gonna be a LOT of food.
Buddy B. ♥
See you in a bit, Carmensita! (I'm totally watching the stream, so don't be late!)

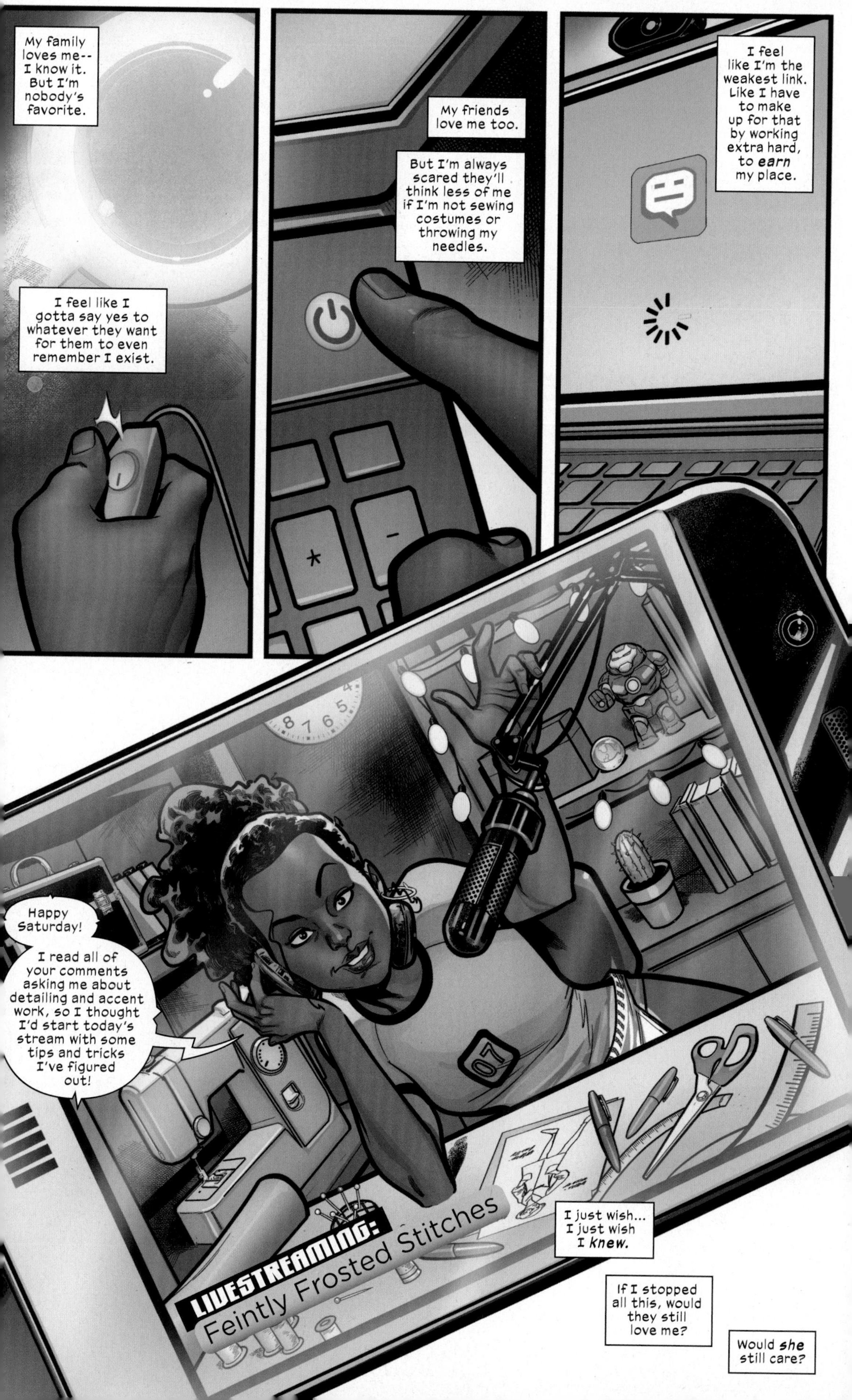
My family loves me-- I know it. But I'm nobody's favorite.
I feel like I gotta say yes to whatever they want for them to even remember I exist.
My friends love me too.
But I'm always scared they'll think less of me if I'm not sewing costumes or throwing my needles.
I feel like I'm the weakest link. Like I have to make up for that by working extra hard, to *earn* my place.
Happy Saturday!
I read all of your comments asking me about detailing and accent work, so I thought I'd start today's stream with some tips and tricks I've figured out!
LIVESTREAMING:
Feintly Frosted Stitches
I just wish... I just wish I *knew.*
If I stopped all this, would they still love me?
Would *she* still care?

DISCOVERING POWER

Mutants around the world have flocked to the island-nation of Krakoa for safety, security and to be part of the first mutant society.

Back in Manhattan, new teen vigilantes CHILDREN OF THE ATOM recently met some of their heroes, the X-MEN, who beckoned the young team to join their fellow mutants on Krakoa. Little did the X-Men know, their absence has not been for a lack of trying...

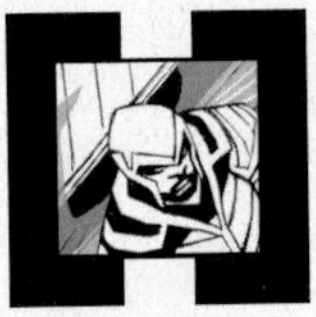

Cherub

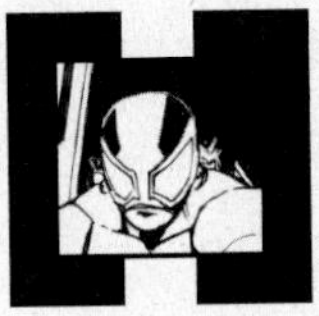

Marvel Guy

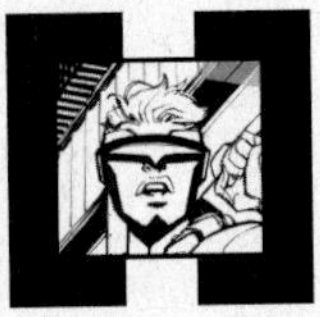

Cyclops-Lass

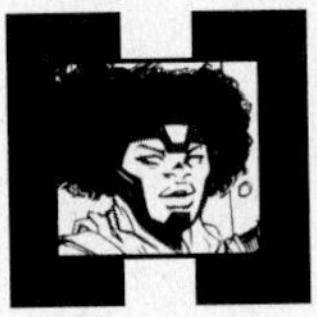

Gimmick

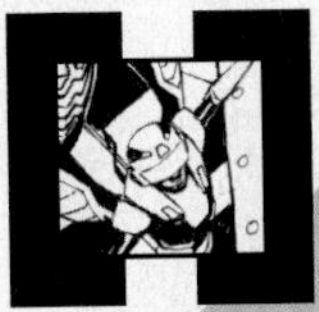

Daycrawler

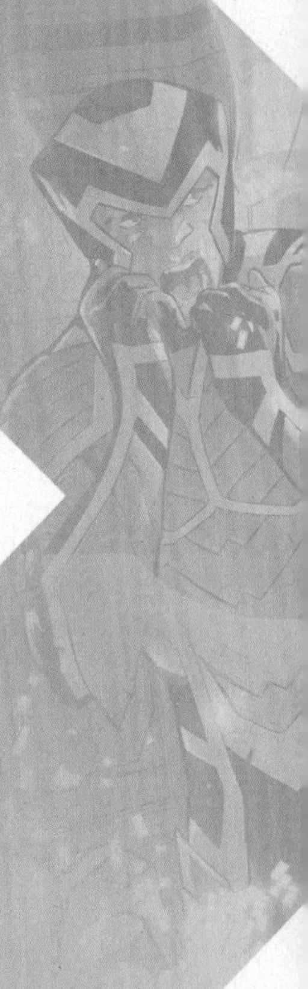

CHILDREN OF THE ATOM
[X_03]

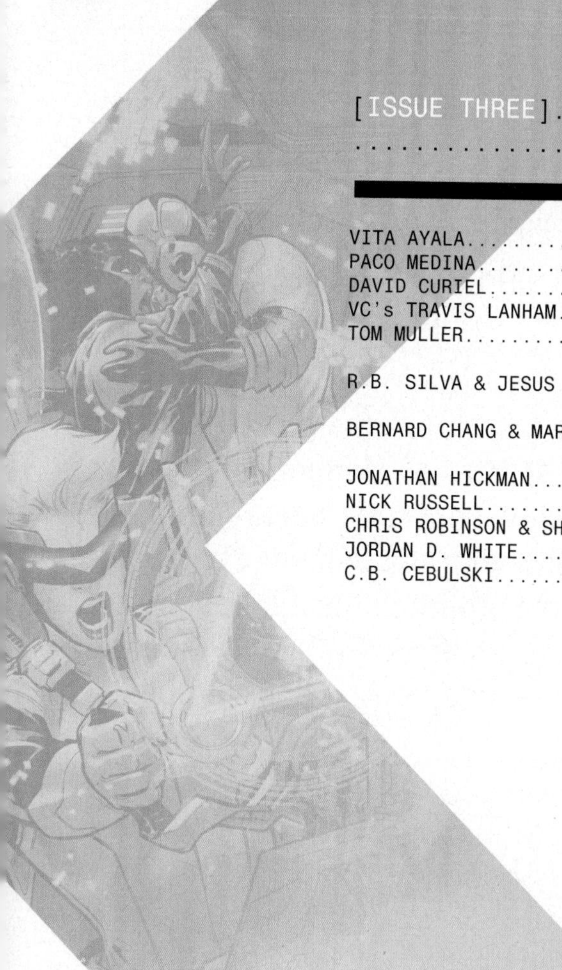

[ISSUE THREE]................................
....................UNUSUAL DINNER GUESTS

VITA AYALA......................................[WRITER]
PACO MEDINA.....................................[ARTIST]
DAVID CURIEL...............................[COLOR ARTIST]
VC's TRAVIS LANHAM............................[LETTERER]
TOM MULLER.....................................[DESIGN]

R.B. SILVA & JESUS ABURTOV.................[COVER ARTISTS]

BERNARD CHANG & MARCELO MAIOLO......[VARIANT COVER ARTISTS]

JONATHAN HICKMAN..............................[HEAD OF X]
NICK RUSSELL.................................[PRODUCTION]
CHRIS ROBINSON & SHANNON ANDREWS BALLESTEROS......[EDITORS]
JORDAN D. WHITE...........................[SENIOR EDITOR]
C.B. CEBULSKI...........................[EDITOR IN CHIEF]

[00_chil__X]
[00_dren__X]

[00_00...0.]
[00_00...3.]

[00_____]
[00_of____]

[00_the___]

[00__atom__]

[XCHA....[mag]_006]
[NGE....[neto]_500]

X-Change

Shop ▼ Search

X-Change > Costumes > Headgear > Magneto >

Broken Helmet. Six Pieces Recovered from Attack on NYC

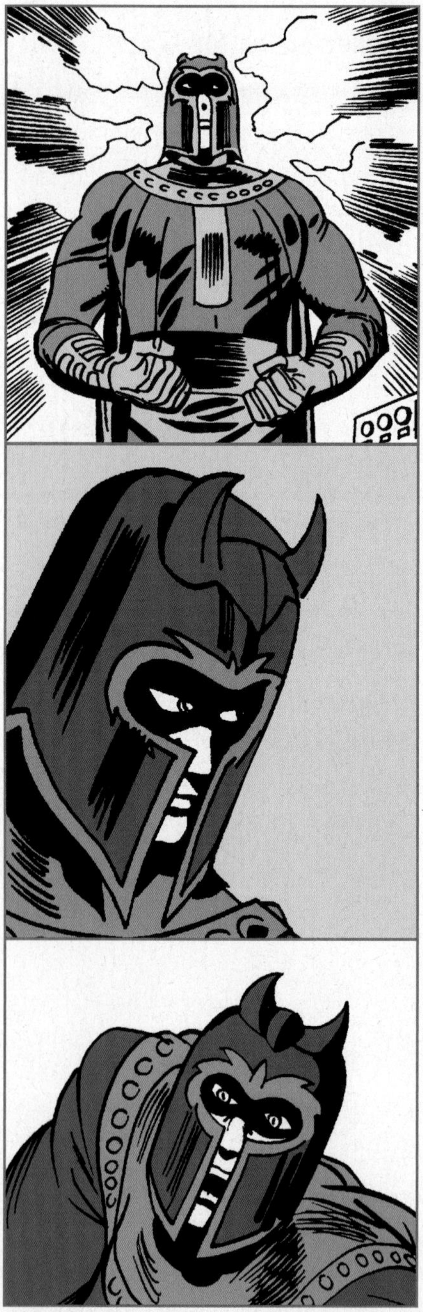

PRICE:

$500.00 USD OR **BEST OFFER**

SHIPPING:

$19.99 USD

DESCRIPTION:

Pre-Krakoa! Authentic artifact from the Master of Magnetism's attack on New York City, damaged in battle with the X-Men! Six pieces from Magneto's iconic helmet, as photographed. The helmet/metal repels telepathic attack/probes!

BUY

** * * [SOLD TO USER: FeintlyFrostedStitches] * * **

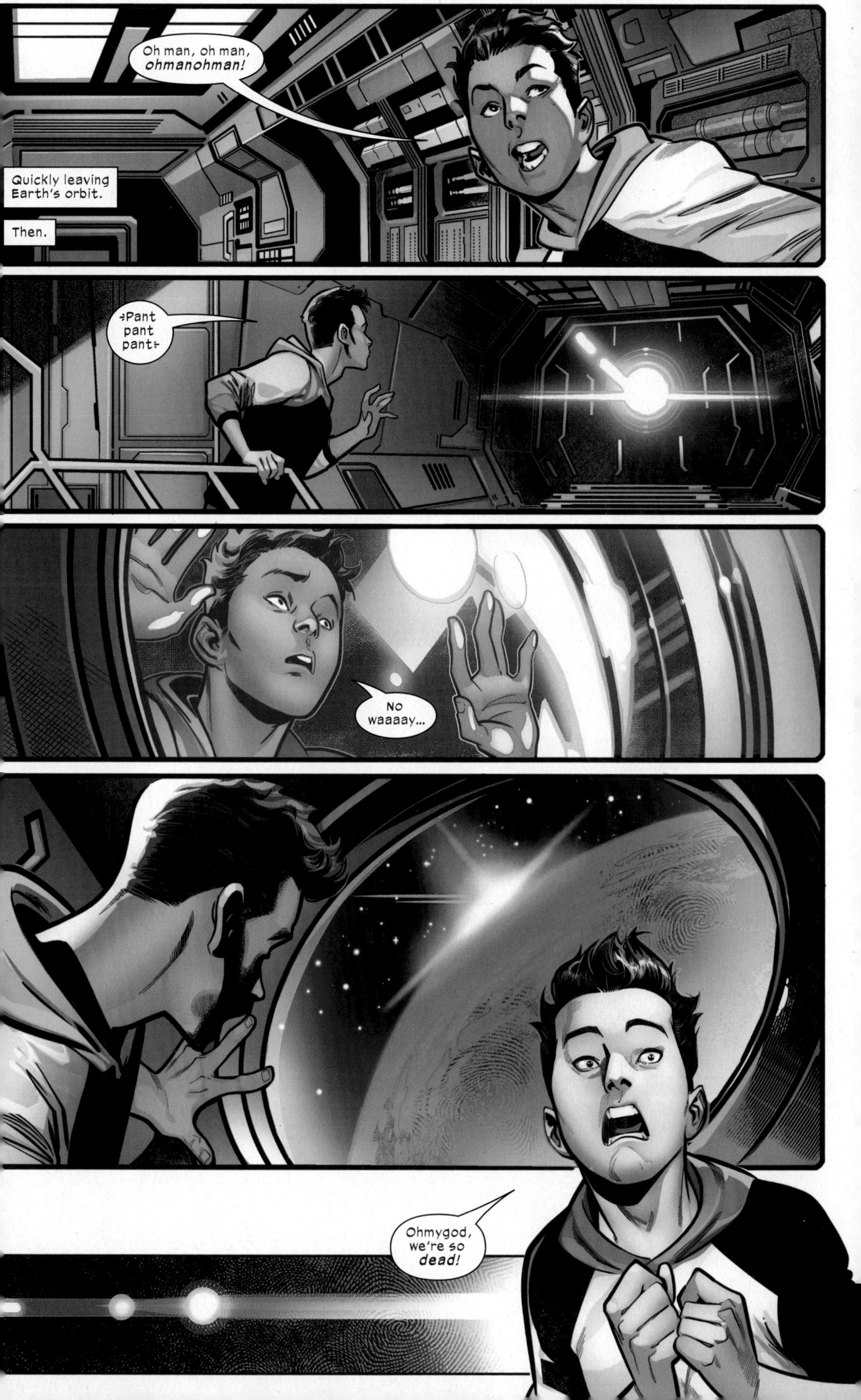
Oh man, oh man, ohmanohman!
Quickly leaving Earth's orbit.
Then.
=Pant pant pant=
No waaaay...
Ohmygod, we're so dead!

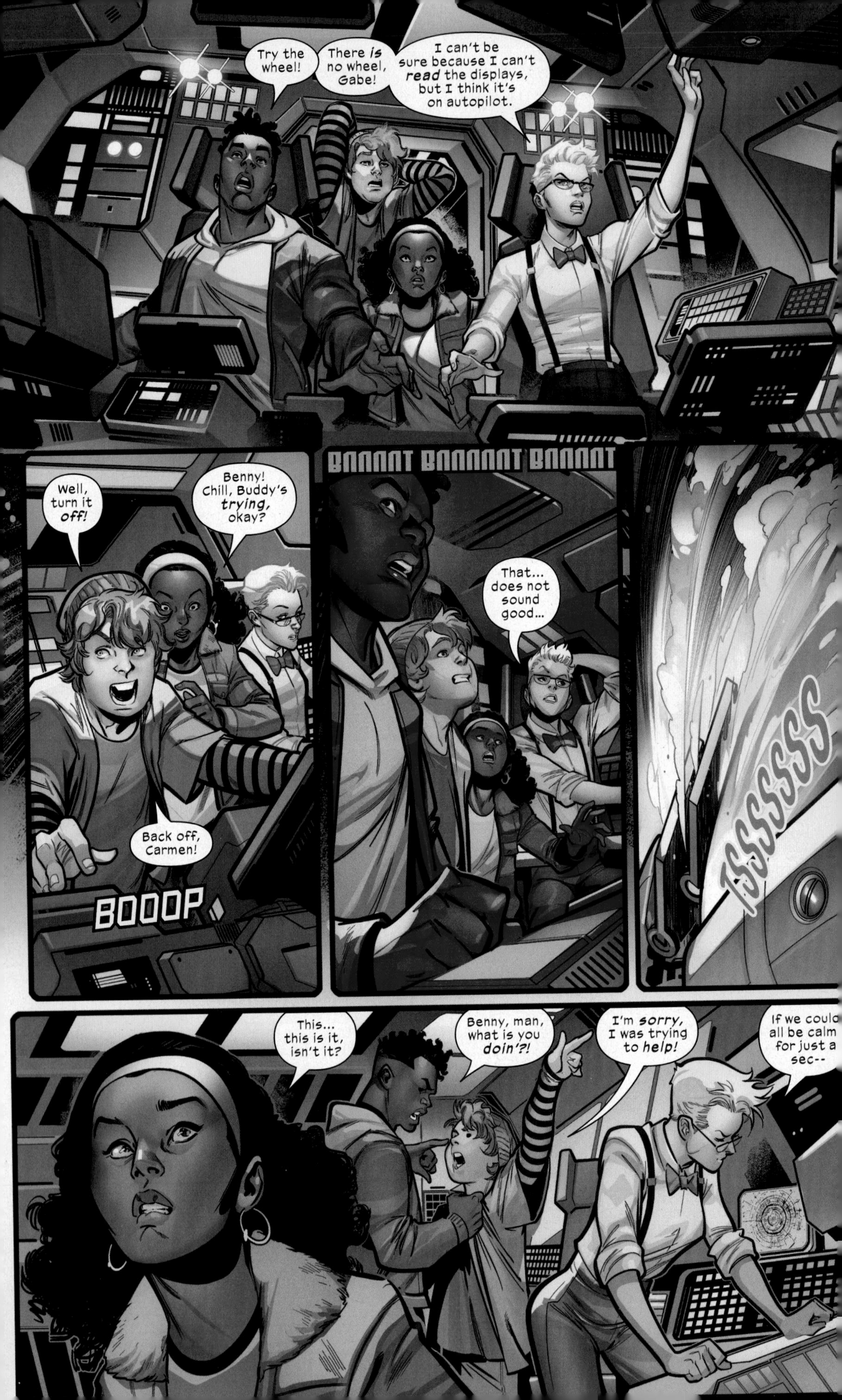

Try the wheel!
There *is* no wheel, Gabe!
I can't be sure because I can't *read* the displays, but I think it's on autopilot.
Well, turn it *off!*
Benny! Chill, Buddy's *trying,* okay?
Back off, Carmen!
BOOOP
BNNNNT BNNNNNT BNNNNT
That... does not sound good...
TSSSSSSS
This... this is it, isn't it?
Benny, man, what is you *doin'?!*
I'm *sorry,* I was trying to *help!*
If we could all be calm for just a sec--

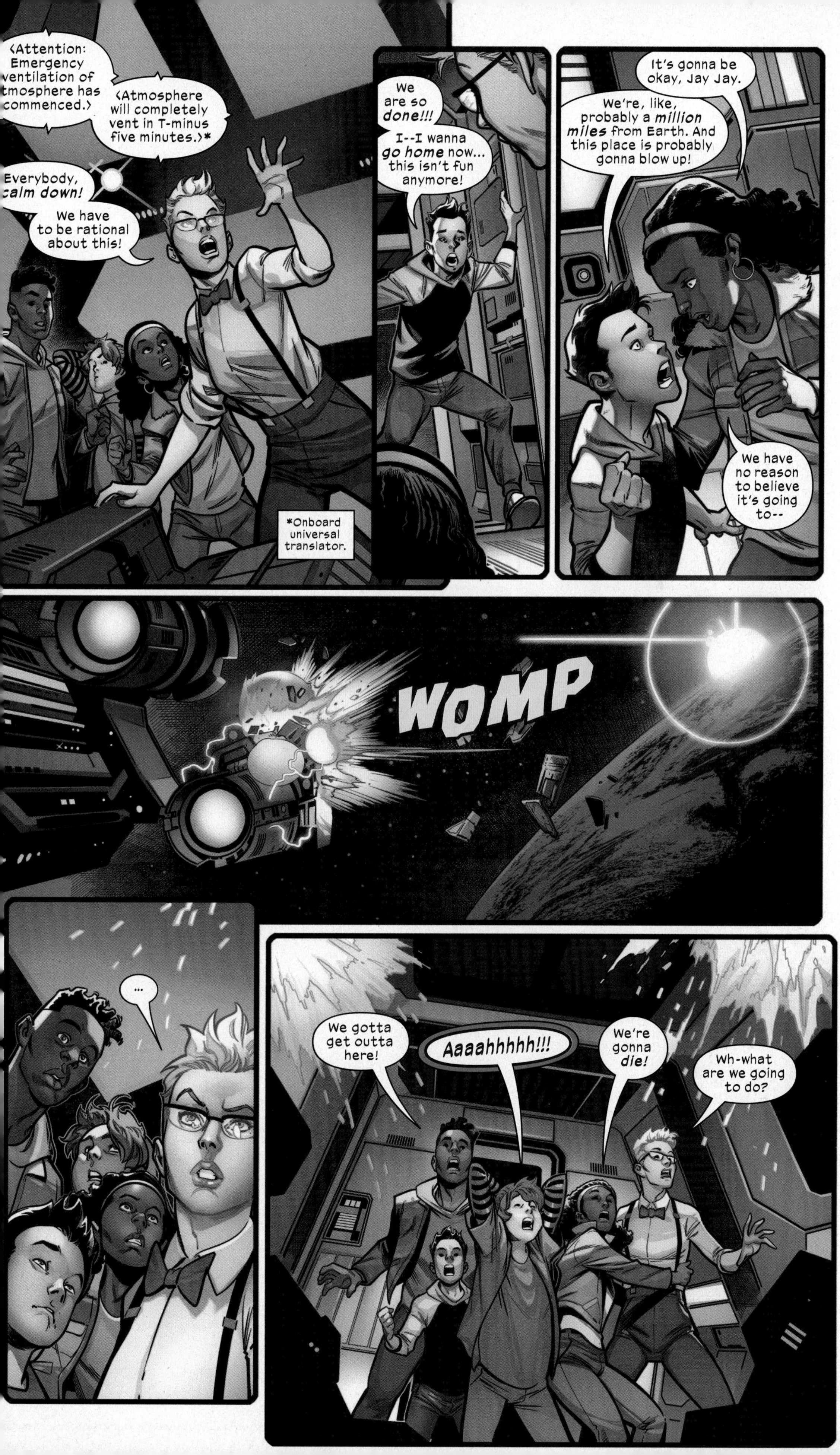

‹Attention: Emergency ventilation of atmosphere has commenced.›
‹Atmosphere will completely vent in T-minus five minutes.›*
Everybody, calm down!
We have to be rational about this!
*Onboard universal translator.
We are so done!!!
I--I wanna go home now... this isn't fun anymore!
It's gonna be okay, Jay Jay.
We're, like, probably a million miles from Earth. And this place is probably gonna blow up!
We have no reason to believe it's going to--
WOMP
...
We gotta get outta here!
Aaaahhhhh!!!
We're gonna die!
Wh-what are we going to do?

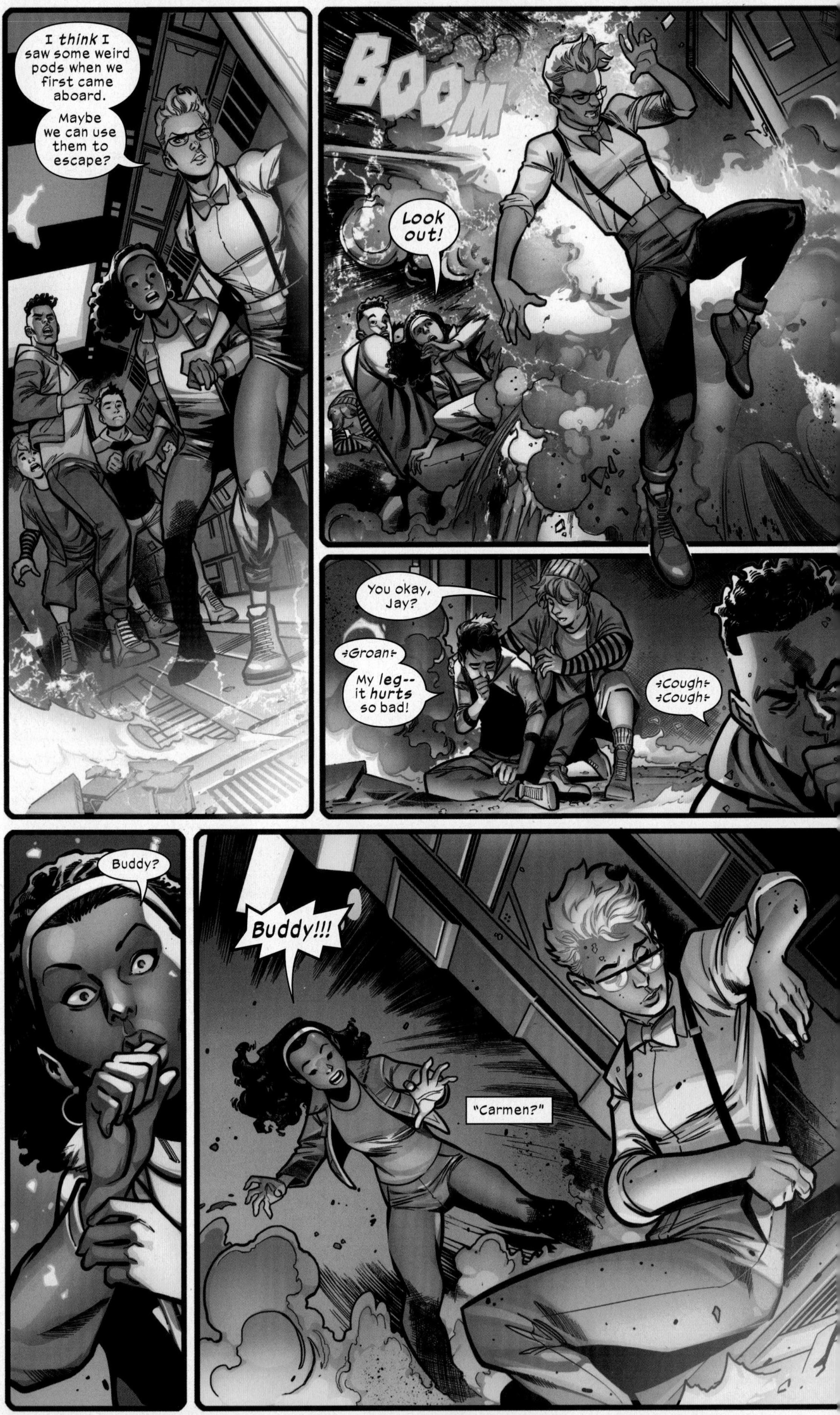
I think I saw some weird pods when we first came aboard.
Maybe we can use them to escape?
BOOM
Look out!
You okay, Jay?
-Groan-
My leg-- it hurts so bad!
-Cough- -Cough-
Buddy?
Buddy!!!
"Carmen?"

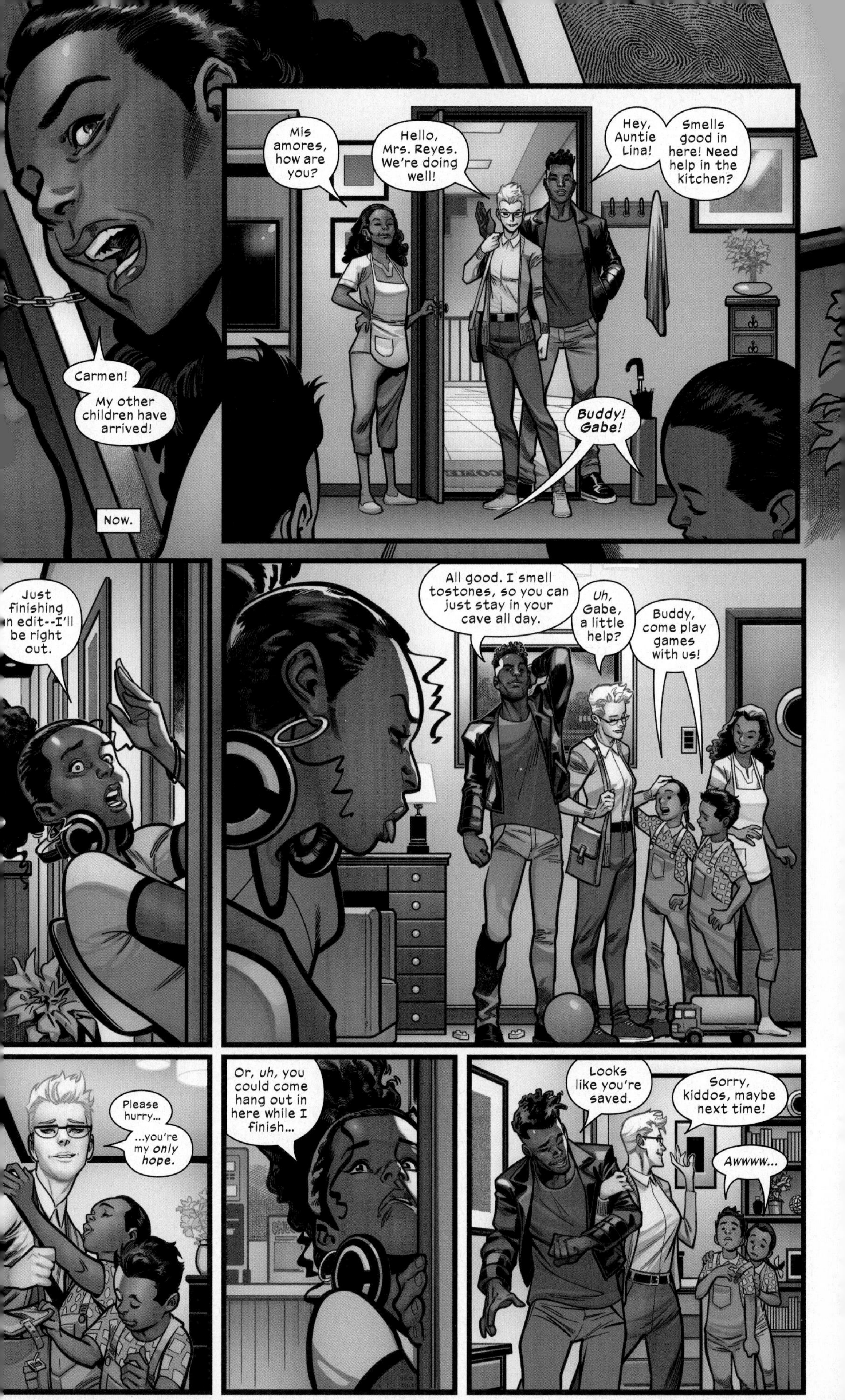
Mis amores, how are you?
Hello, Mrs. Reyes. We're doing well!
Hey, Auntie Lina!
Smells good in here! Need help in the kitchen?
Carmen!
My other children have arrived!
Buddy! Gabe!
Now.
Just finishing n edit--I'll be right out.
All good. I smell tostones, so you can just stay in your cave all day.
Uh, Gabe, a little help?
Buddy, come play games with us!
Please hurry...
...you're my only hope.
Or, uh, you could come hang out in here while I finish...
Looks like you're saved.
Sorry, kiddos, maybe next time!
Awwww...

FEINTLY FROSTED STITCHES UPDATE

DETAILS AND ACCENTS

I've gotten a bunch of comments praising (thank you!!!) the accents on some of my more recent pieces and asking all kinds of questions about my process.

I decided to do a live Q and A on my stream and break down my thinking on the issue. Check out the video.

I think something that isn't discussed enough in conversations about cosplay -- and making your own clothes from patterns in general -- is that the details that make a piece unique are what makes a piece shine.

*** TO BE CLEAR: There is NOTHING wrong with replicating things exactly or with wanting something to be exactly like the original! ***

BUT, that being said, I see a lot of y'all talking about reproducing things exactly -- how that's what makes a piece valid. And while that works for some people, I think the strength of DIY is that makers put themselves in their work! The little details and accents that speak to you? That set your piece apart? That's what makes it special!

The reason I got into this wasn't just because learning to repair and repurpose old clothes is cheaper than buying (though that is important) or because I wanted to make money (I wish!!!), but also because sewing and cosplay give people a place to express themselves and to play. Sometimes this is the only way folks can be completely open -- to be themselves -- and I want to encourage that!

SO! I hope that anyone reading this who may have been nervous to put themselves into their work gets a boost in confidence. You are what makes your work special! Celebrate that!

And to folks who were asking what my next pattern is/ when I'm dropping it, watch this space!

[Hint: Drip worthy of a queen! :3]

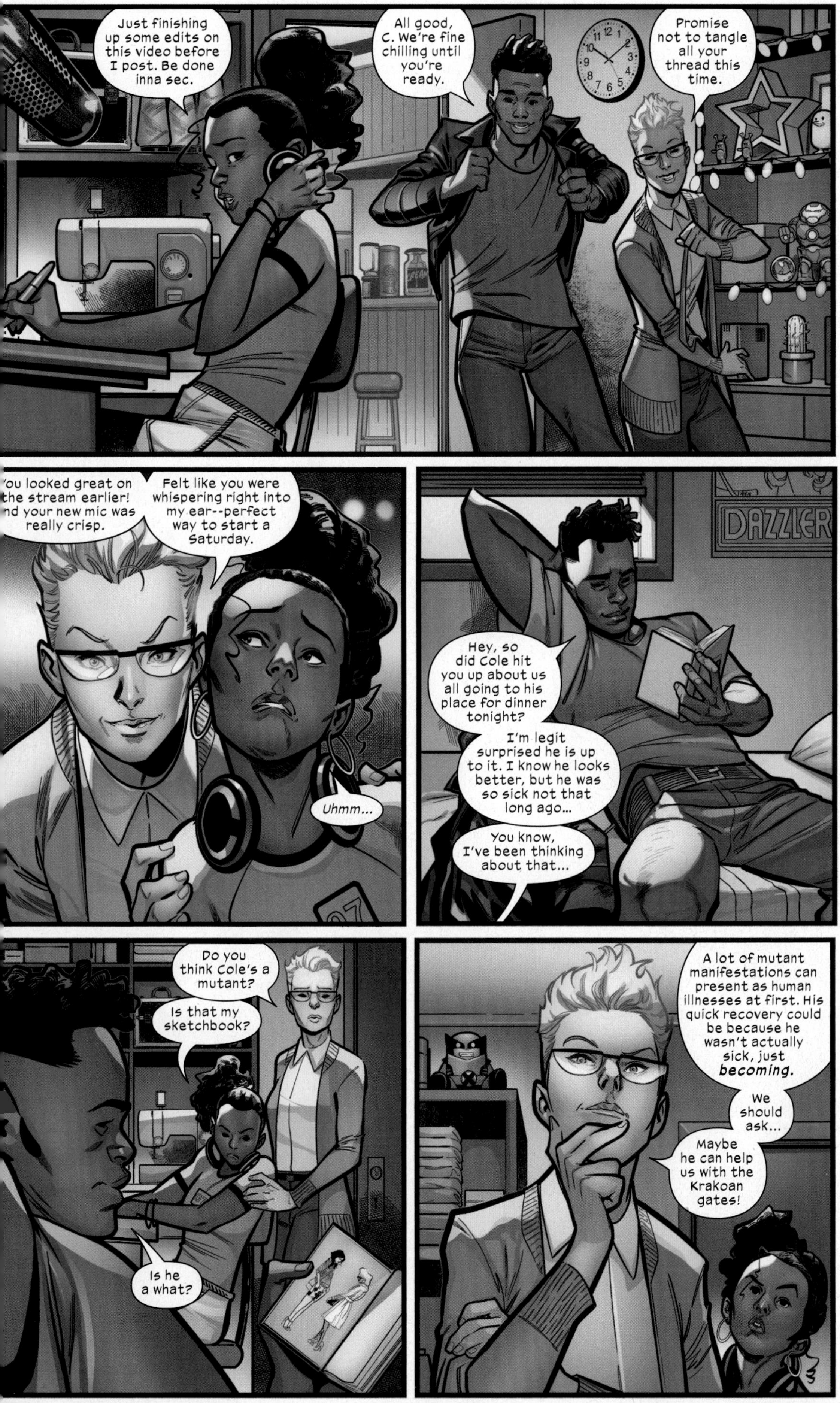
Just finishing up some edits on this video before I post. Be done inna sec.
All good, C. We're fine chilling until you're ready.
Promise not to tangle all your thread this time.
You looked great on the stream earlier! And your new mic was really crisp.
Felt like you were whispering right into my ear--perfect way to start a Saturday.
Uhmm...
DAZZLER
Hey, so did Cole hit you up about us all going to his place for dinner tonight?
I'm legit surprised he is up to it. I know he looks better, but he was so sick not that long ago...
You know, I've been thinking about that...
Do you think Cole's a mutant?
Is that my sketchbook?
Is he a what?
A lot of mutant manifestations can present as human illnesses at first. His quick recovery could be because he wasn't actually sick, just *becoming.*
We should ask...
Maybe he can help us with the Krakoan gates!

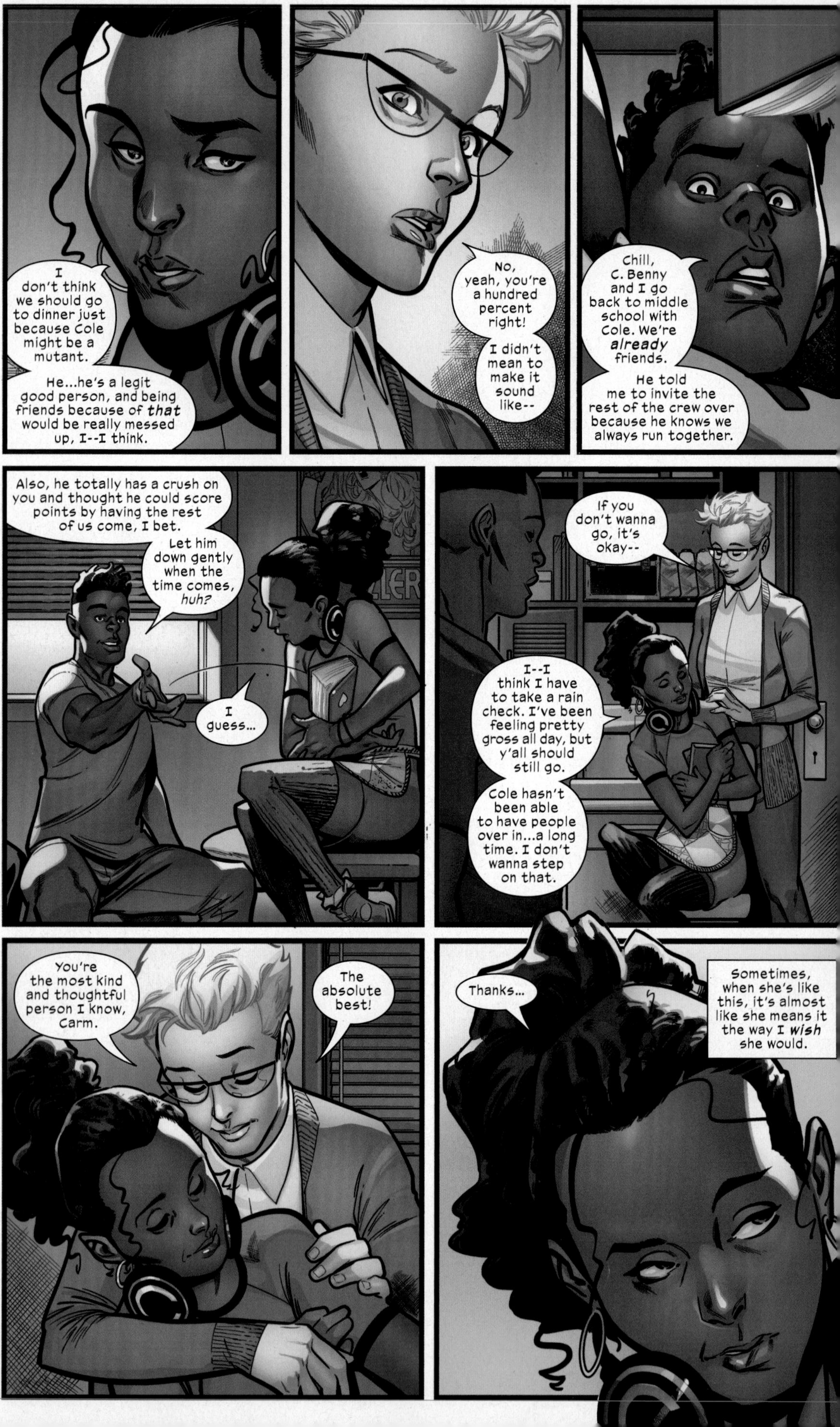

I don't think we should go to dinner just because Cole might be a mutant.
He...he's a legit good person, and being friends because of *that* would be really messed up, I--I think.
No, yeah, you're a hundred percent right!
I didn't mean to make it sound like--
Chill, C. Benny and I go back to middle school with Cole. We're *already* friends.
He told me to invite the rest of the crew over because he knows we always run together.
Also, he totally has a crush on you and thought he could score points by having the rest of us come, I bet.
Let him down gently when the time comes, *huh?*
I guess...
If you don't wanna go, it's okay--
I--I think I have to take a rain check. I've been feeling pretty gross all day, but y'all should still go.
Cole hasn't been able to have people over in...a long time. I don't wanna step on that.
You're the most kind and thoughtful person I know, Carm.
The absolute best!
Thanks...
Sometimes, when she's like this, it's almost like she means it the way I *wish* she would.

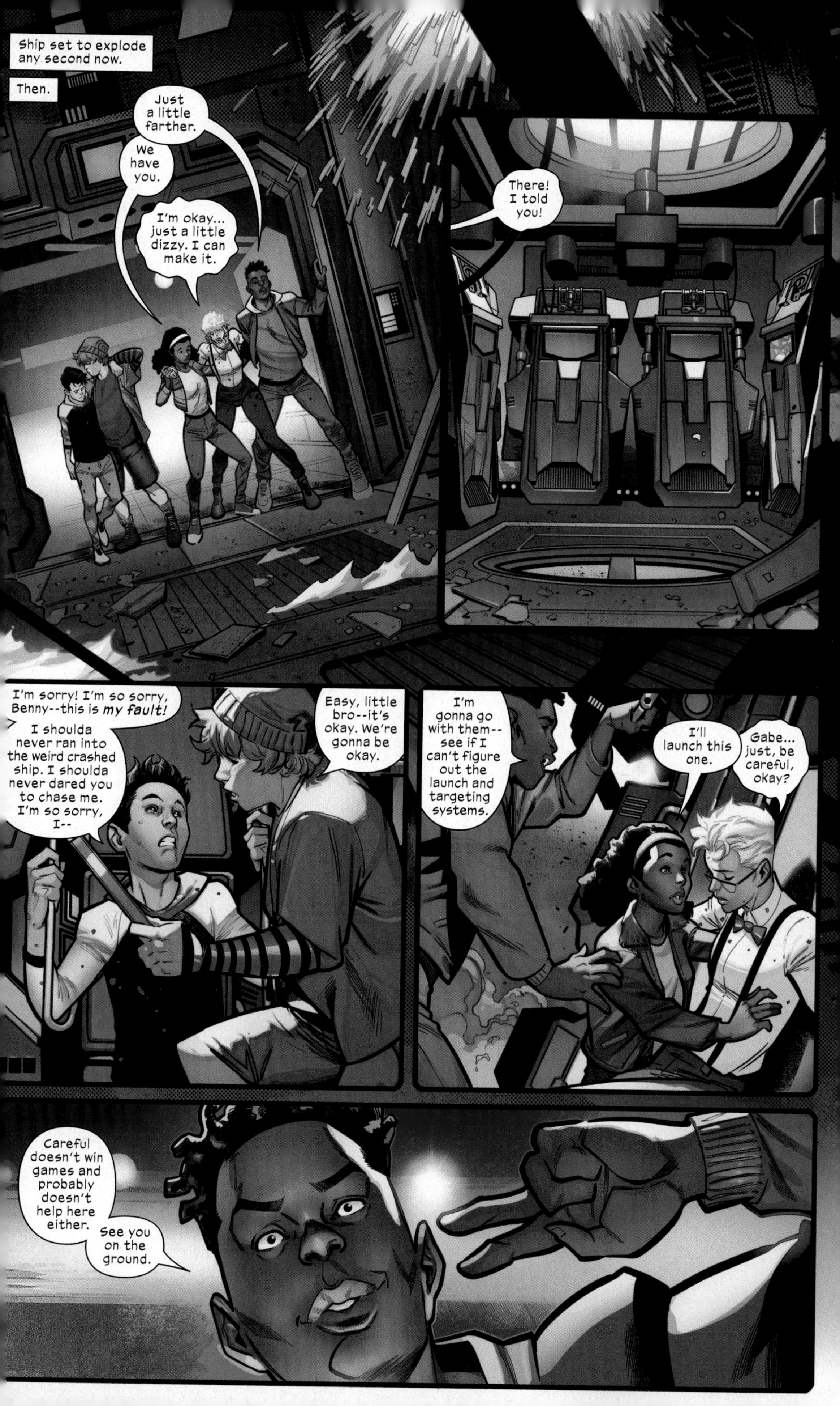
Ship set to explode any second now.
Then.
Just a little farther.
We have you.
I'm okay... just a little dizzy. I can make it.
There! I told you!
I'm sorry! I'm so sorry, Benny--this is *my fault!*
I shoulda never ran into the weird crashed ship. I shoulda never dared you to chase me. I'm so sorry, I--
Easy, little bro--it's okay. We're gonna be okay.
I'm gonna go with them--see if I can't figure out the launch and targeting systems.
I'll launch this one.
Gabe... just, be careful, okay?
Careful doesn't win games and probably doesn't help here either.
See you on the ground.

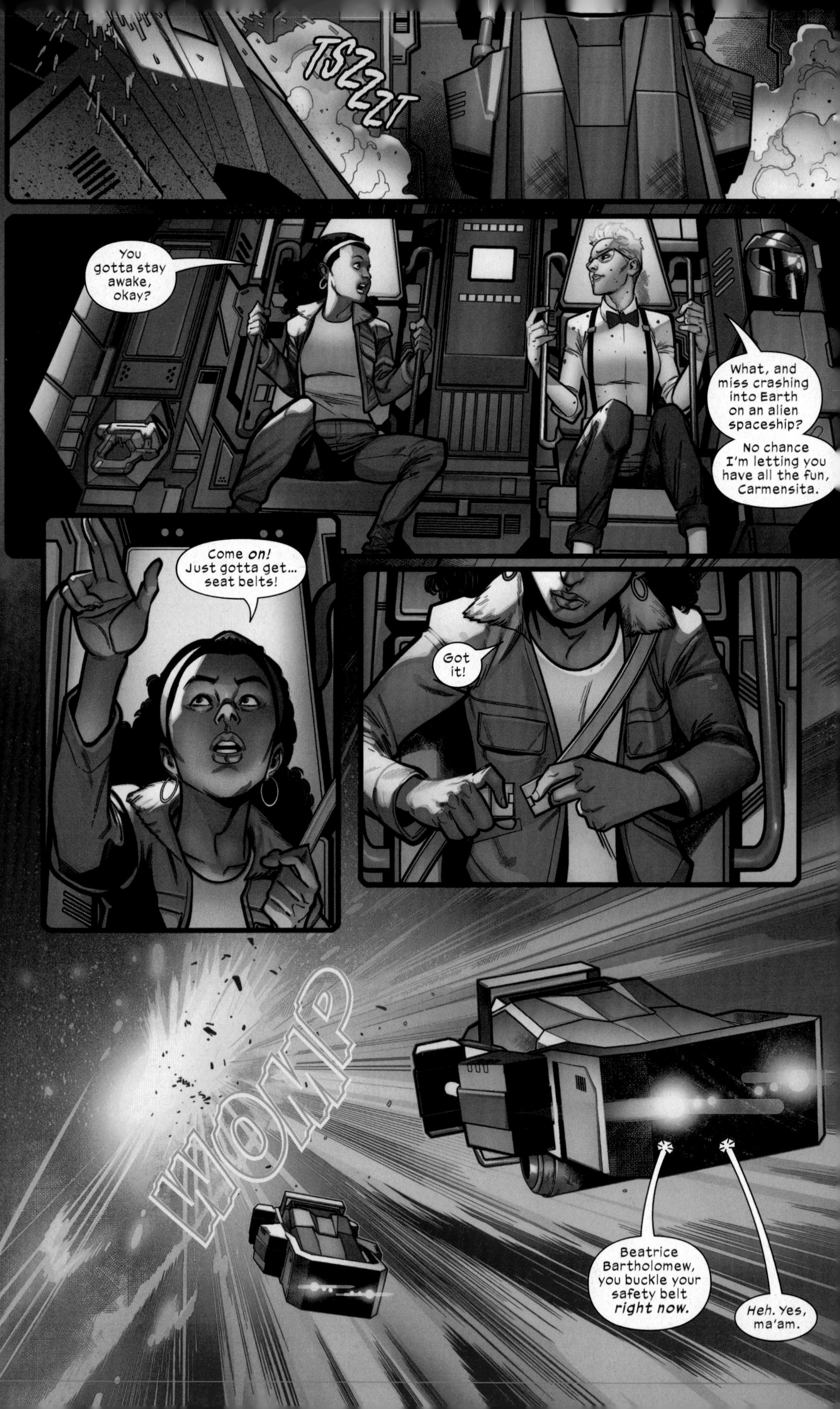
TSZZZT
You gotta stay awake, okay?
What, and miss crashing into Earth on an alien spaceship?
No chance I'm letting you have all the fun, Carmensita.
Come *on!* Just gotta get... seat belts!
Got it!
WOMP
Beatrice Bartholomew, you buckle your safety belt ***right now.***
Heh. Yes, ma'am.

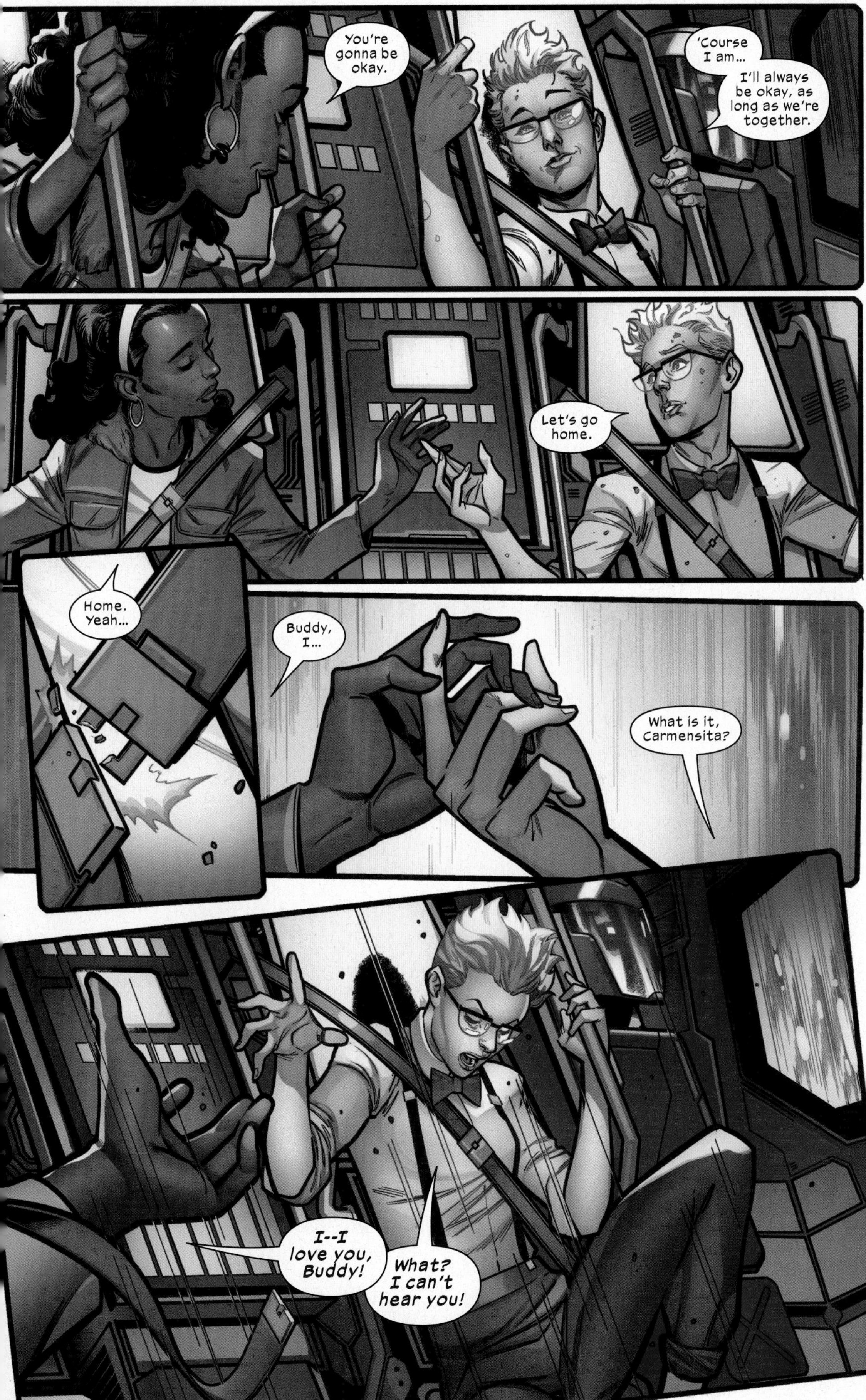
You're gonna be okay.
'Course I am...
I'll always be okay, as long as we're together.
Let's go home.
Home. Yeah...
Buddy, I...
What is it, Carmensita?
I--I love you, Buddy!
What? I can't hear you!

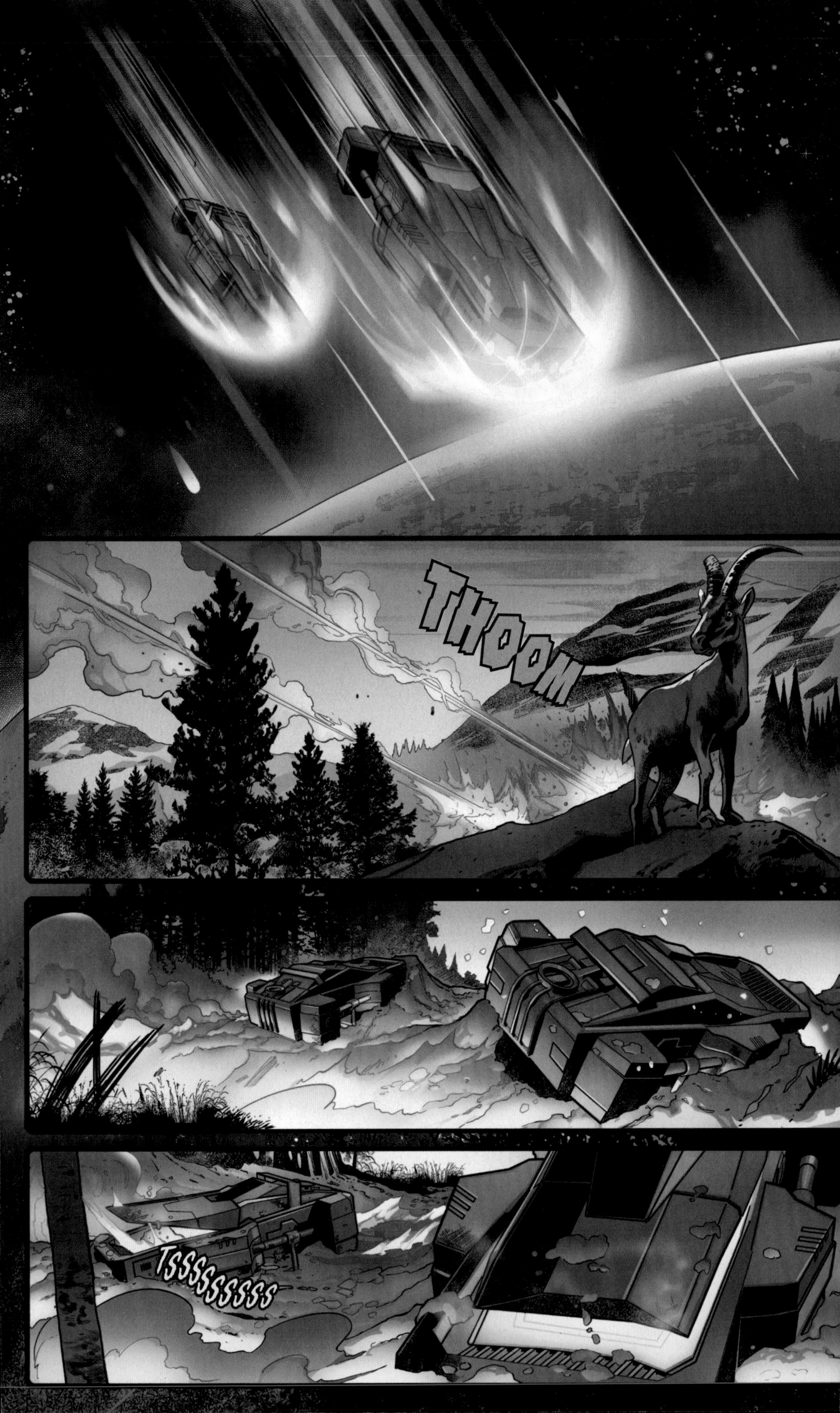
THOOM
TSSSSSSSSSS

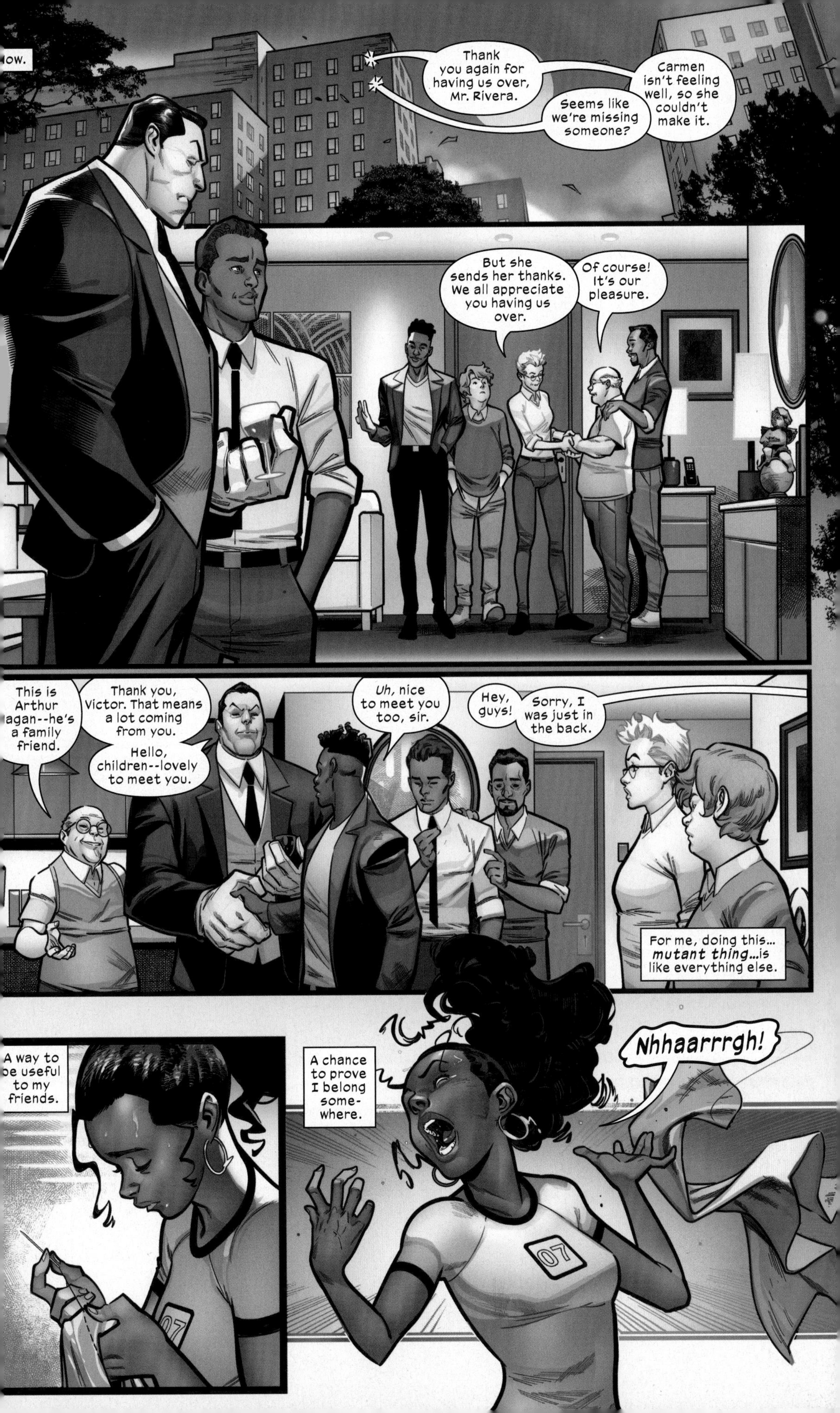

ow.
Thank you again for having us over, Mr. Rivera.
Seems like we're missing someone?
Carmen isn't feeling well, so she couldn't make it.
But she sends her thanks. We all appreciate you having us over.
Of course! It's our pleasure.
This is Arthur agan--he's a family friend.
Thank you, Victor. That means a lot coming from you.
Hello, children--lovely to meet you.
Uh, nice to meet you too, sir.
Hey, guys!
Sorry, I was just in the back.
For me, doing this... *mutant thing*...is like everything else.
A way to oe useful to my friends.
A chance to prove I belong some-where.
Nhhaarrrgh!
07
07

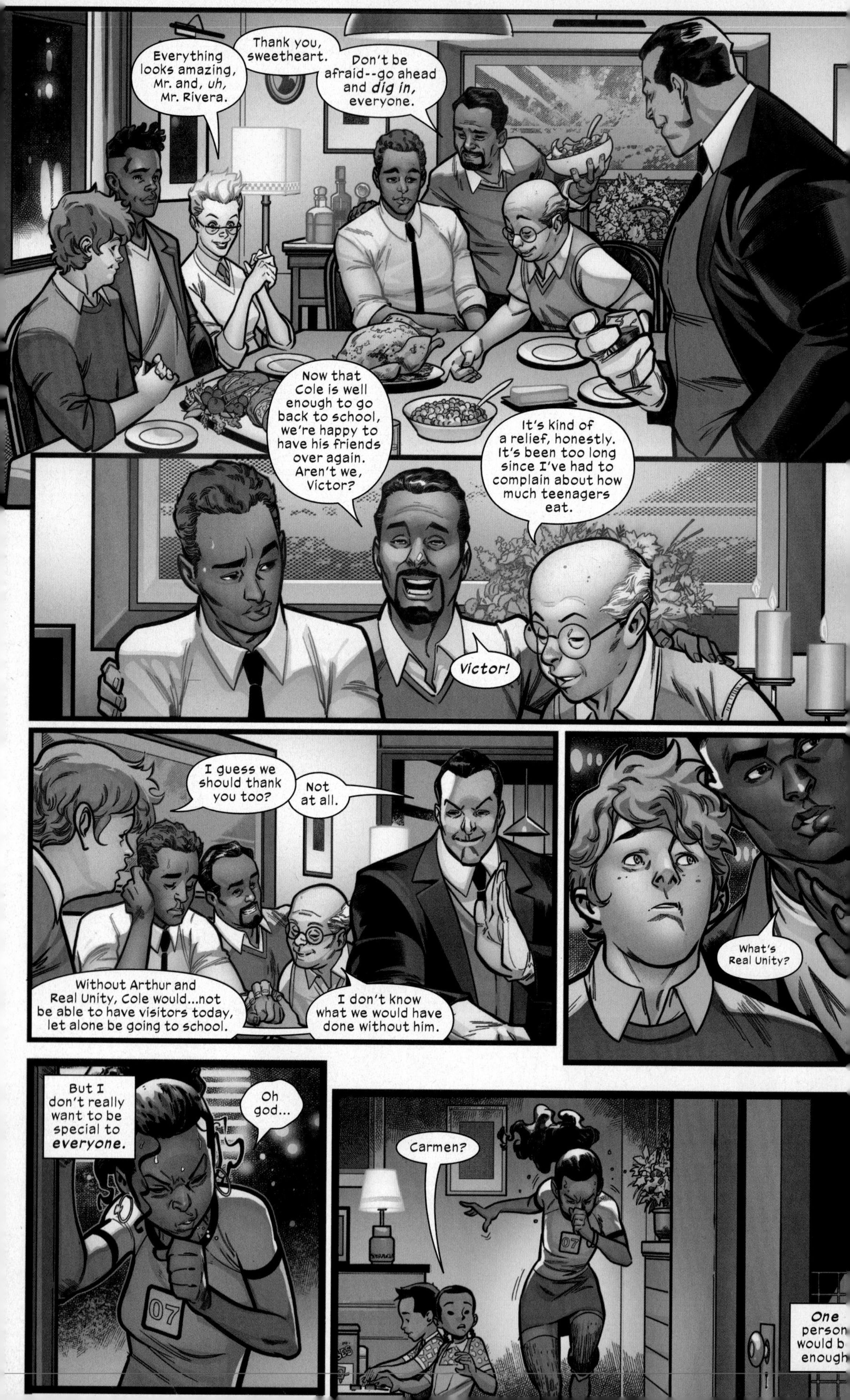

Everything looks amazing, Mr. and, *uh*, Mr. Rivera.
Thank you, sweetheart.
Don't be afraid--go ahead and *dig in*, everyone.
Now that Cole is well enough to go back to school, we're happy to have his friends over again. Aren't we, Victor?
It's kind of a relief, honestly. It's been too long since I've had to complain about how much teenagers eat.
Victor!
I guess we should thank you too?
Not at all.
Without Arthur and Real Unity, Cole would...not be able to have visitors today, let alone be going to school.
I don't know what we would have done without him.
What's Real Unity?
But I don't really want to be special to *everyone*.
Oh god...
Carmen?
One person would b enough

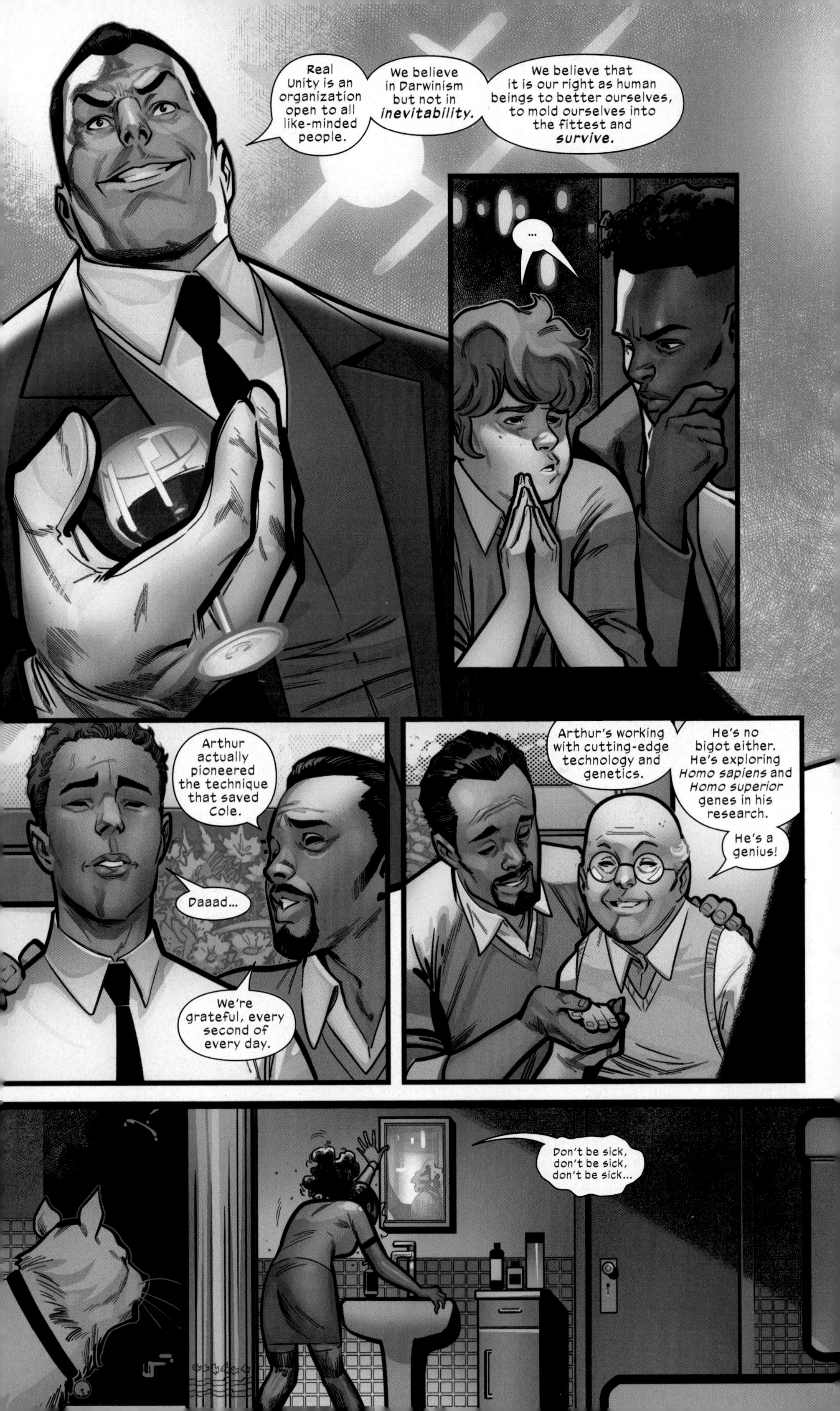

Real Unity is an organization open to all like-minded people.
We believe in Darwinism but not in *inevitability.*
We believe that it is our right as human beings to better ourselves, to mold ourselves into the fittest and *survive.*
...
Arthur actually pioneered the technique that saved Cole.
Daaad...
We're grateful, every second of every day.
Arthur's working with cutting-edge technology and genetics.
He's no bigot either. He's exploring *Homo sapiens* and *Homo superior* genes in his research.
He's a genius!
Don't be sick, don't be sick, don't be sick...

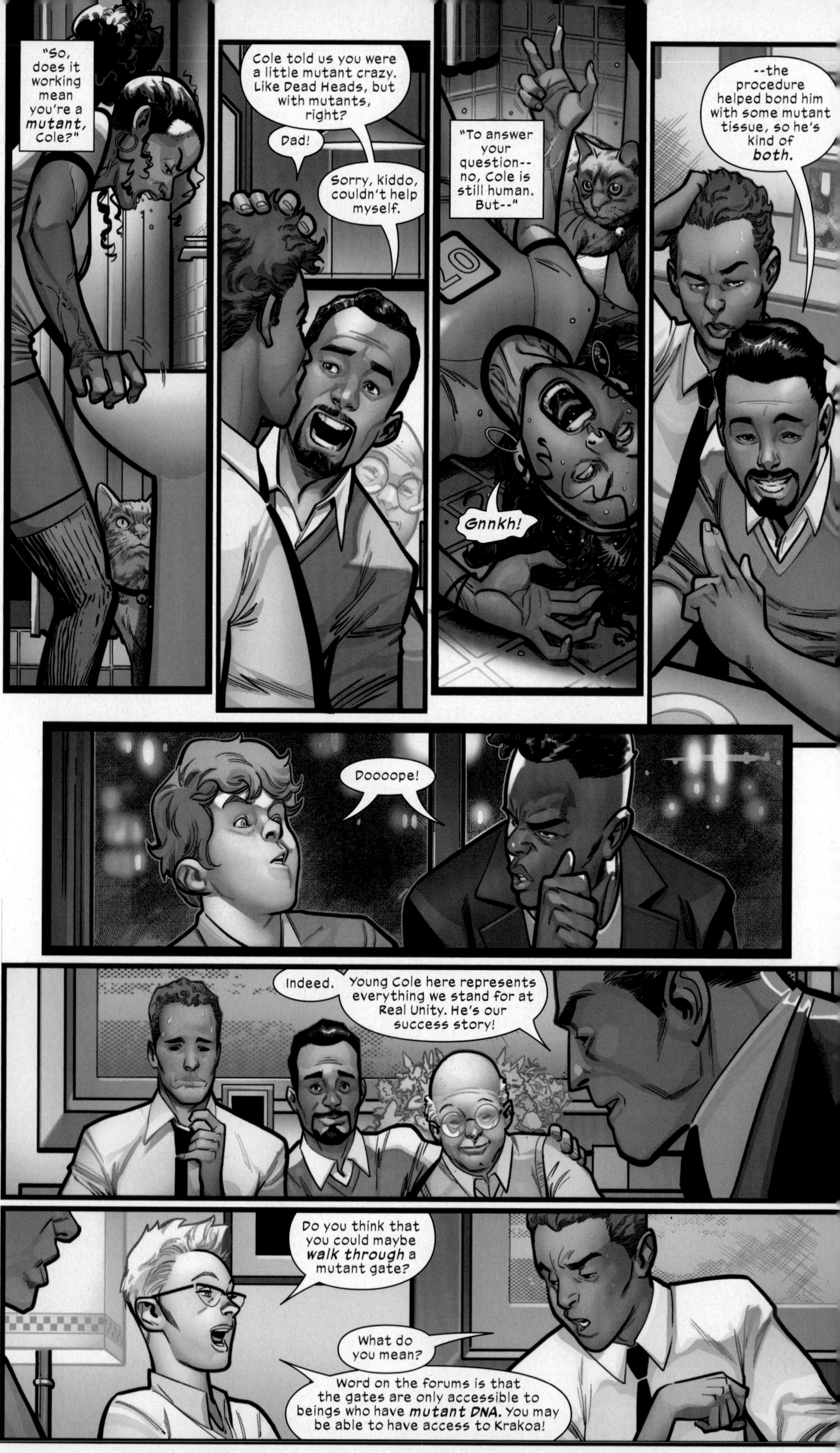
"So, does it working mean you're a *mutant,* Cole?"
Cole told us you were a little mutant crazy. Like Dead Heads, but with mutants, right?
Dad!
Sorry, kiddo, couldn't help myself.
"To answer your question--no, Cole is still human. But--"
Gnnkh!
--the procedure helped bond him with some mutant tissue, so he's kind of *both.*
Doooope!
Indeed.
Young Cole here represents everything we stand for at Real Unity. He's our success story!
Do you think that you could maybe *walk through* a mutant gate?
What do you mean?
Word on the forums is that the gates are only accessible to beings who have *mutant DNA.* You may be able to have access to Krakoa!

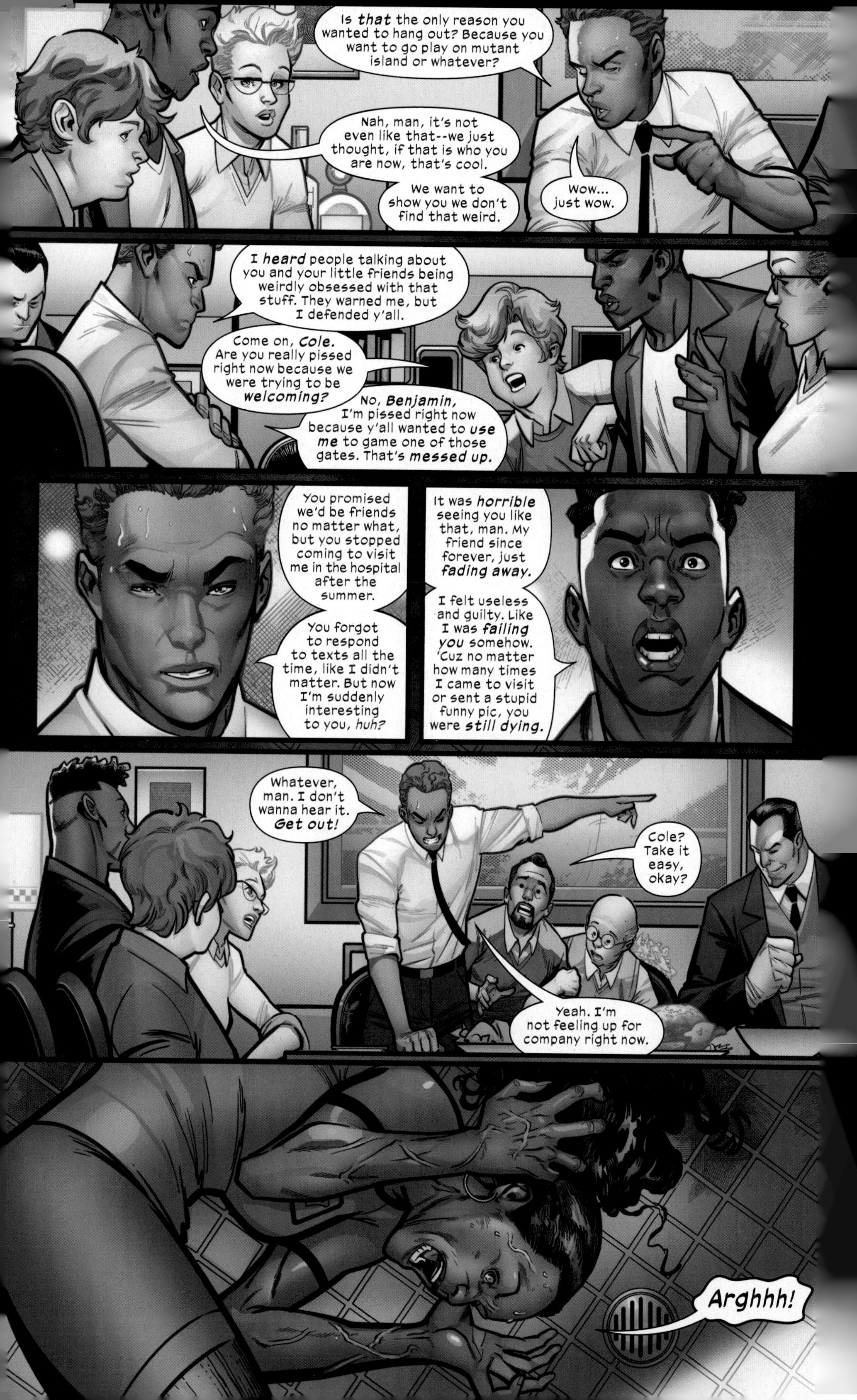
Is *that* the only reason you wanted to hang out? Because you want to go play on mutant island or whatever?
Nah, man, it's not even like that--we just thought, if that is who you are now, that's cool.
We want to show you we don't find that weird.
Wow... just wow.
I *heard* people talking about you and your little friends being weirdly obsessed with that stuff. They warned me, but I defended y'all.
Come on, *Cole.* Are you really pissed right now because we were trying to be *welcoming?*
No, *Benjamin,* I'm pissed right now because y'all wanted to *use me* to game one of those gates. That's *messed up.*
You promised we'd be friends no matter what, but you stopped coming to visit me in the hospital after the summer.
You forgot to respond to texts all the time, like I didn't matter. But now I'm suddenly interesting to you, *huh?*
It was *horrible* seeing you like that, man. My friend since forever, just *fading away.*
I felt useless and guilty. Like I was *failing you* somehow. 'Cuz no matter how many times I came to visit or sent a stupid funny pic, you were *still dying.*
Whatever, man. I don't wanna hear it. *Get out!*
Cole? Take it easy, okay?
Yeah. I'm not feeling up for company right now.
Arghhh!

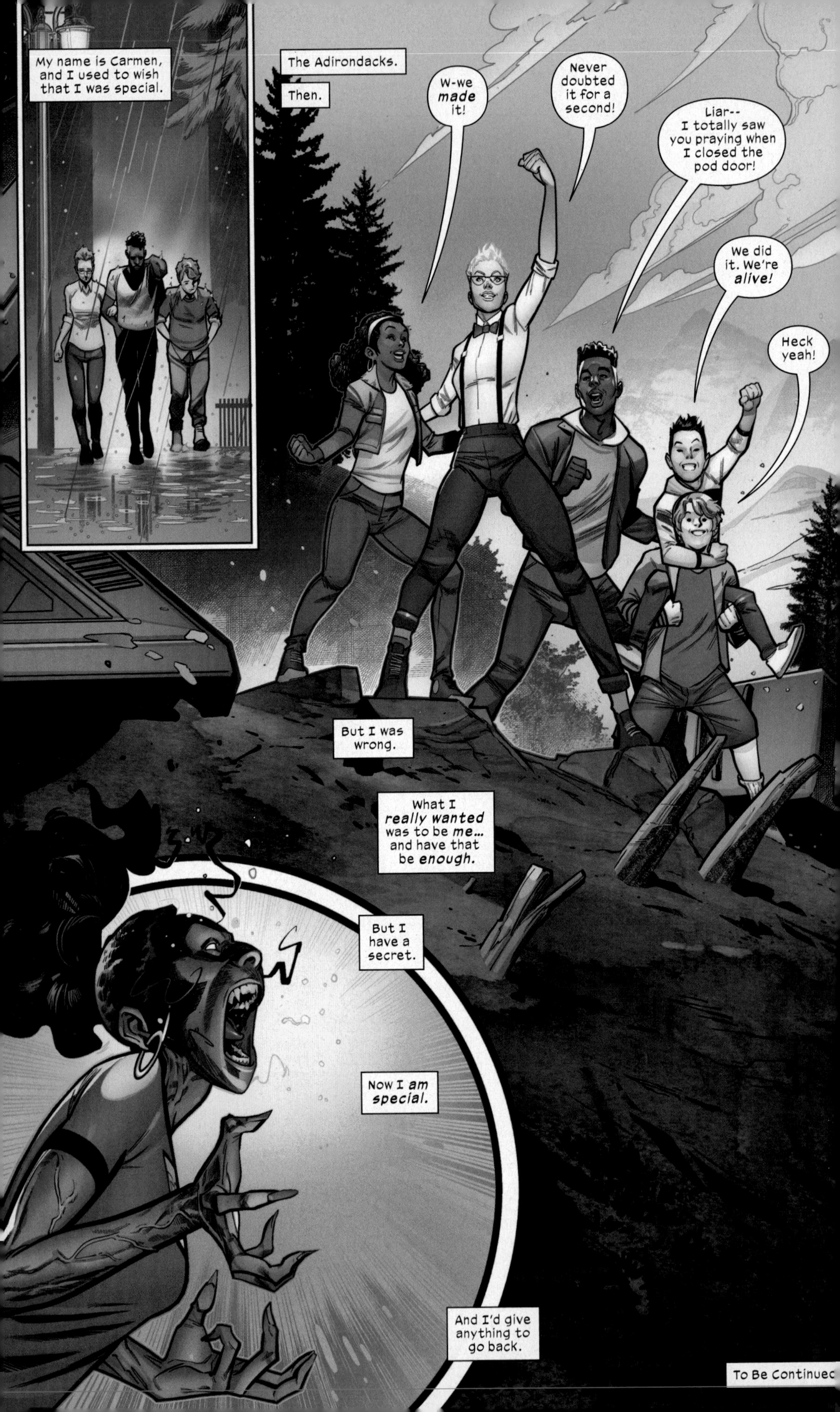

My name is Carmen, and I used to wish that I was special.
The Adirondacks.
Then.
W-we *made* it!
Never doubted it for a second!
Liar-- I totally saw you praying when I closed the pod door!
We did it. We're *alive!*
Heck yeah!
But I was wrong.
What I *really wanted* was to be *me*... and have that be *enough.*
But I have a secret.
Now I *am special.*
And I'd give anything to go back.
To Be Continuec

[reign_of_x]

[kra_]
[koa_]

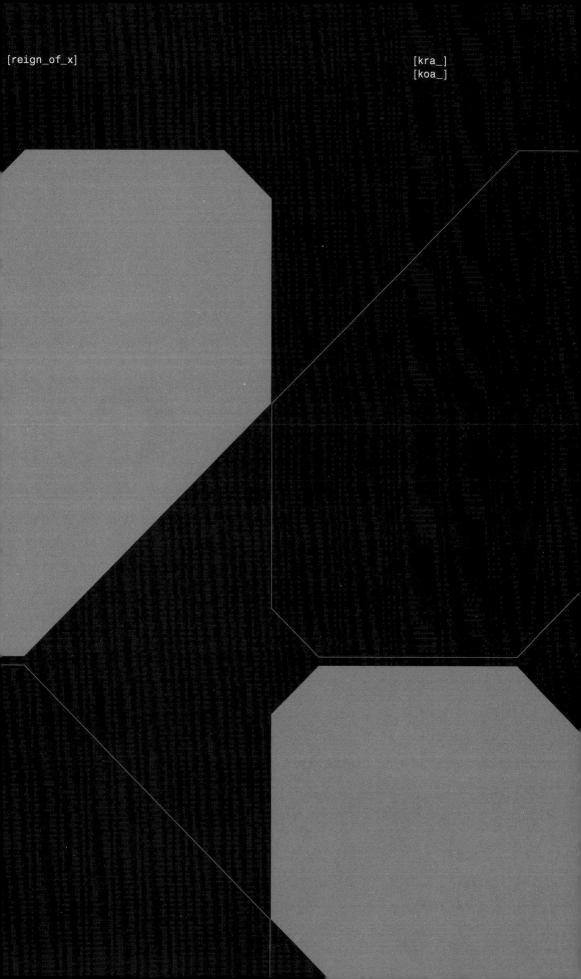

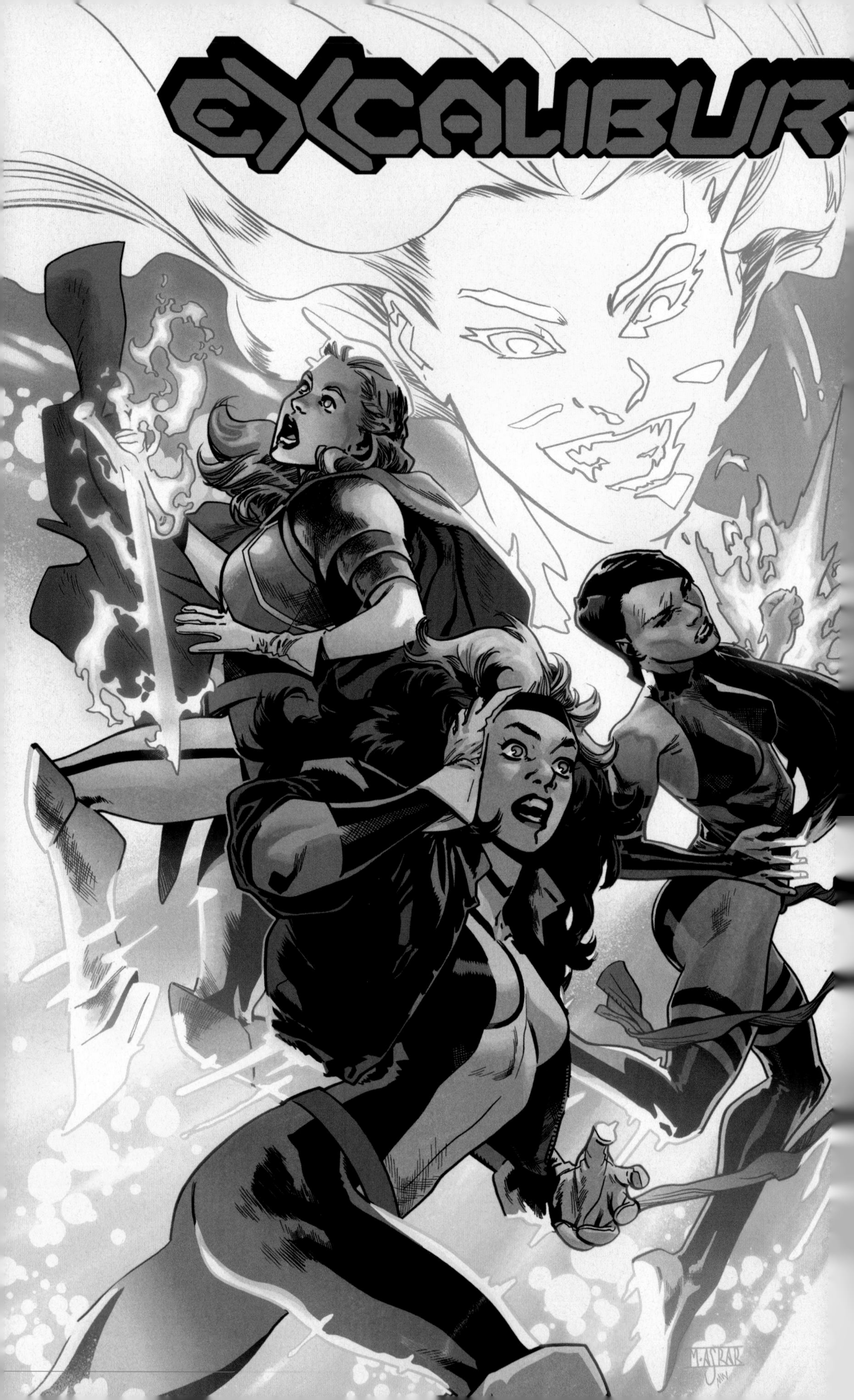
EXCALIBUR

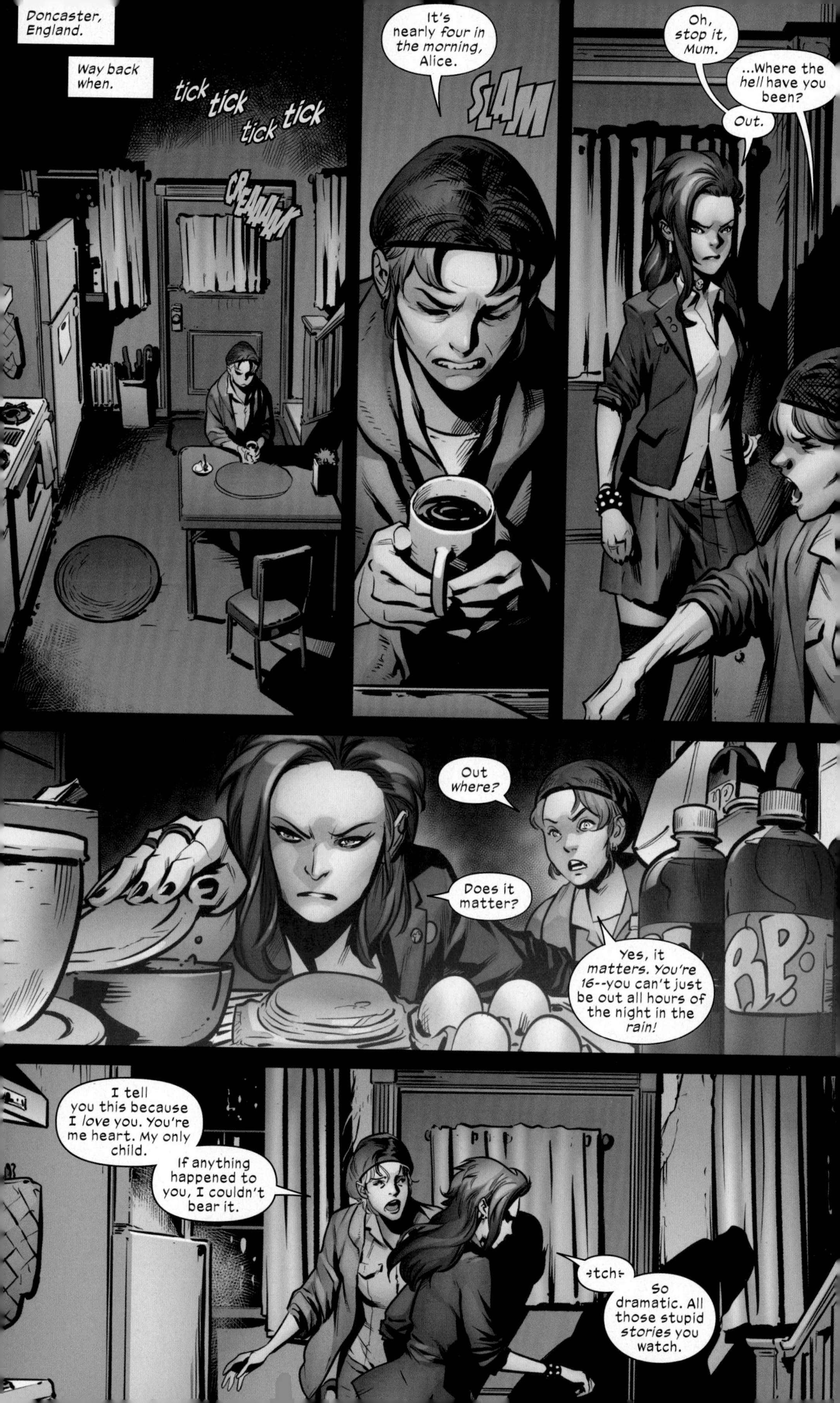

Doncaster, England.
Way back when.
tick tick tick tick
CREAAAAK
It's nearly four in the morning, Alice.
SLAM
Oh, stop it, Mum.
...Where the hell have you been?
Out.
Out where?
Does it matter?
Yes, it matters. You're 16--you can't just be out all hours of the night in the rain!
I tell you this because I love you. You're me heart. My only child.
If anything happened to you, I couldn't bear it.
-tch-
So dramatic. All those stupid stories you watch.

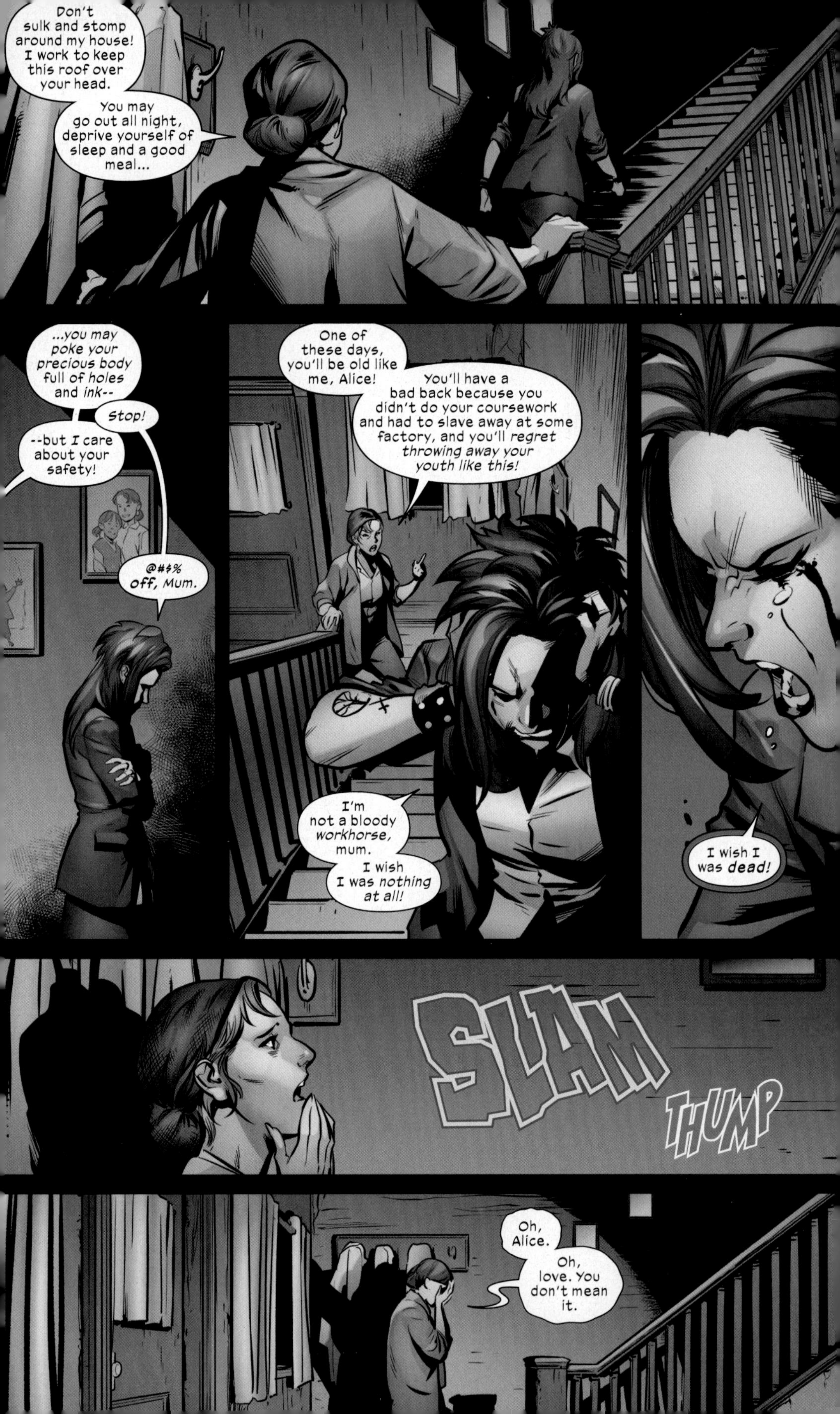
Don't sulk and stomp around my house! I work to keep this roof over your head.
You may go out all night, deprive yourself of sleep and a good meal...
...you may poke your precious body full of holes and ink--
Stop!
--but I care about your safety!
@#$% off, Mum.
One of these days, you'll be old like me, Alice!
You'll have a bad back because you didn't do your coursework and had to slave away at some factory, and you'll regret throwing away your youth like this!
I'm not a bloody workhorse, mum.
I wish I was nothing at all!
I wish I was dead!
SLAM
THUMP
Oh, Alice.
Oh, love. You don't mean it.

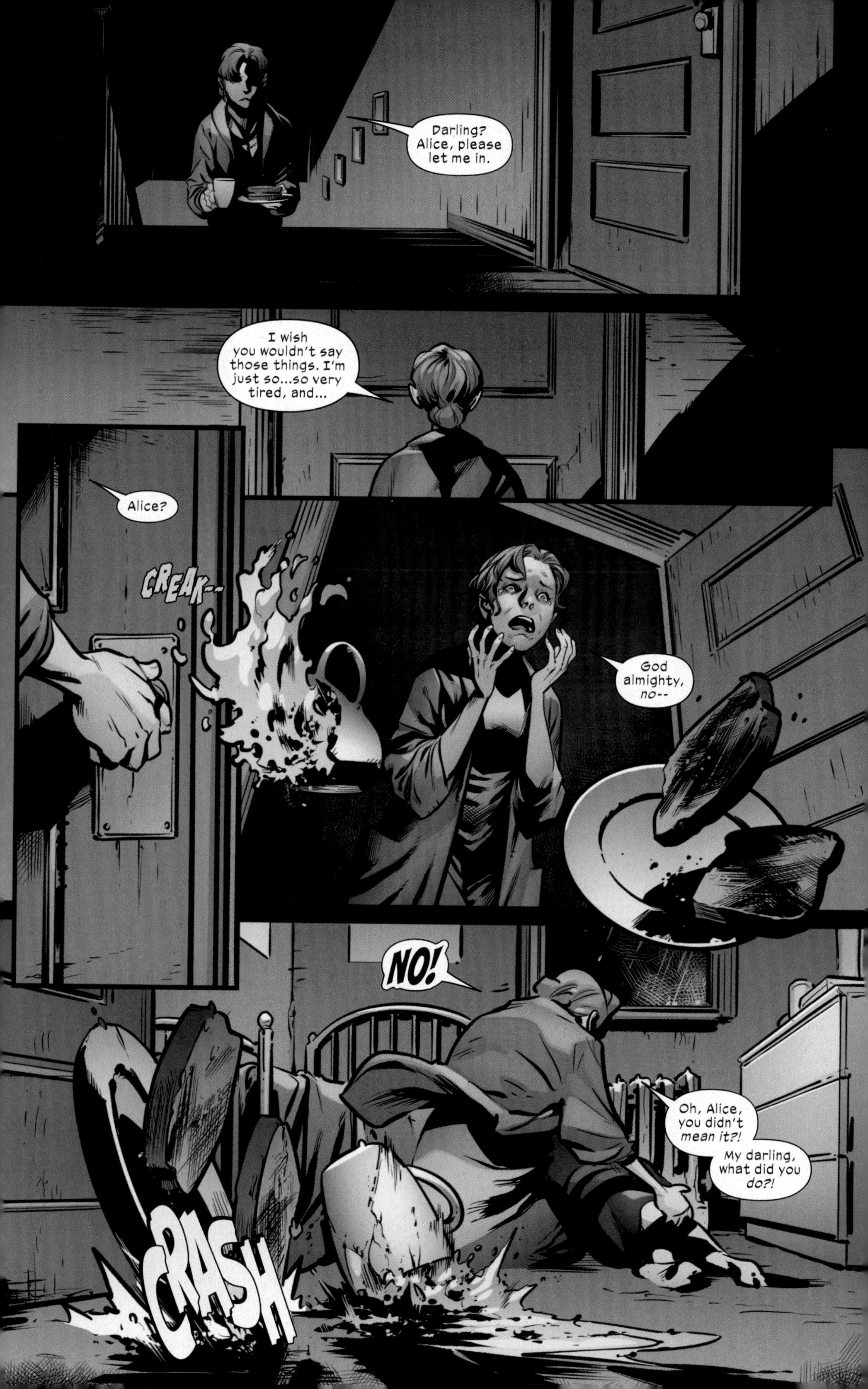
Darling? Alice, please let me in.
I wish you wouldn't say those things. I'm just so...so very tired, and...
Alice?
CREAK--
God almighty, no--
NO!
Oh, Alice, you didn't mean it?!
My darling, what did you do?!
CRASH

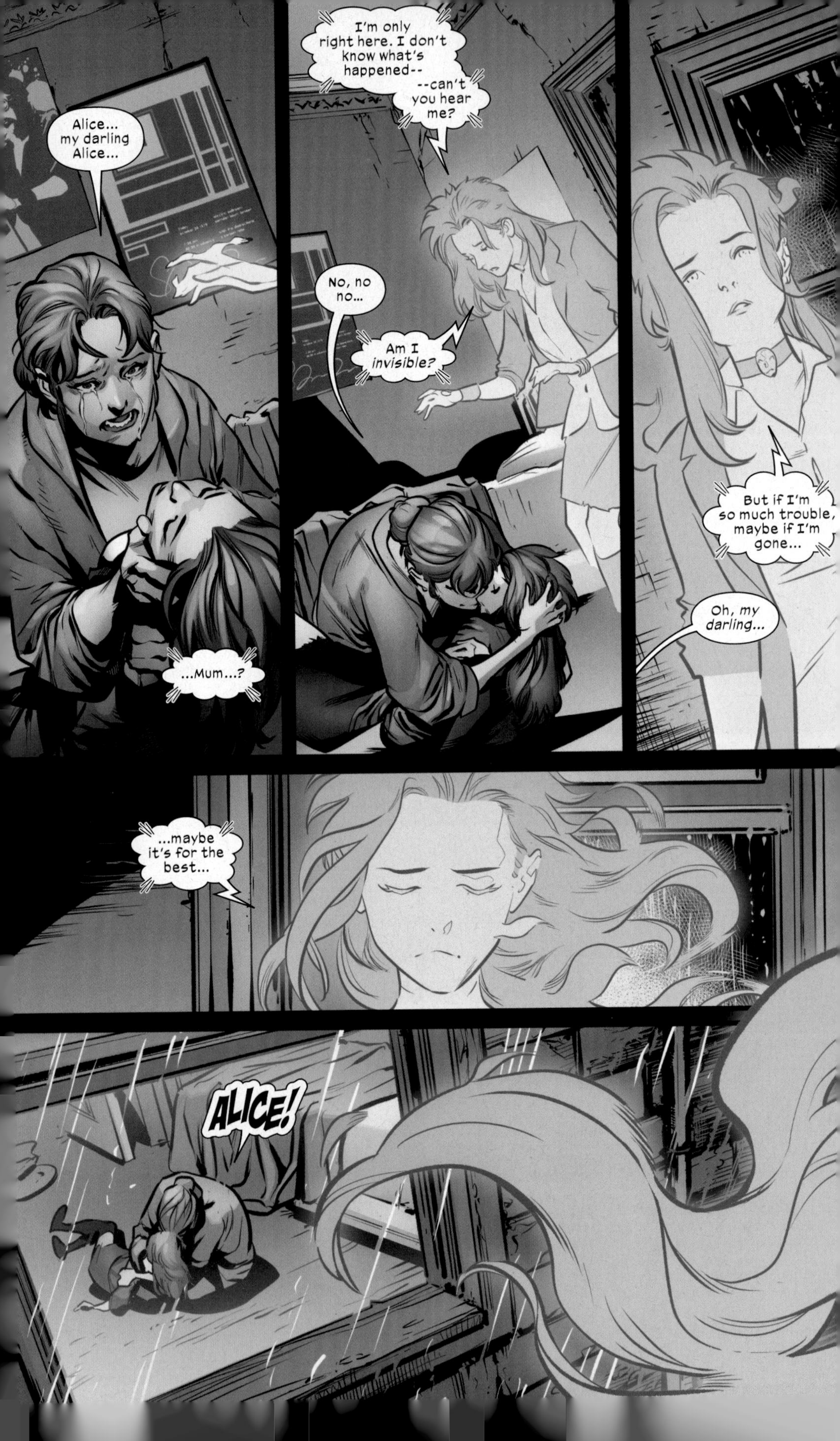
Alice... my darling Alice...
...Mum...?
I'm only right here. I don't know what's happened--
--can't you hear me?
No, no no...
Am I *invisible?*
But if I'm so much trouble, maybe if I'm gone...
Oh, my darling...
...maybe it's for the best...
ALICE!

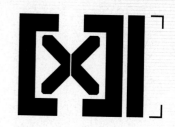

MALICE (ALICE MacALLISTER)

ORIGIN: DONCASTER, ENGLAND

KNOWN AFFILIATIONS: Marauders, Nathaniel Essex (past)

MUTANT ABILITIES: Malice has heretofore been observed as a sentient being of pure psychic energy, only able to manifest corporeally via physical possession. Her origins are unknown, but it is believed if she ever had a body, she has been detached from it for a long time.

Her acts of possession are aggressive, suppressing the mind of the target completely in favor of Malice's control. She has historically used these possessions in harmful and violent ways, acting against other mutants.

Figure 1

Malice's previous targets report that she is resistant to typical psychic prying and elusive to their efforts. Current theories from her past targets seem to imply that Malice is not herself **psionic** -- her possession is not **_psychic_** but **"emotional,"** an unscientific term that may later prove incomplete. (See: _Astral projection._)

PREVIOUS TARGETS FOR MONITORING: Polaris, Storm, Wolverine, Rogue, Dazzler, others.

IDENTIFYING FACTORS: Malice's targets are known to be identifiable by a **necklace** (fig. 1) appearing on the throat of the target, but recent activity has proven that she has found ways to conceal the necklace on the body, such as removing and swallowing the item.

MALICIOUS INTENT

When Captain Britain went missing, EXCALIBUR leaped into action to find her -- and while they thought she was back...The thing inside Betsy's body was *not* her.

In fact, Betsy was being possessed by a mutant psychic entity called Malice...and now that Betsy's free, Malice is loose on Krakoa.

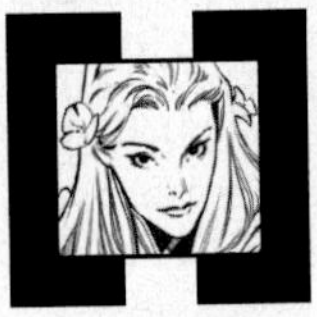

Captain Britain

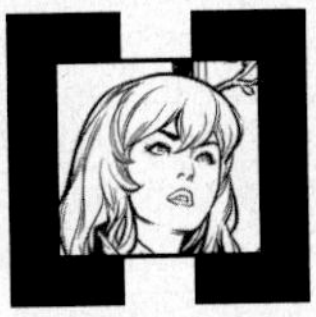

Rogue

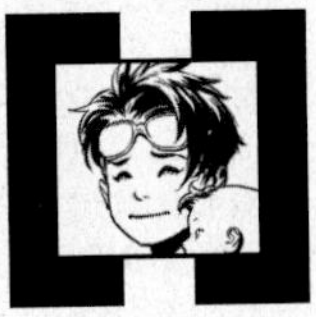

Jubilee

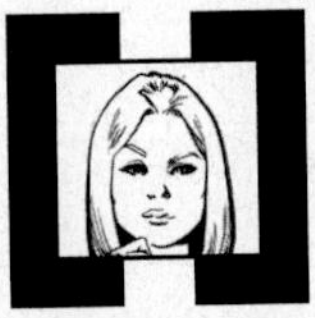

Emma Frost

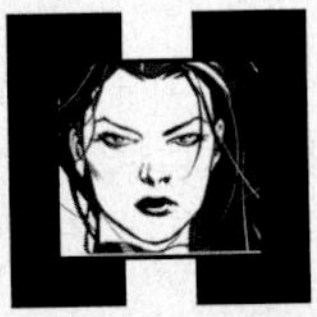

Psylocke

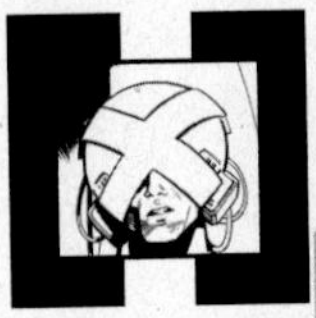

Charles Xavier

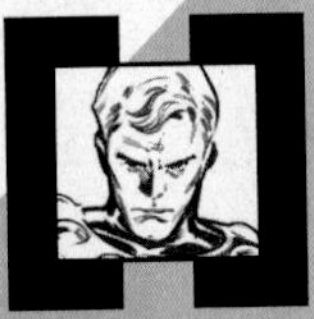

Magneto

[00_Reign]
[00___ofX]

EXCALIBUR [X_20]

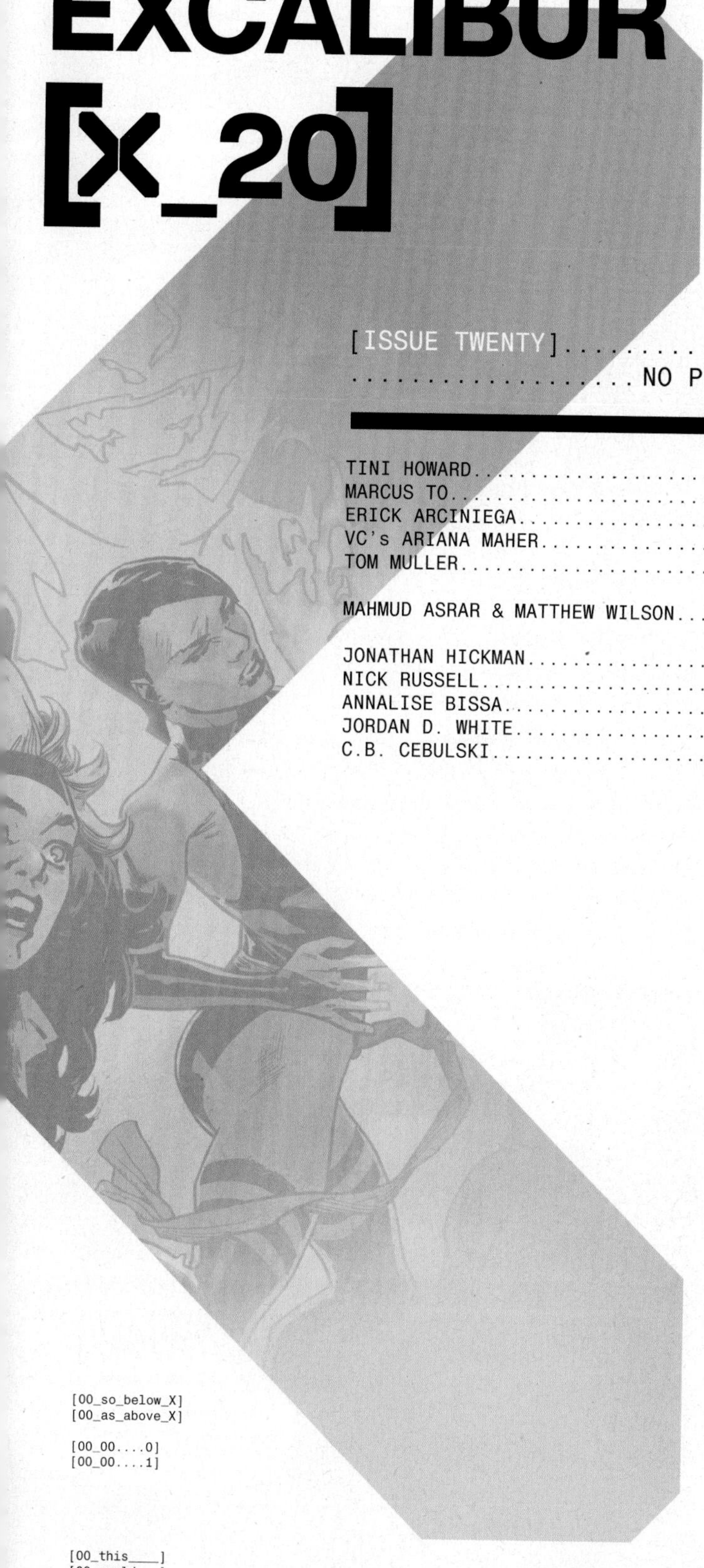

[ISSUE TWENTY].................................
.....................NO PITY FROM YOUR FRIENDS

TINI HOWARD..[WRITER]
MARCUS TO..[ARTIST]
ERICK ARCINIEGA.............................[COLOR ARTIST]
VC's ARIANA MAHER................................[LETTERER]
TOM MULLER...[DESIGN]

MAHMUD ASRAR & MATTHEW WILSON...............[COVER ARTISTS]

JONATHAN HICKMAN..................................[HEAD OF X]
NICK RUSSELL....................................[PRODUCTION]
ANNALISE BISSA............................[ASSOCIATE EDITOR]
JORDAN D. WHITE....................................[EDITOR]
C.B. CEBULSKI.............................[EDITOR IN CHIEF]

[00_so_below_X]
[00_as_above_X]

[00_00....0]
[00_00....1]

[00_this____]
[00_world___]

[00_and_the_]

[00___other_]

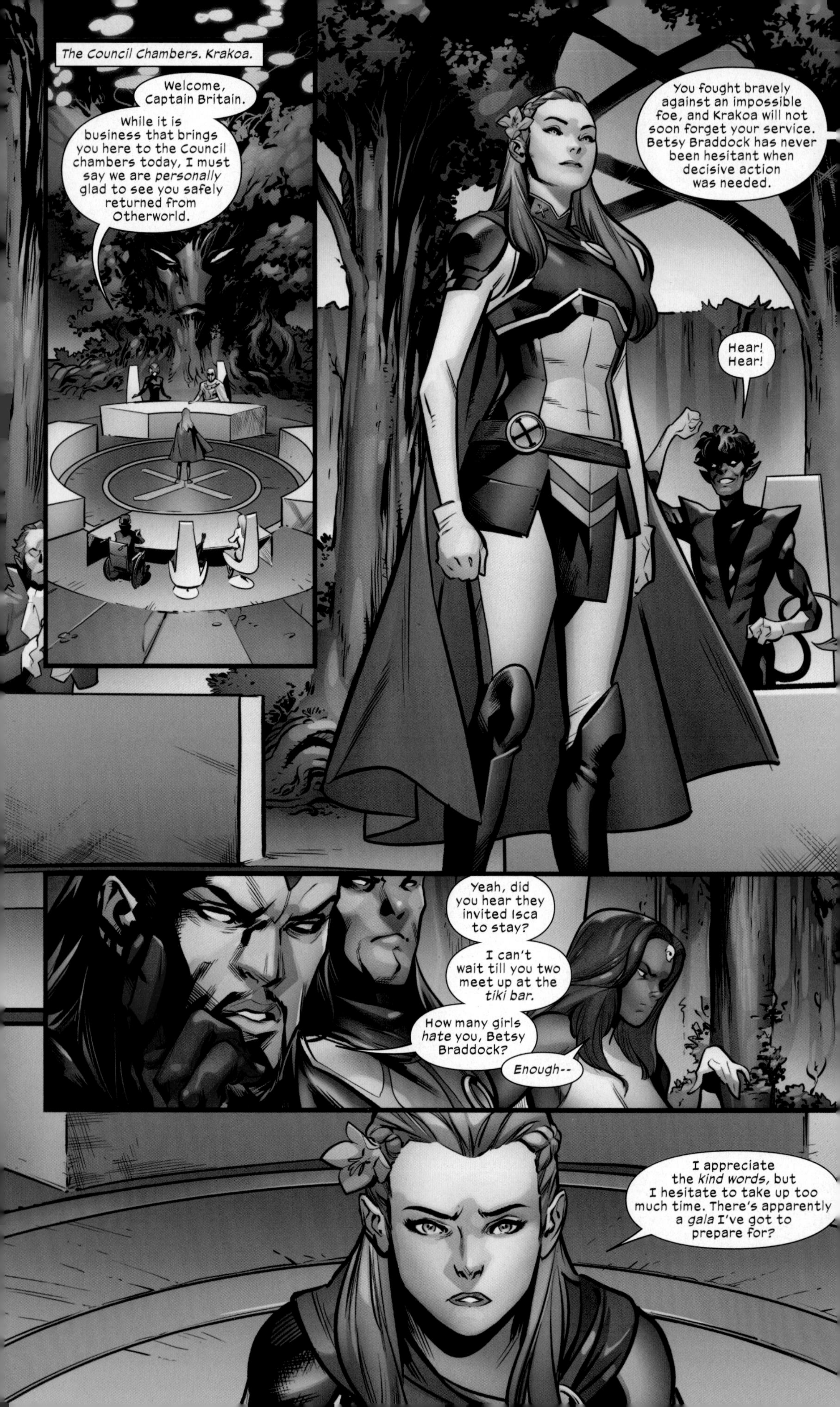

The Council Chambers. Krakoa.
Welcome, Captain Britain.
While it is business that brings you here to the Council chambers today, I must say we are *personally* glad to see you safely returned from Otherworld.
You fought bravely against an impossible foe, and Krakoa will not soon forget your service. Betsy Braddock has never been hesitant when decisive action was needed.
Hear! Hear!
Yeah, did you hear they invited Isca to stay?
I can't wait till you two meet up at the *tiki bar.*
How many girls *hate* you, Betsy Braddock?
Enough--
I appreciate the *kind words,* but I hesitate to take up too much time. There's apparently a *gala* I've got to prepare for?

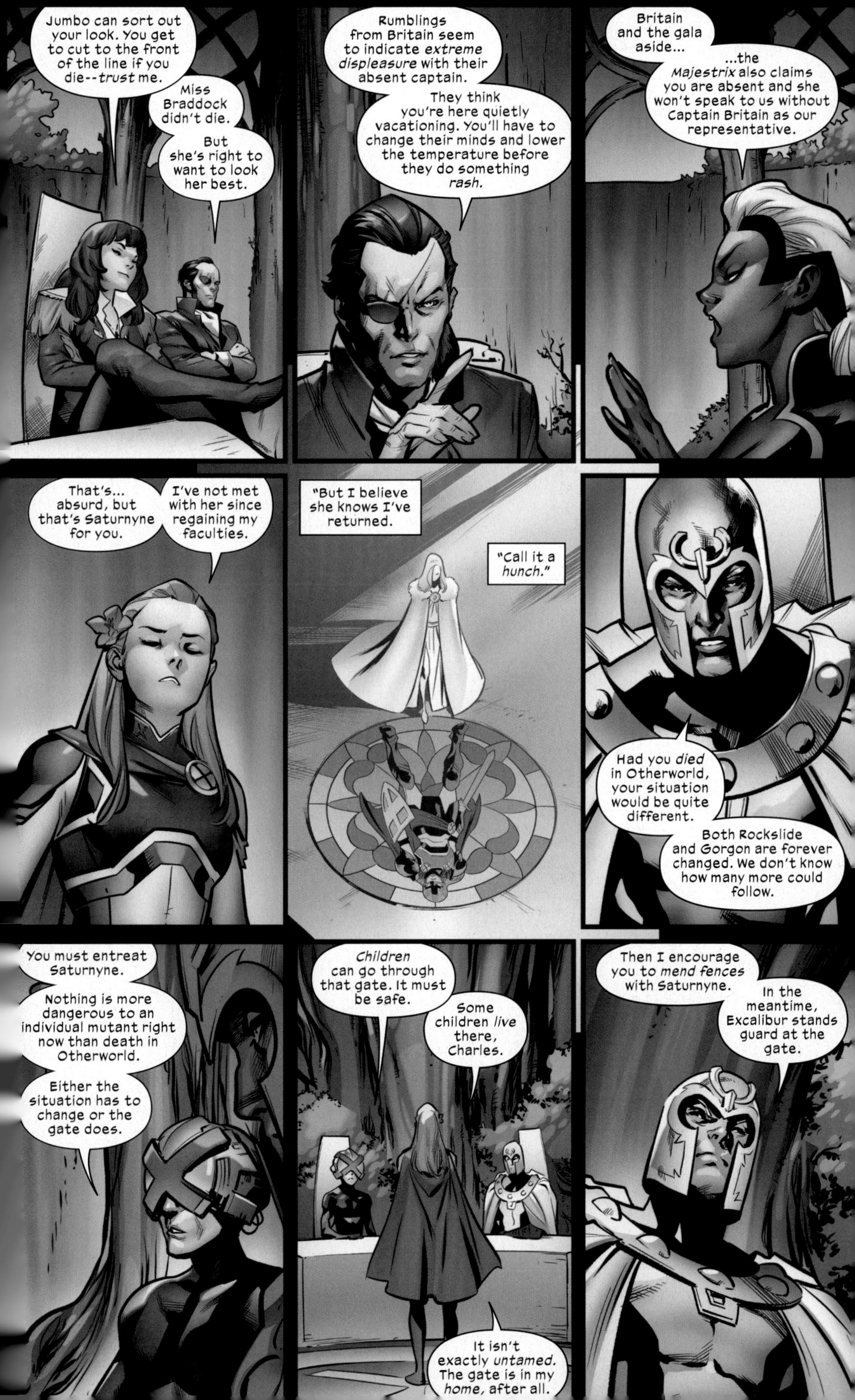

Jumbo can sort out your look. You get to cut to the front of the line if you die--*trust* me.
Miss Braddock didn't die.
But she's right to want to look her best.
Rumblings from Britain seem to indicate *extreme displeasure* with their absent captain.
They think you're here quietly vacationing. You'll have to change their minds and lower the temperature before they do something *rash.*
Britain and the gala aside...
...the *Majestrix* also claims you are absent and she won't speak to us without Captain Britain as our representative.
That's... absurd, but that's Saturnyne for you.
I've not met with her since regaining my faculties.
"But I believe she knows I've returned.
"Call it a *hunch.*"
Had you *died* in Otherworld, your situation would be quite different.
Both Rockslide and Gorgon are forever changed. We don't know how many more could follow.
You must entreat Saturnyne.
Nothing is more dangerous to an individual mutant right now than death in Otherworld.
Either the situation has to change or the gate does.
Children can go through that gate. It must be safe.
Some children *live* there, Charles.
It isn't exactly *untamed.* The gate is in my *home,* after all.
Then I encourage you to *mend fences* with Saturnyne.
In the meantime, Excalibur stands guard at the gate.

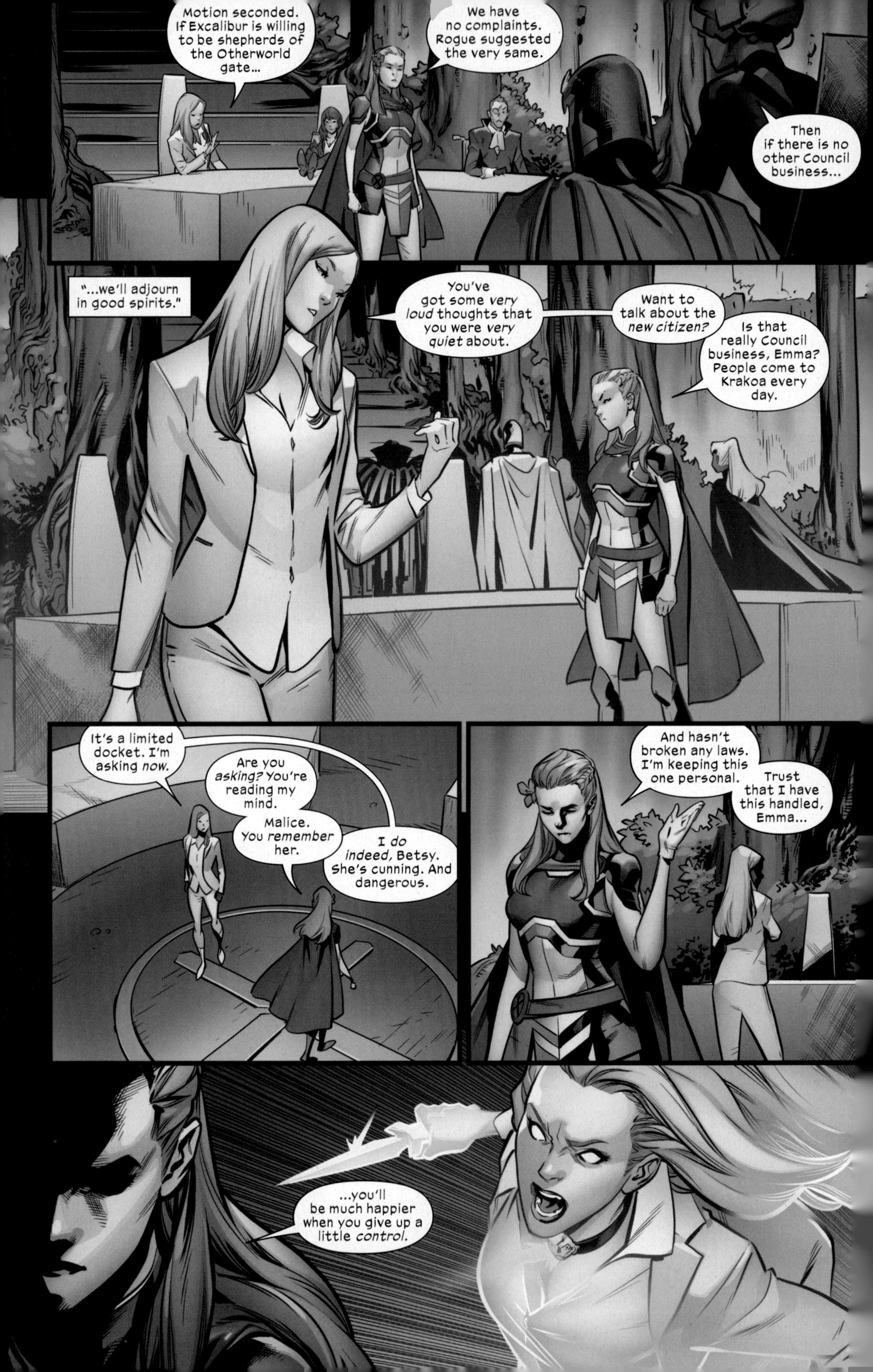

Motion seconded. If Excalibur is willing to be shepherds of the Otherworld gate...
We have no complaints. Rogue suggested the very same.
Then if there is no other Council business...
"...we'll adjourn in good spirits."
You've got some *very loud* thoughts that you were *very quiet* about.
Want to talk about the *new citizen?*
Is that really Council business, Emma? People come to Krakoa every day.
It's a limited docket. I'm asking *now.*
Are you *asking?* You're reading my mind.
Malice. You *remember* her.
I *do indeed,* Betsy. She's cunning. And dangerous.
And hasn't broken any laws. I'm keeping this one personal.
Trust that I have this handled, Emma...
...you'll be much happier when you give up a little *control.*

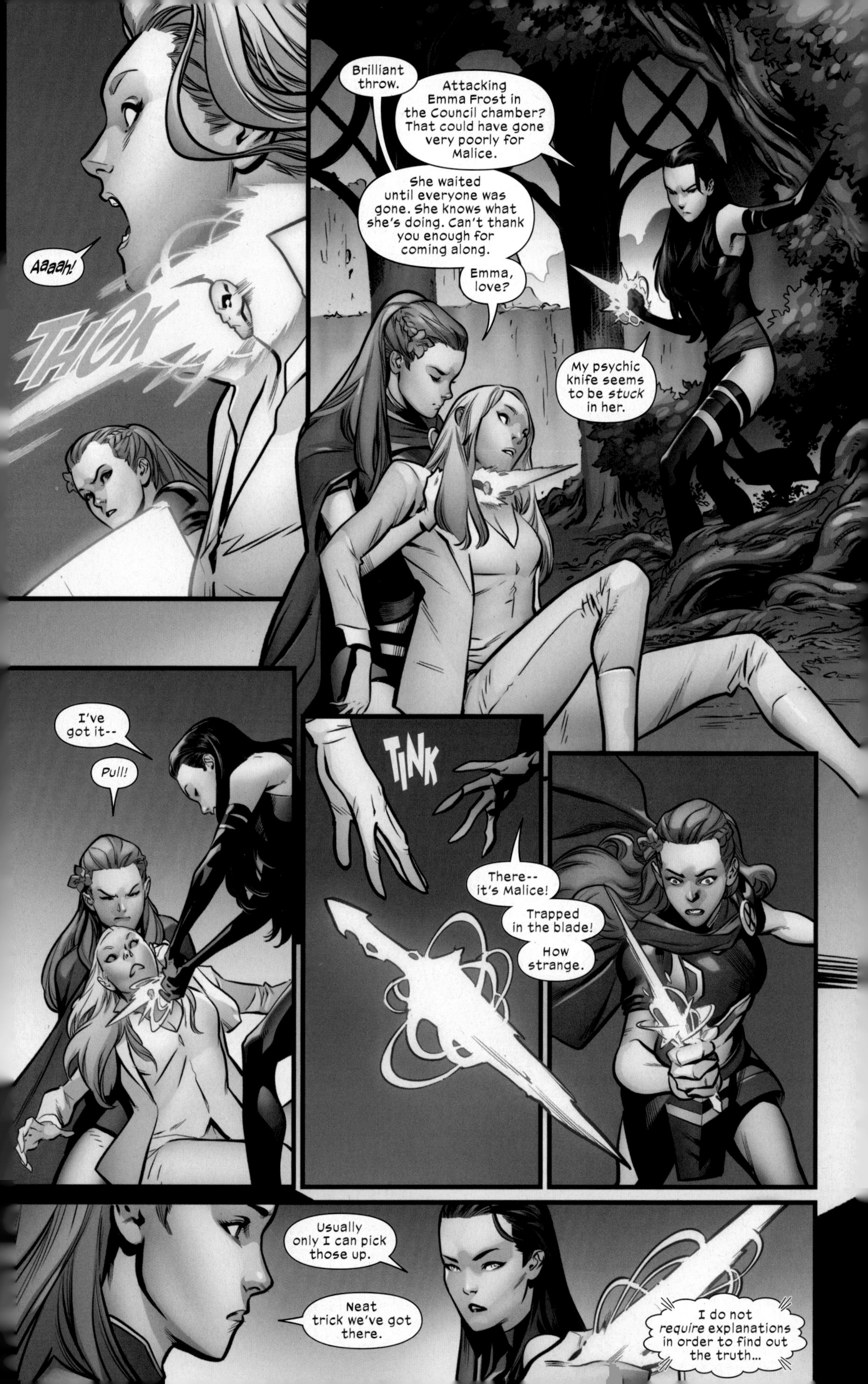
Aaaah!
THOK
Brilliant throw.
Attacking Emma Frost in the Council chamber? That could have gone very poorly for Malice.
She waited until everyone was gone. She knows what she's doing. Can't thank you enough for coming along.
Emma, love?
My psychic knife seems to be *stuck* in her.
I've got it--
Pull!
TINK
There-- it's Malice!
Trapped in the blade!
How strange.
Usually only I can pick those up.
Neat trick we've got there.
I do not *require* explanations in order to find out the truth...

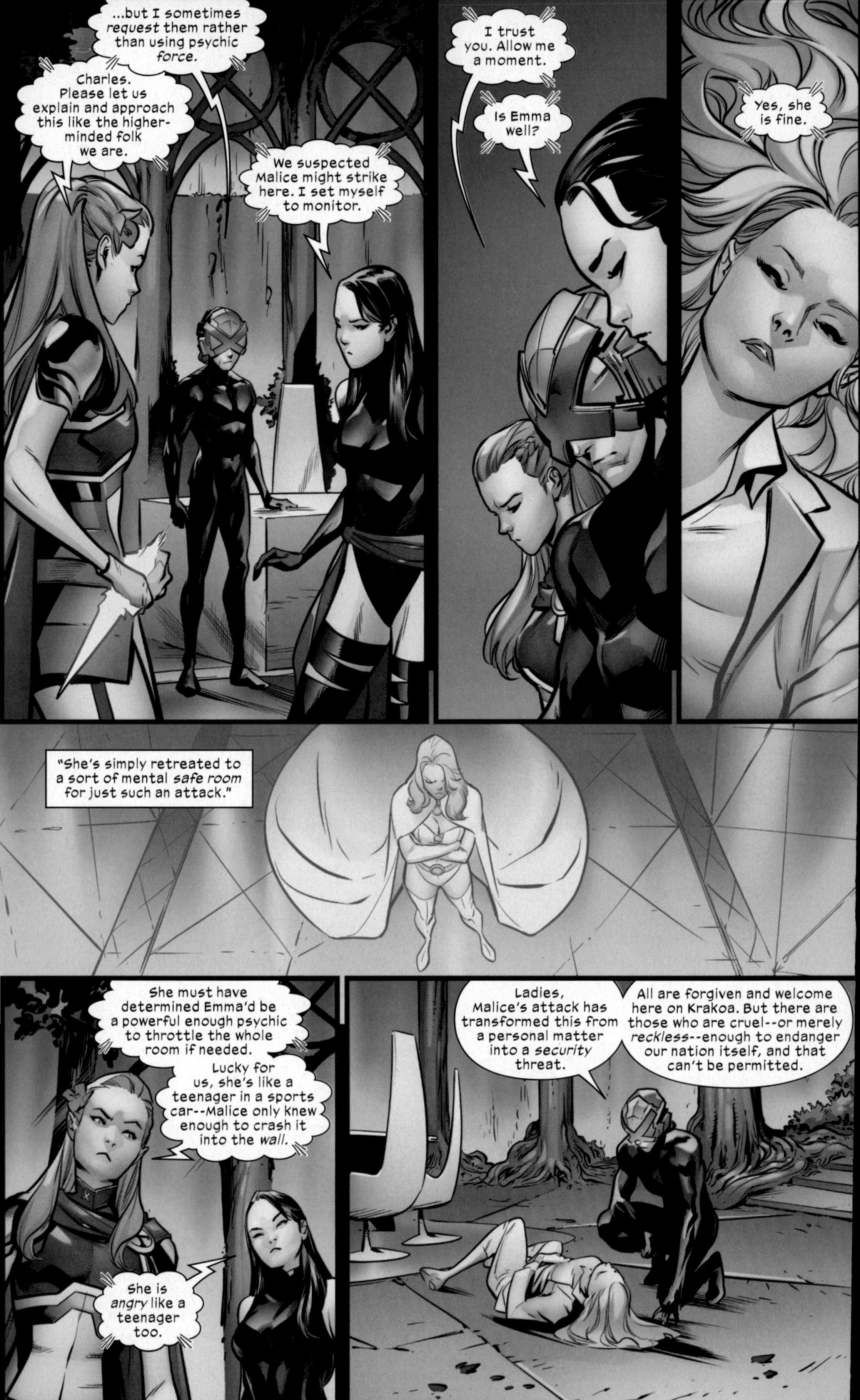
...but I sometimes *request* them rather than using psychic *force.*
Charles. Please let us explain and approach this like the higher-minded folk we are.
We suspected Malice might strike here. I set myself to monitor.
I trust you. Allow me a moment.
Is Emma well?
Yes, she is fine.
"She's simply retreated to a sort of mental *safe room* for just such an attack."
She must have determined Emma'd be a powerful enough psychic to throttle the whole room if needed.
Lucky for us, she's like a teenager in a sports car--Malice only knew enough to crash it into the *wall.*
She is *angry* like a teenager too.
Ladies, Malice's attack has transformed this from a personal matter into a *security* threat.
All are forgiven and welcome here on Krakoa. But there are those who are cruel--or merely *reckless*--enough to endanger our nation itself, and that can't be permitted.

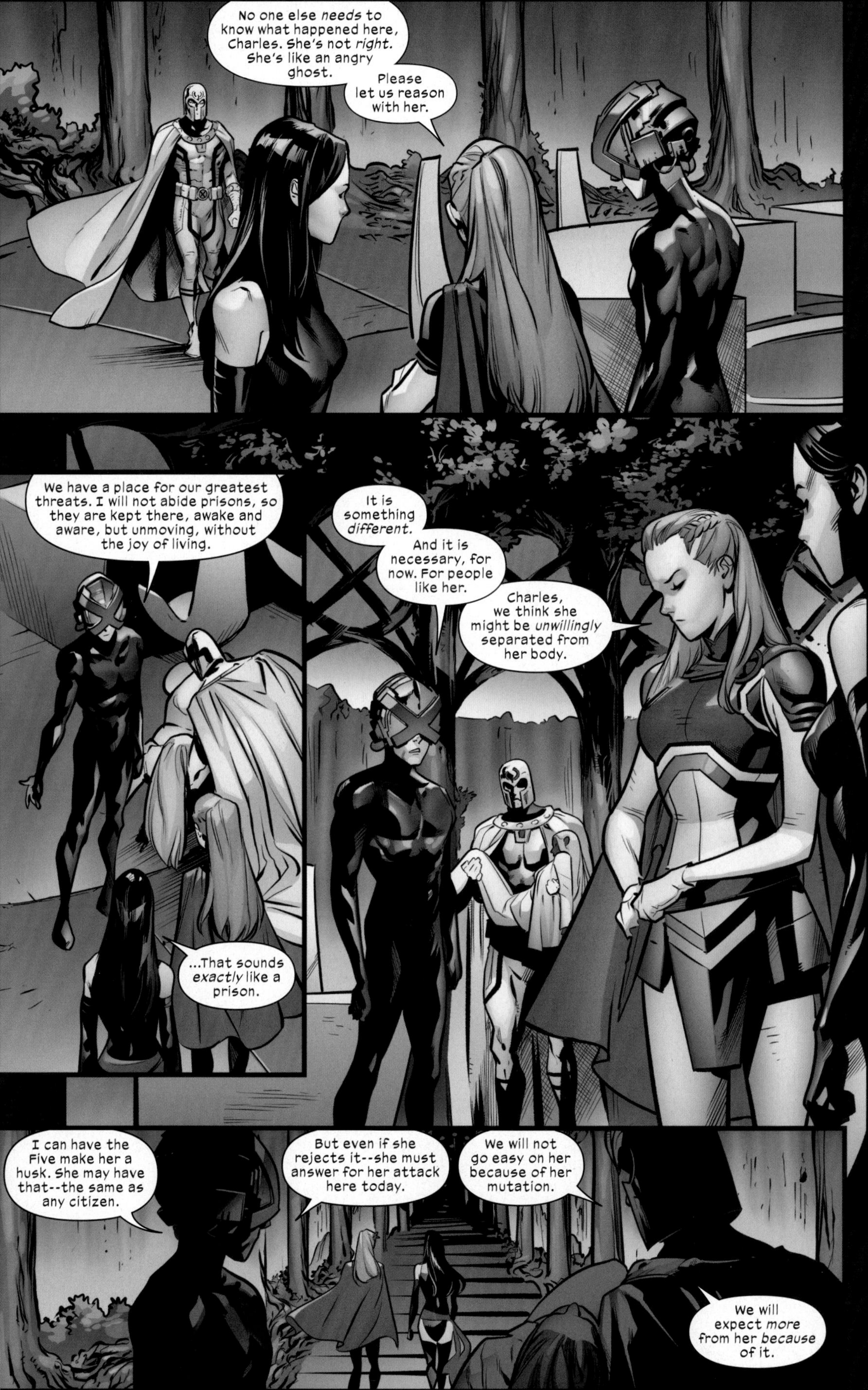
No one else *needs* to know what happened here, Charles. She's not *right*. She's like an angry ghost.
Please let us reason with her.
We have a place for our greatest threats. I will not abide prisons, so they are kept there, awake and aware, but unmoving, without the joy of living.
...That sounds *exactly* like a prison.
It is something *different*.
And it is necessary, for now. For people like her.
Charles, we think she might be *unwillingly* separated from her body.
I can have the Five make her a husk. She may have that--the same as any citizen.
But even if she rejects it--she must answer for her attack here today.
We will not go easy on her because of her mutation.
We will expect *more* from her *because* of it.

"WISDOM" 1711 GMT
Betsy, call me x

"WISDOM" 1832 GMT
I'm not on the pull, honestly, please call me back
before the gala

"WISDOM" 1913 GMT
would prefer to talk about this on the phone if
you're around

"WISDOM" 2101 GMT
I'm not asking you to the gala - you would say no
and I have to go with someone else that's why I
need you to call me

"WISDOM" 0245 GMT
My DATES are breathing down my neck about you

"WISDOM" 0310 GMT
My DATES are Reuben and his coven

"WISDOM" 0311 GMT
Fine you dont have to call me i wouldn't call me
either. I don't like the way they've been talking
about you and Reuben is there for something big

"WISDOM" 0314 GMT
bin this phone, i'm binning mine

"WISDOM" 0342 GMT
Be careful x

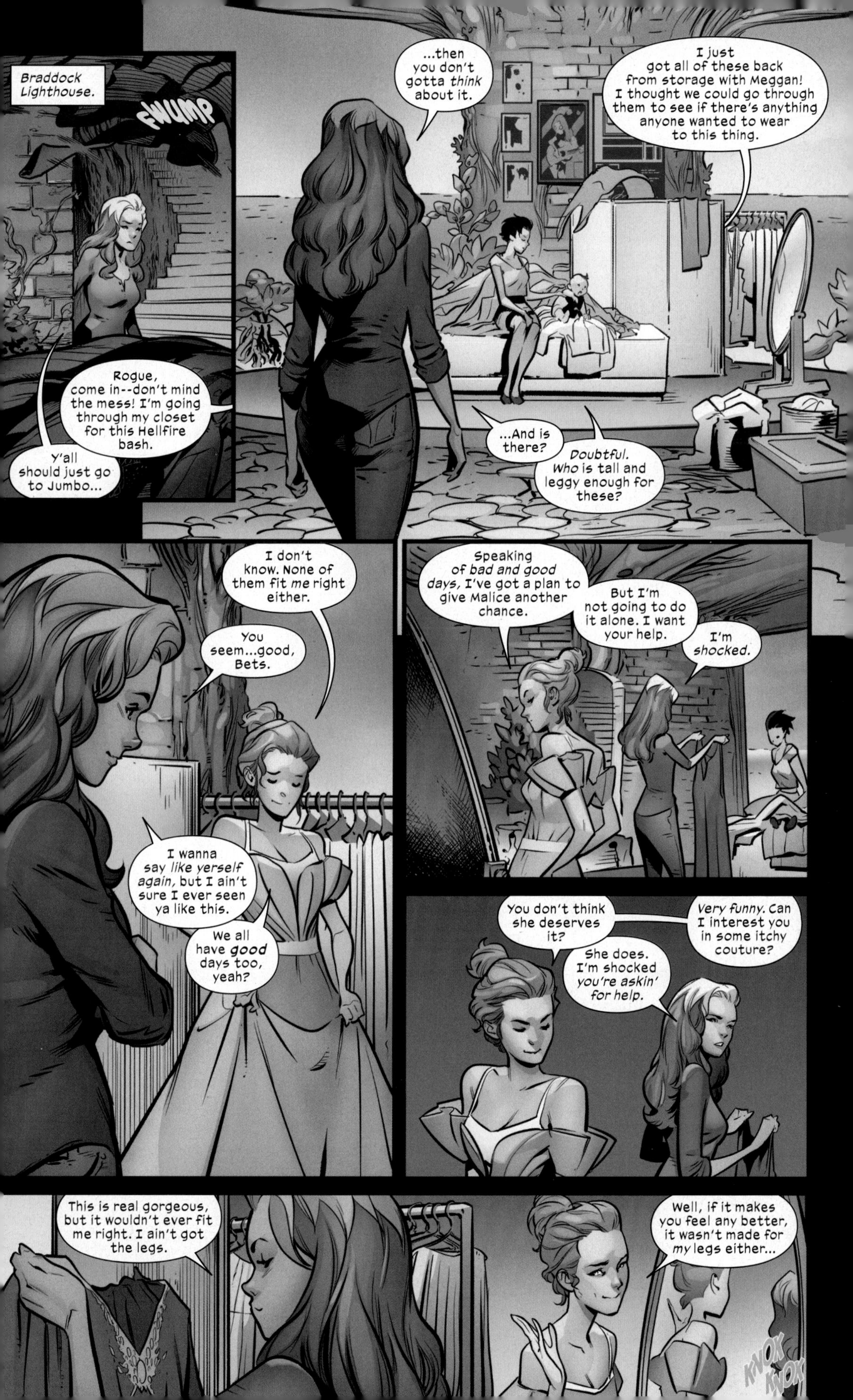
Braddock Lighthouse.
FWUMP
Y'all should just go to Jumbo...
Rogue, come in--don't mind the mess! I'm going through my closet for this Hellfire bash.
...then you don't gotta *think* about it.
I just got all of these back from storage with Meggan! I thought we could go through them to see if there's anything anyone wanted to wear to this thing.
...And is there?
Doubtful. Who is tall and leggy enough for these?
I don't know. None of them fit *me* right either.
You seem...good, Bets.
I wanna say *like yerself again,* but I ain't sure I ever seen ya like this.
We all have *good* days too, yeah?
Speaking of *bad and good days,* I've got a plan to give Malice another chance.
But I'm not going to do it alone. I want your help.
I'm *shocked.*
You don't think she deserves it?
She does. I'm shocked *you're askin'* for help.
Very funny. Can I interest you in some itchy couture?
This is real gorgeous, but it wouldn't ever fit me right. I ain't got the legs.
Well, if it makes you feel any better, it wasn't made for *my* legs either...
KNOK KNOK

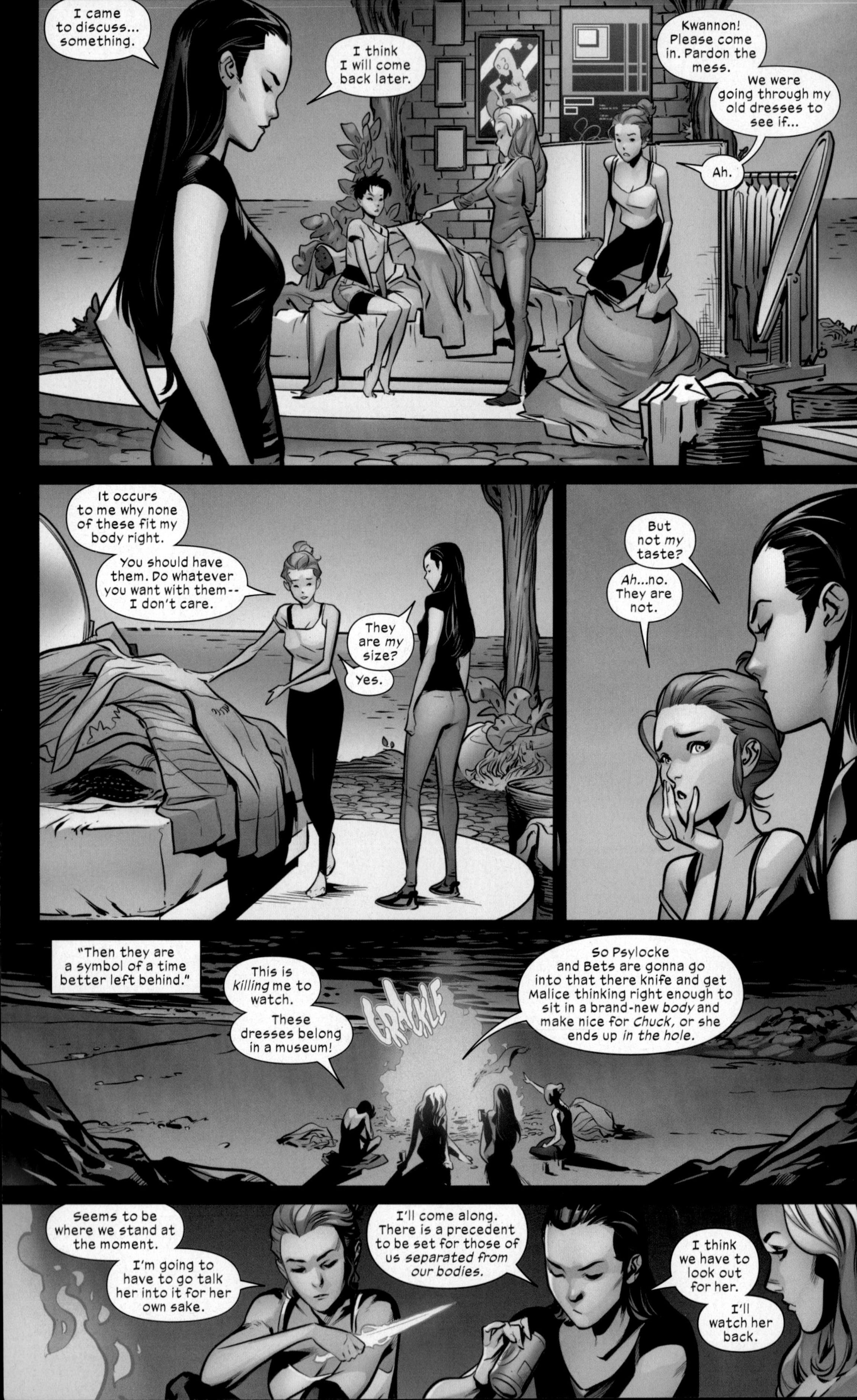
I came to discuss... something.
I think I will come back later.
Kwannon! Please come in. Pardon the mess.
We were going through my old dresses to see if...
Ah.
It occurs to me why none of these fit my body right.
You should have them. Do whatever you want with them-- I don't care.
They are *my* size?
Yes.
But not *my* taste?
Ah...no. They are not.
"Then they are a symbol of a time better left behind."
This is *killing* me to watch.
These dresses belong in a museum!
CRACKLE
So Psylocke and Bets are gonna go into that there knife and get Malice thinking right enough to sit in a brand-new *body* and make nice for *Chuck*, or she ends up *in the hole*.
Seems to be where we stand at the moment.
I'm going to have to go talk her into it for her own sake.
I'll come along. There is a precedent to be set for those of us *separated from our bodies*.
I think we have to look out for her.
I'll watch her back.

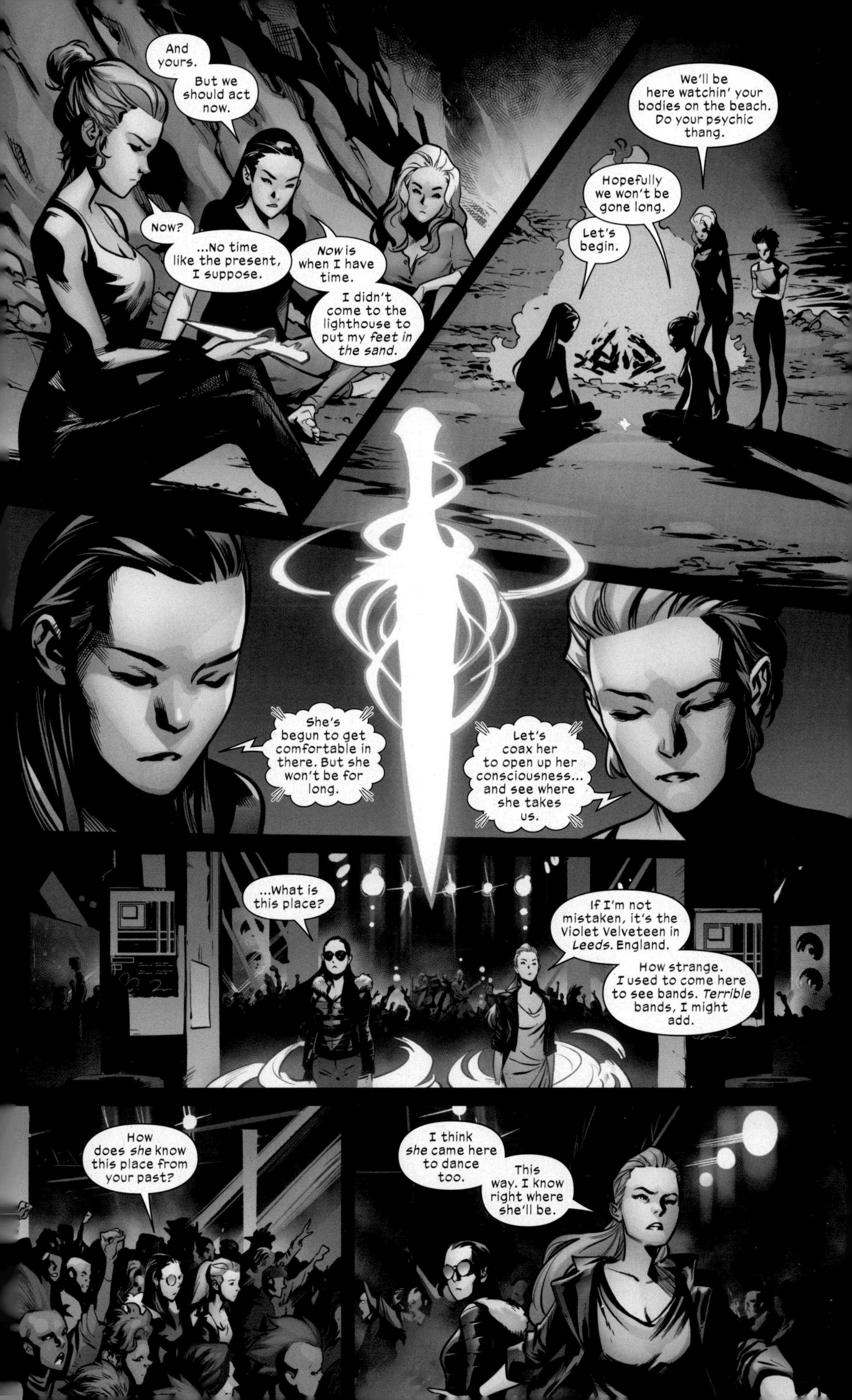

And yours.
But we should act now.
Now?
...No time like the present, I suppose.
Now is when I have time.
I didn't come to the lighthouse to put my *feet in the sand.*
We'll be here watchin' your bodies on the beach. Do your psychic thang.
Hopefully we won't be gone long.
Let's begin.
She's begun to get comfortable in there. But she won't be for long.
Let's coax her to open up her consciousness... and see where she takes us.
...What is this place?
If I'm not mistaken, it's the Violet Velveteen in *Leeds.* England.
How strange. *I* used to come here to see bands. *Terrible* bands, I might add.
How does *she* know this place from your past?
I think *she* came here to dance too.
This way. I know right where she'll be.

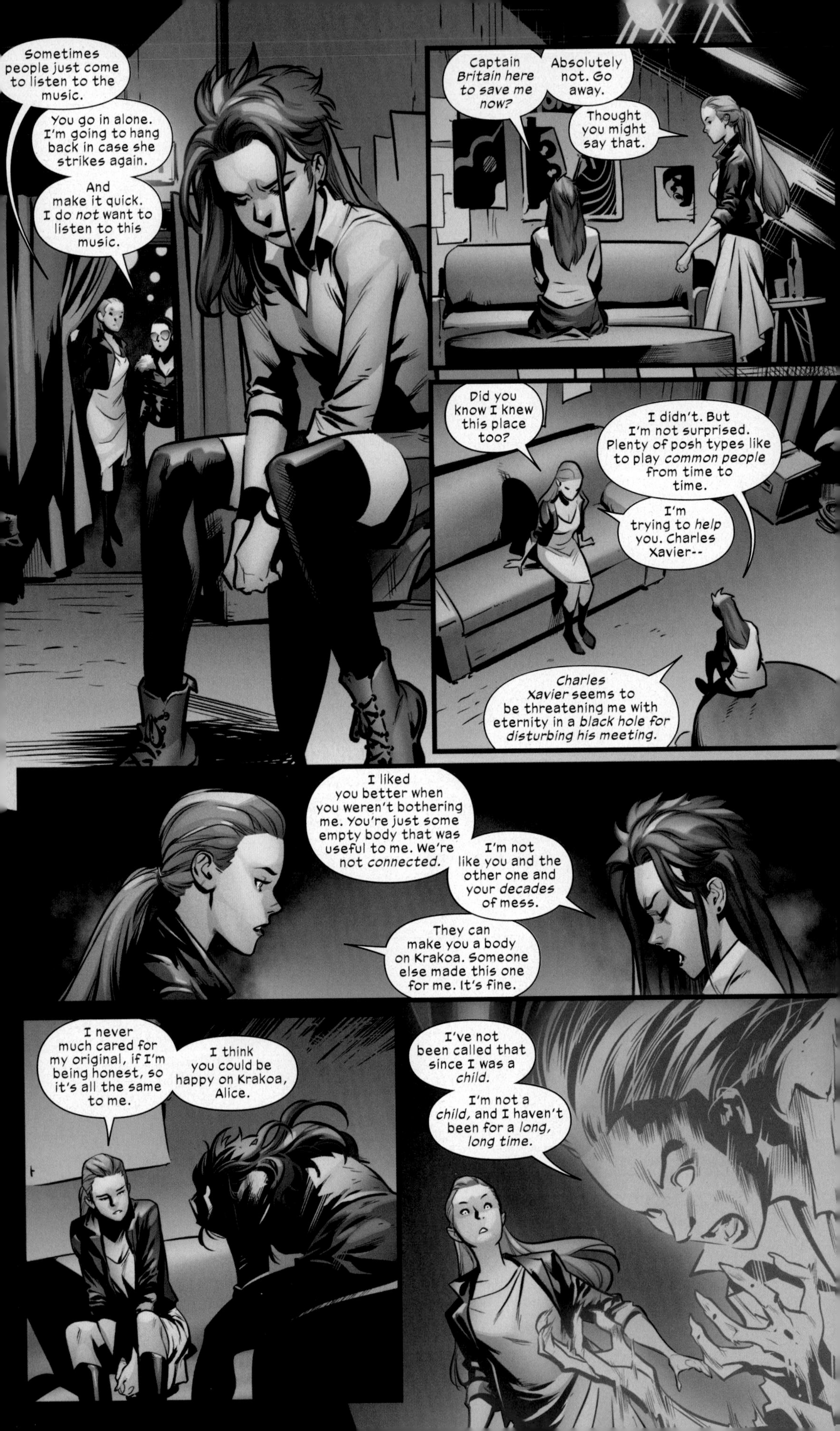
Sometimes people just come to listen to the music.
You go in alone. I'm going to hang back in case she strikes again.
And make it quick. I do *not* want to listen to this music.
Captain *Britain here to save me now?*
Absolutely not. Go away.
Thought you might say that.
Did you know I knew this place too?
I didn't. But I'm not surprised. Plenty of posh types like to play *common people* from time to time.
I'm trying to *help* you. Charles Xavier--
Charles Xavier seems to be threatening me with eternity in a black hole for disturbing his meeting.
I liked you better when you weren't bothering me. You're just some empty body that was useful to me. We're not *connected.*
I'm not like you and the other one and your *decades* of mess.
They can make you a body on Krakoa. Someone else made this one for me. It's fine.
I never much cared for my original, if I'm being honest, so it's all the same to me.
I think you could be happy on Krakoa, Alice.
I've not been called that since I was a *child.*
I'm not a *child,* and I haven't been for a *long, long* time.

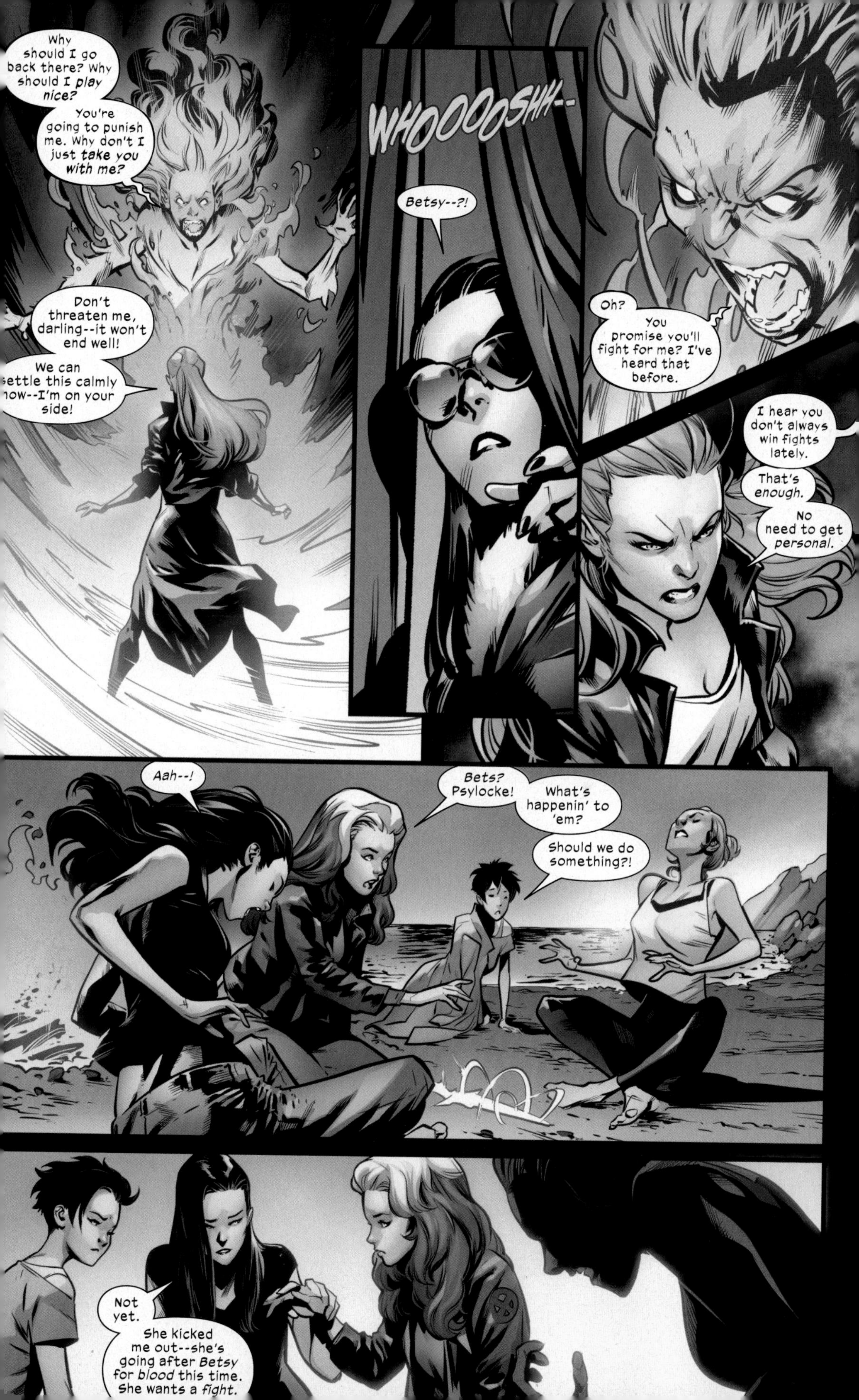
Why should I go back there? Why should I *play nice?*
You're going to punish me. Why don't I just *take you with me?*
Don't threaten me, darling--it won't end well!
We can settle this calmly now--I'm on your side!
WHOOOOOSHH--
Betsy--?!
Oh?
You promise you'll fight for me? I've heard that before.
I hear you don't always win fights lately.
That's *enough.*
No need to get *personal.*
Aah--!
Bets? Psylocke!
What's happenin' to 'em?
Should we do something?!
Not yet.
She kicked me out--she's going after *Betsy* for *blood* this time. She wants a *fight.*

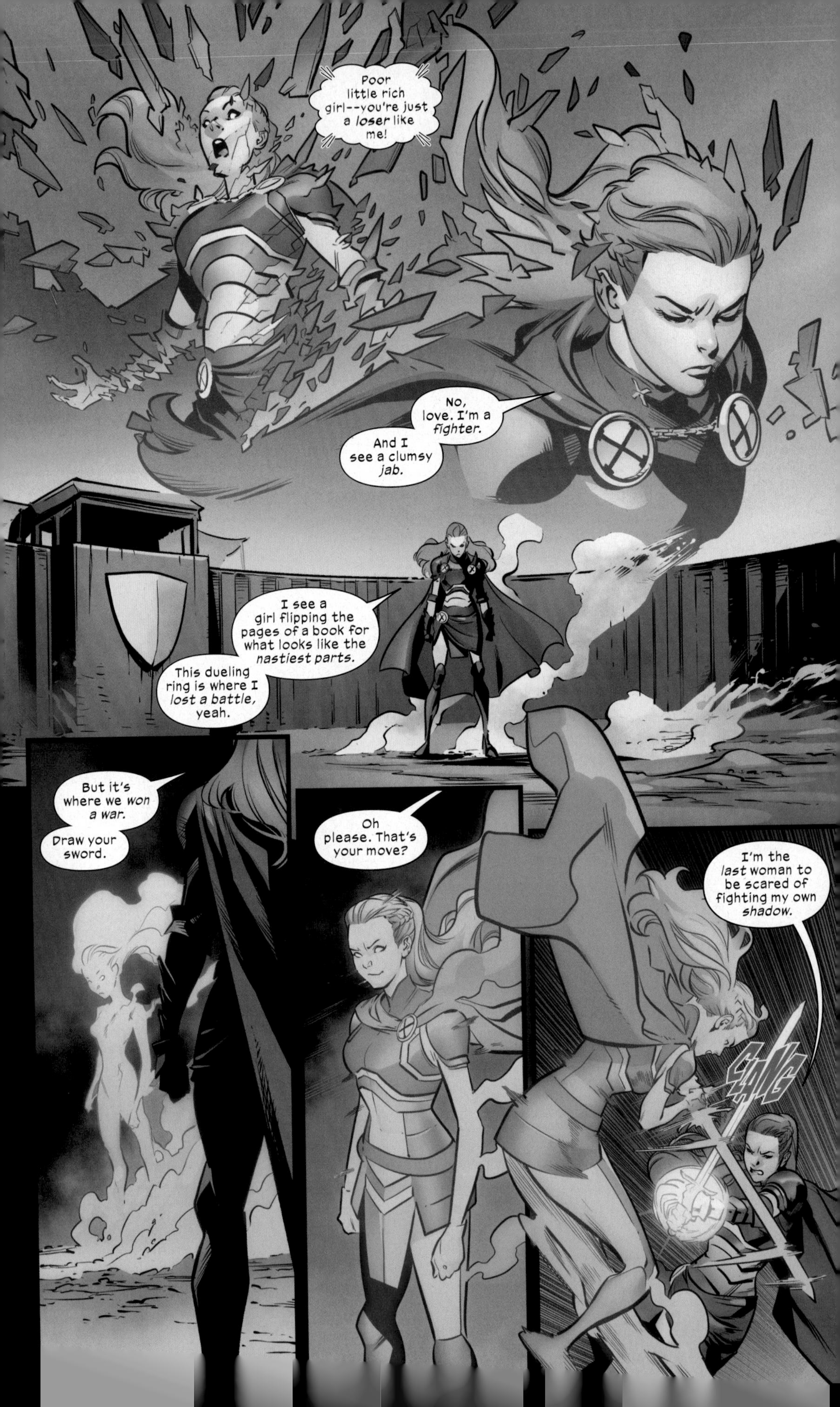
Poor little rich girl--you're just a *loser* like me!
No, love. I'm a *fighter.*
And I see a clumsy *jab.*
I see a girl flipping the pages of a book for what looks like the *nastiest parts.*
This dueling ring is where I *lost a battle,* yeah.
But it's where we *won* a war.
Draw your sword.
Oh please. That's your move?
I'm the *last* woman to be scared of fighting my own *shadow.*
CLANG

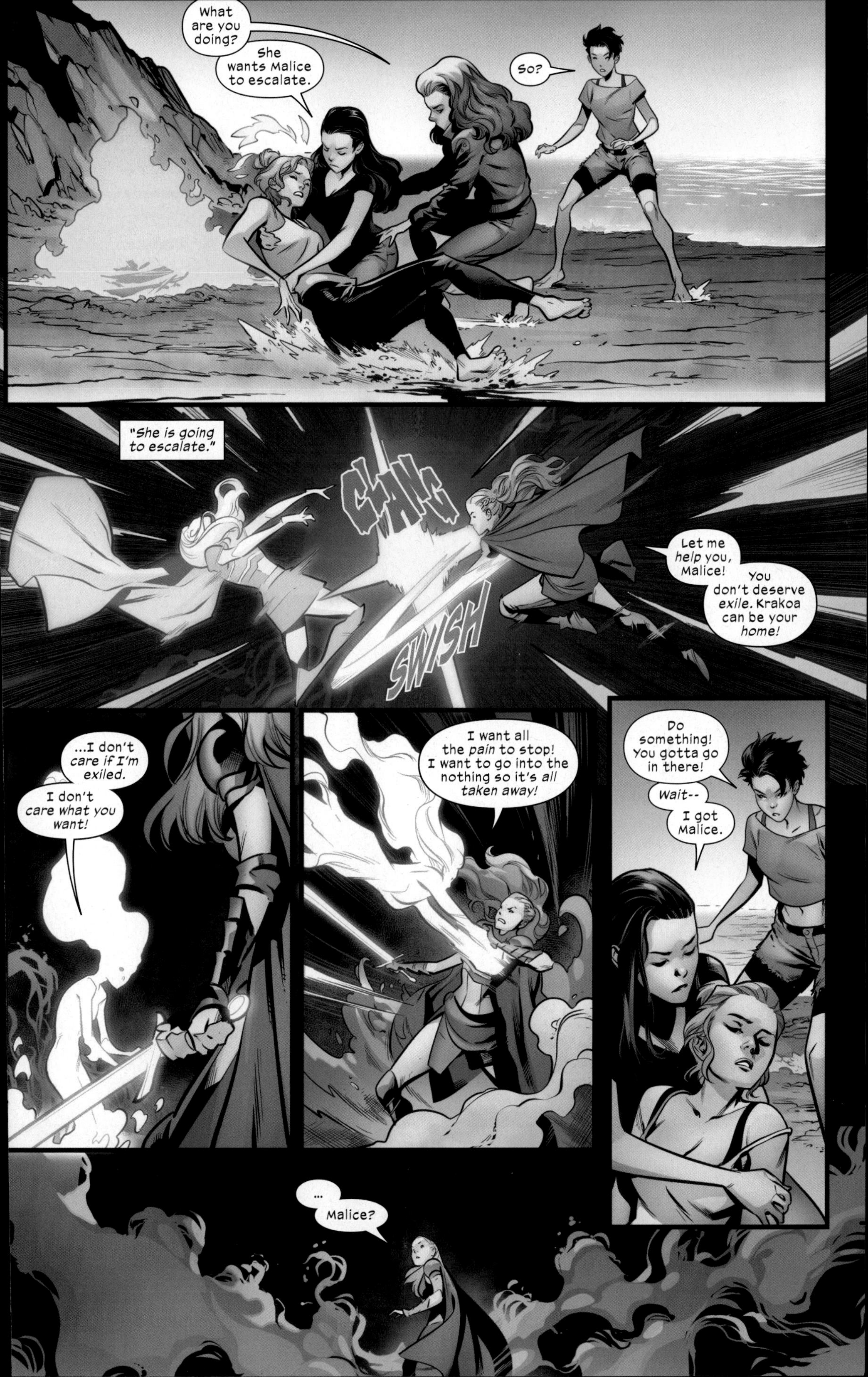
What are you doing?
She wants Malice to escalate.
So?
"She is going to escalate."
CLANG
SWISH
Let me help you, Malice!
You don't deserve exile. Krakoa can be your home!
...I don't care if I'm exiled.
I don't care what you want!
I want all the pain to stop! I want to go into the nothing so it's all taken away!
Do something! You gotta go in there!
Wait--
I got Malice.
...
Malice?

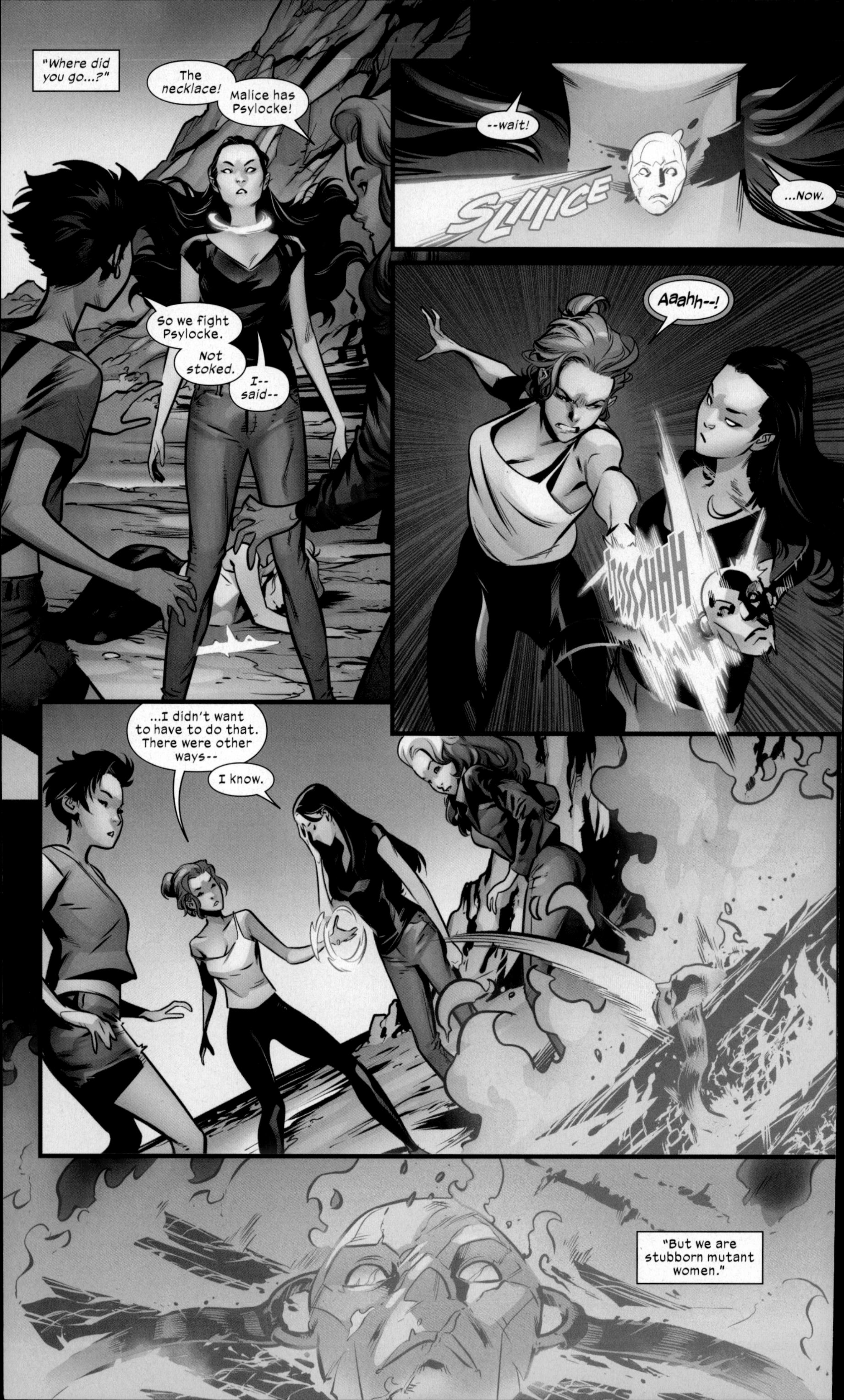
"Where did you go...?"
The necklace!
Malice has Psylocke!
So we fight Psylocke.
Not stoked.
I-- said--
--wait!
SLIIIICE
...NOW.
Aaahh--!
...I didn't want to have to do that. There were other ways--
I know.
"But we are stubborn mutant women."

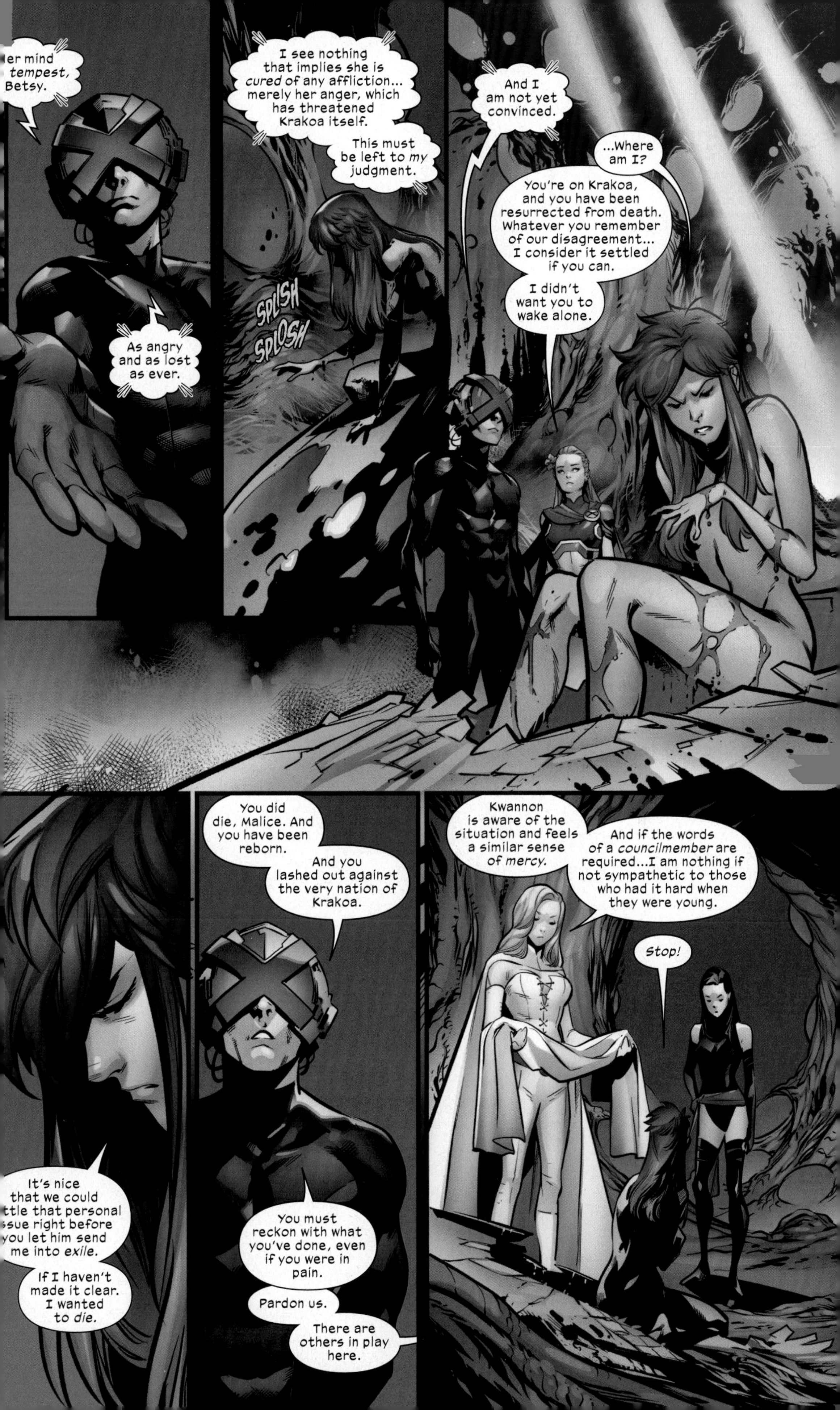

er mind tempest, Betsy.
I see nothing that implies she is *cured* of any affliction... merely her anger, which has threatened Krakoa itself.
This must be left to *my* judgment.
SPLISH
SPLOSH
As angry and as lost as ever.
And I am not yet convinced.
...Where am I?
You're on Krakoa, and you have been resurrected from death. Whatever you remember of our disagreement... I consider it settled if you can.
I didn't want you to wake alone.
It's nice that we could ttle that personal ssue right before you let him send me into *exile*.
If I haven't made it clear. I wanted to *die*.
You did die, Malice. And you have been reborn.
And you lashed out against the very nation of Krakoa.
You must reckon with what you've done, even if you were in pain.
Pardon us.
There are others in play here.
Kwannon is aware of the situation and feels a similar sense of *mercy*.
And if the words of a *councilmember* are required...I am nothing if not sympathetic to those who had it hard when they were young.
Stop!

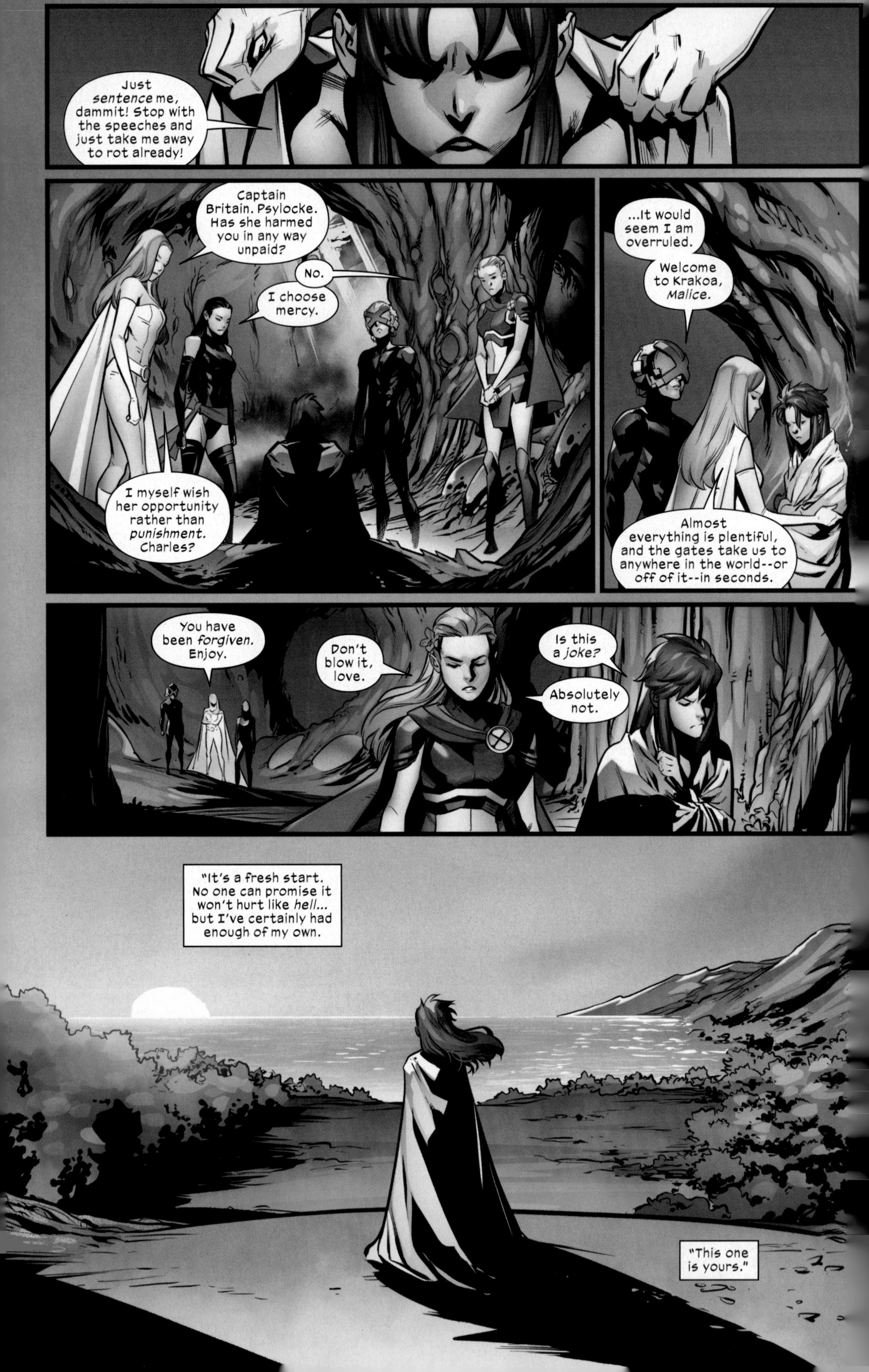
Just sentence me, dammit! Stop with the speeches and just take me away to rot already!
Captain Britain. Psylocke. Has she harmed you in any way unpaid?
No.
I choose mercy.
I myself wish her opportunity rather than punishment. Charles?
...It would seem I am overruled.
Welcome to Krakoa, Malice.
Almost everything is plentiful, and the gates take us to anywhere in the world--or off of it--in seconds.
You have been forgiven. Enjoy.
Don't blow it, love.
Is this a joke?
Absolutely not.
"It's a fresh start. No one can promise it won't hurt like hell... but I've certainly had enough of my own.
"This one is yours."

[kra_]
[koa_]

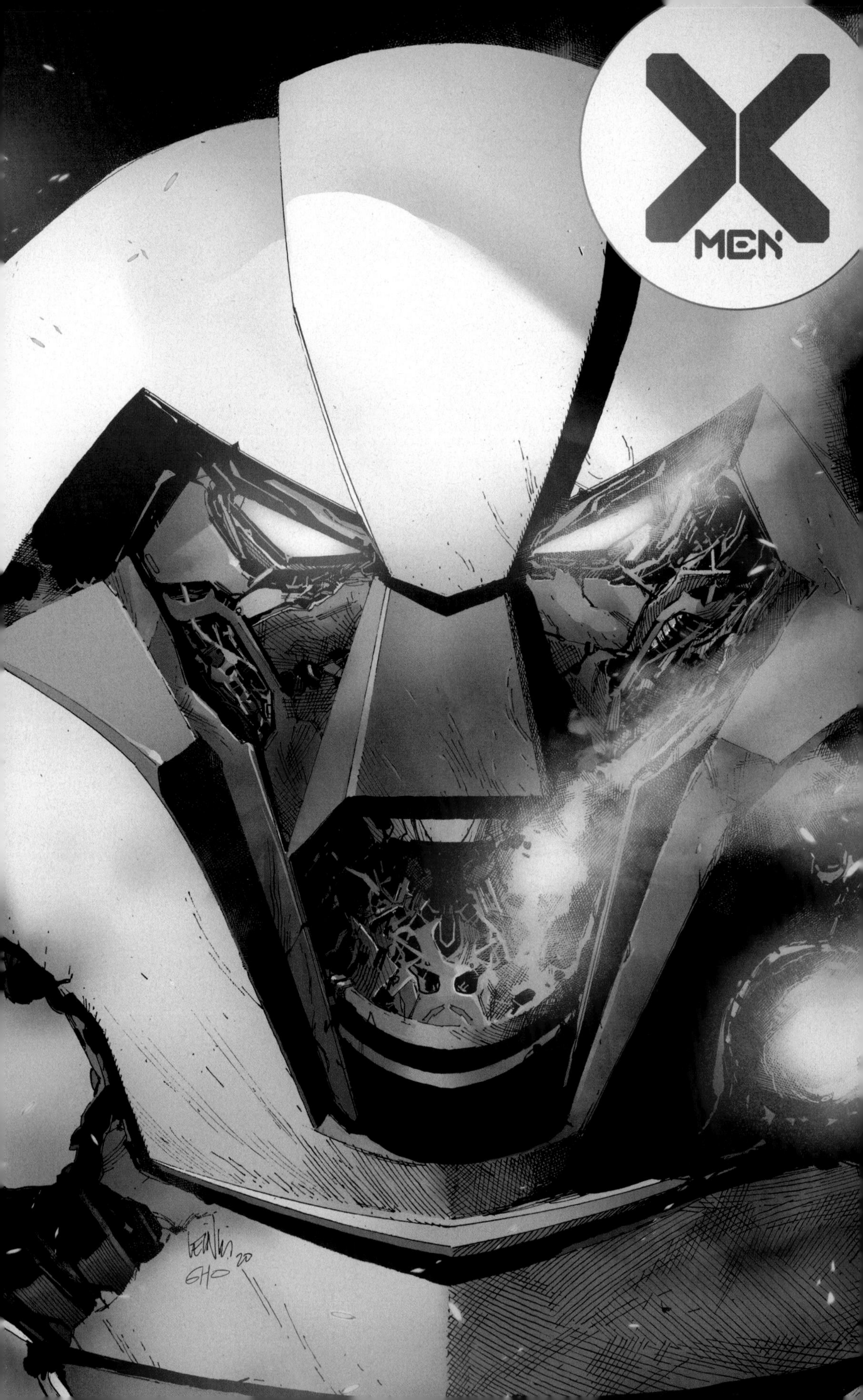
X
MEN

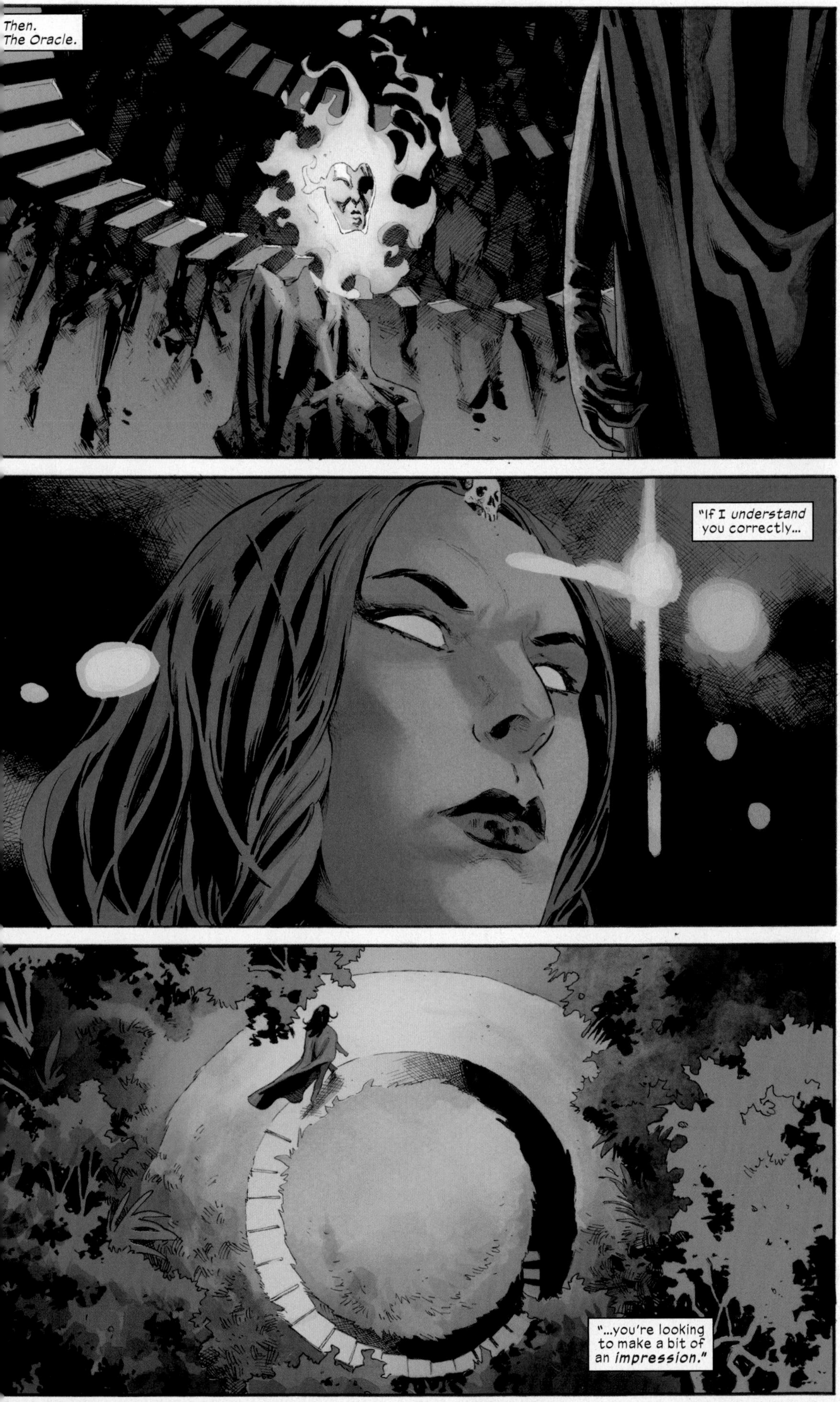
Then.
The Oracle.
"If I *understand* you correctly...
"...you're looking to make a bit of an *impression*."

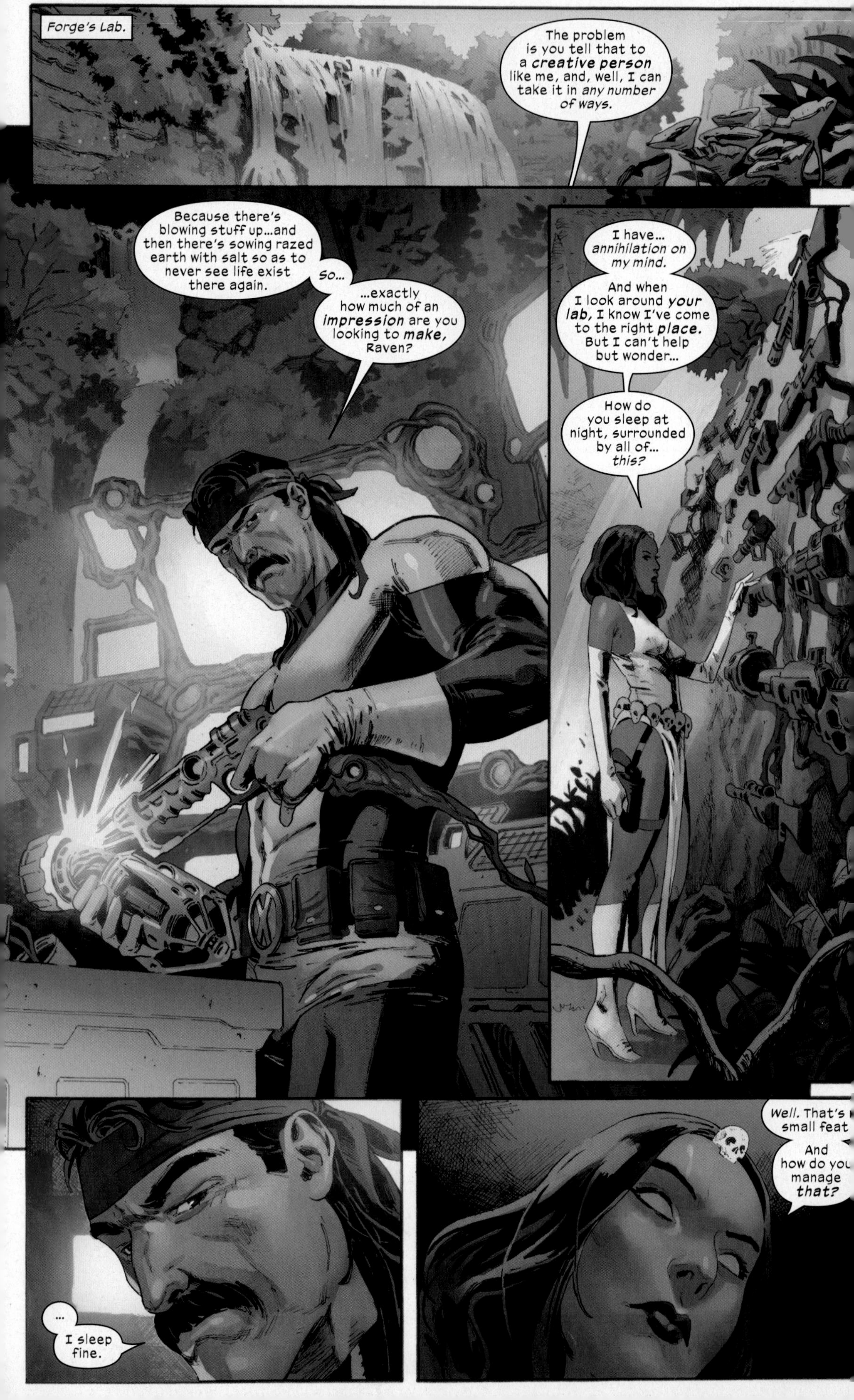

Forge's Lab.
The problem is you tell that to a *creative person* like me, and, well, I can take it in *any number of ways.*
Because there's blowing stuff up...and then there's sowing razed earth with salt so as to never see life exist there again.
So...
...exactly how much of an *impression* are you looking to *make,* Raven?
I have... *annihilation on my mind.*
And when I look around *your lab,* I know I've come to the right *place.* But I can't help but wonder...
How do you sleep at night, surrounded by all of... *this?*
...
I sleep fine.
Well. That's small feat
And how do you manage *that?*

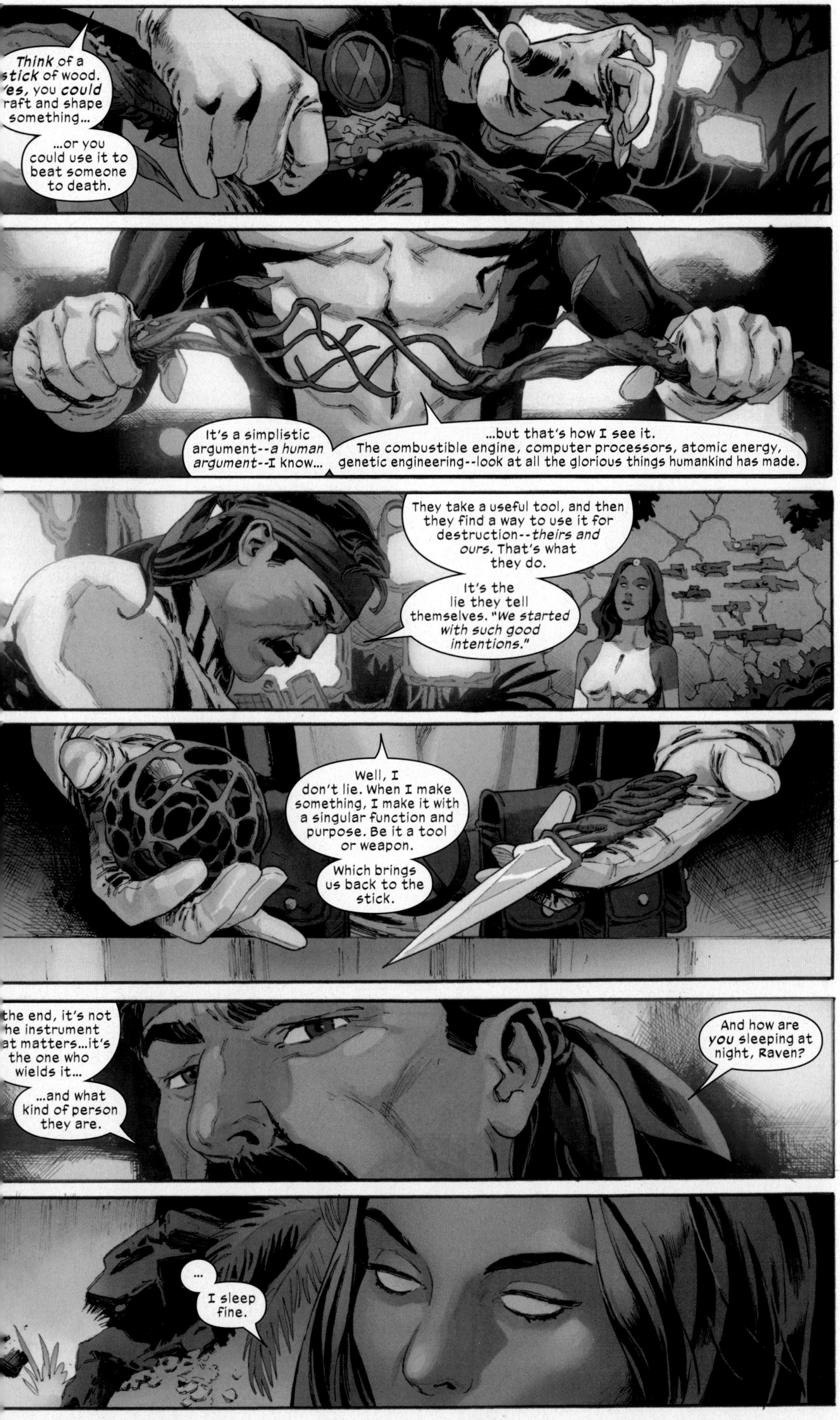
Think of a stick of wood. Yes, you could craft and shape something...
...or you could use it to beat someone to death.
It's a simplistic argument--a human argument--I know...
...but that's how I see it. The combustible engine, computer processors, atomic energy, genetic engineering--look at all the glorious things humankind has made.
They take a useful tool, and then they find a way to use it for destruction--theirs and ours. That's what they do.
It's the lie they tell themselves. "We started with such good intentions."
Well, I don't lie. When I make something, I make it with a singular function and purpose. Be it a tool or weapon.
Which brings us back to the stick.
the end, it's not he instrument at matters...it's the one who wields it...
...and what kind of person they are.
And how are you sleeping at night, Raven?
...
I sleep fine.

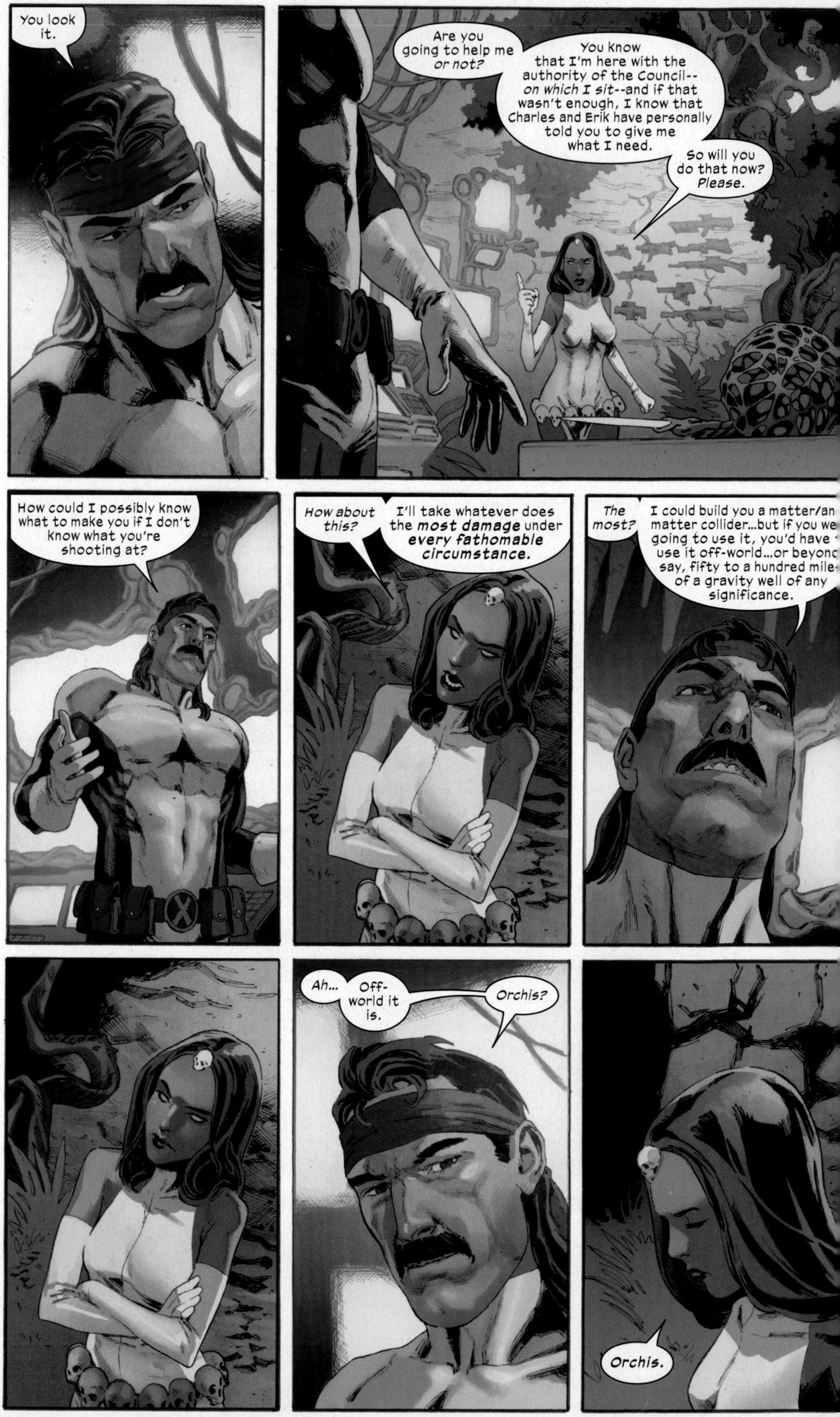

You look it.
Are you going to help me *or not?*
You know that I'm here with the authority of the Council-- *on which I sit*--and if that wasn't enough, I know that Charles and Erik have personally told you to give me what I need.
So will you do that now? *Please.*
How could I possibly know what to make you if I don't know what you're shooting at?
How about this?
I'll take whatever does the ***most damage*** under ***every fathomable circumstance.***
The most?
I could build you a matter/an matter collider...but if you we going to use it, you'd have use it off-world...or beyonc say, fifty to a hundred mile of a gravity well of any significance.
Ah...
Off-world it is.
Orchis?
Orchis.

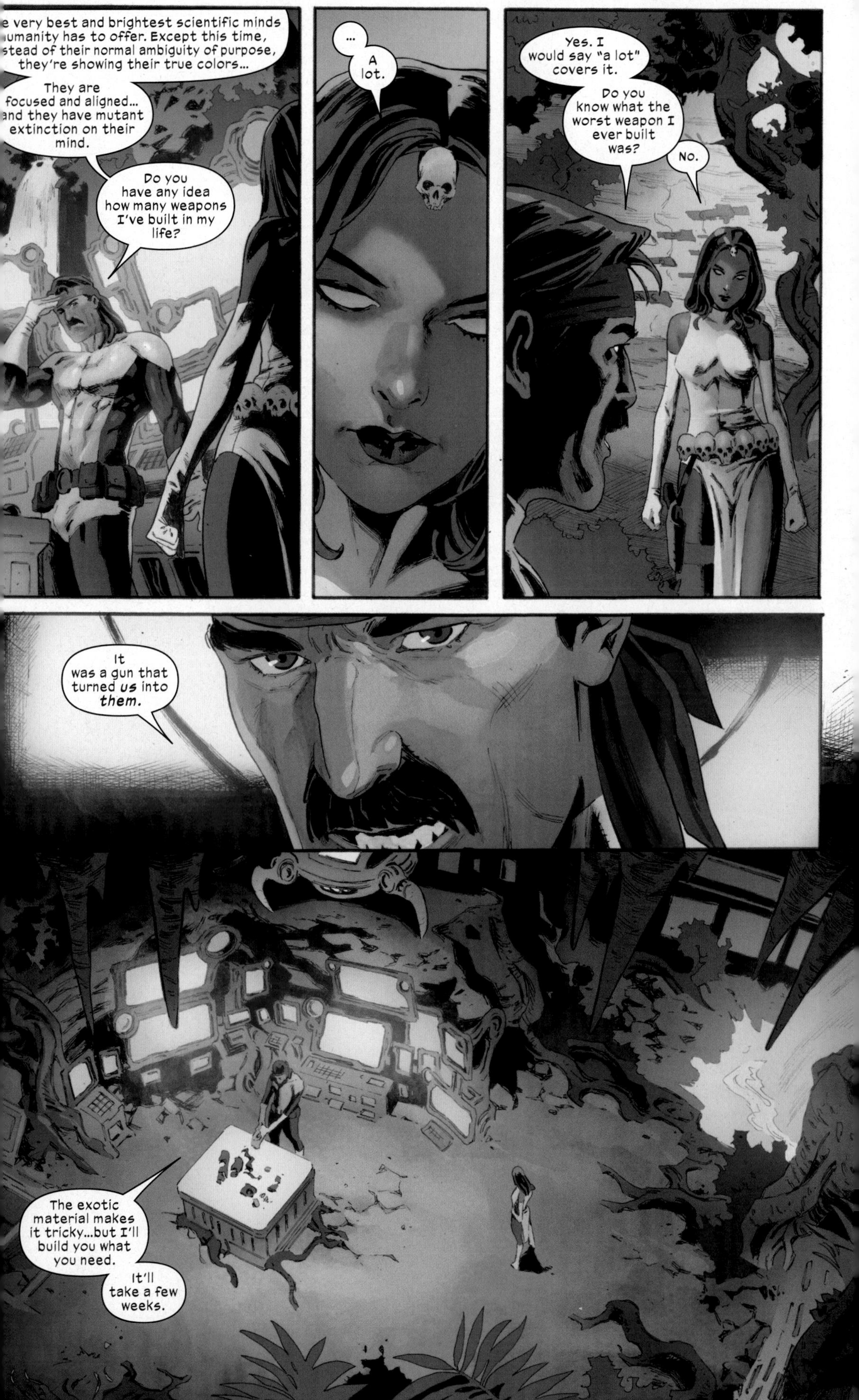
e very best and brightest scientific minds ıumanity has to offer. Except this time, stead of their normal ambiguity of purpose, they're showing their true colors...
They are focused and aligned... and they have mutant extinction on their mind.
Do you have any idea how many weapons I've built in my life?
... A lot.
Yes. I would say "a lot" covers it.
Do you know what the worst weapon I ever built was?
No.
It was a gun that turned *us* into *them.*
The exotic material makes it tricky...but I'll build you what you need.
It'll take a few weeks.

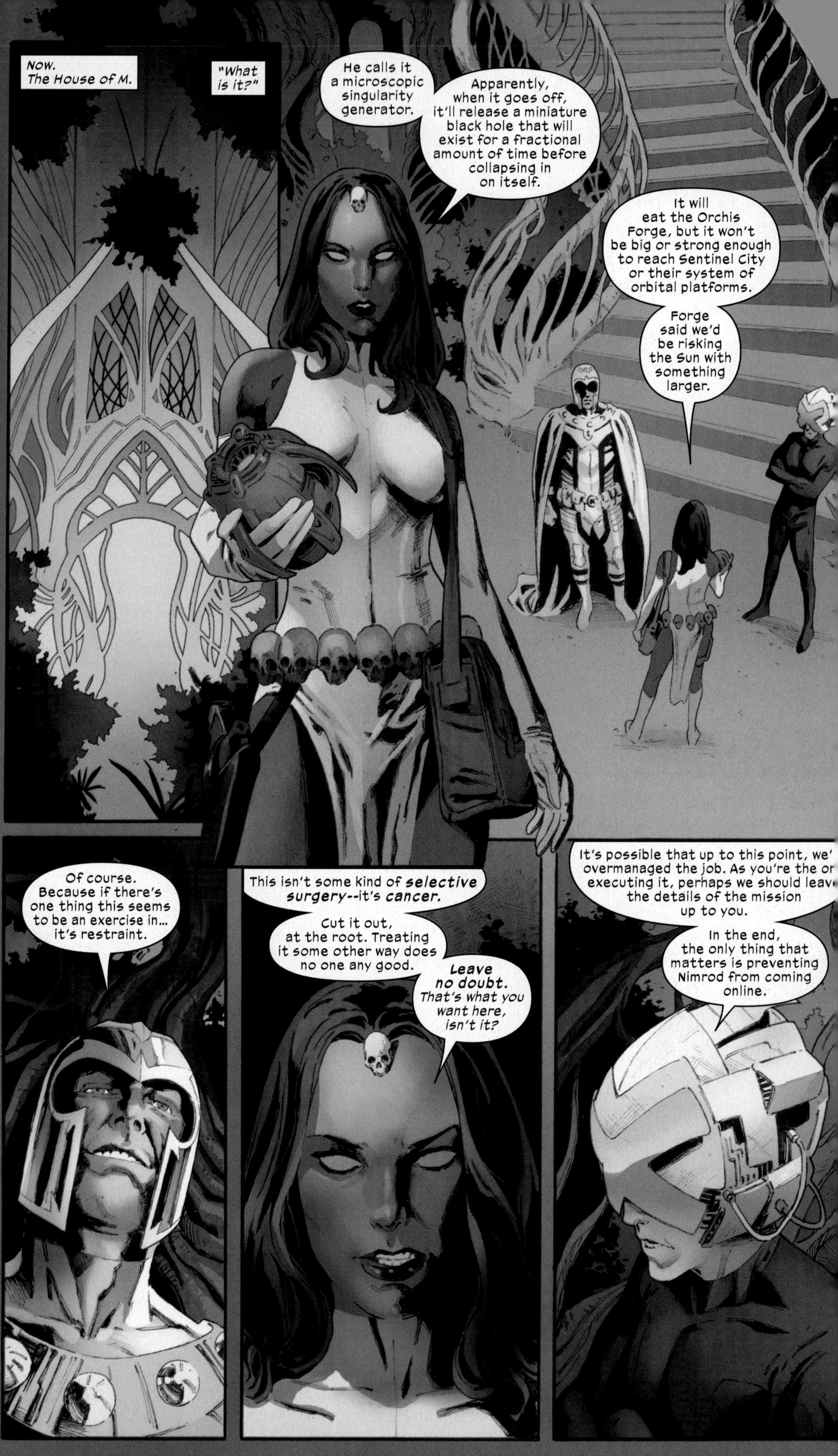
Now.
The House of M.
"What is it?"
He calls it a microscopic singularity generator.
Apparently, when it goes off, it'll release a miniature black hole that will exist for a fractional amount of time before collapsing in on itself.
It will eat the Orchis Forge, but it won't be big or strong enough to reach Sentinel City or their system of orbital platforms.
Forge said we'd be risking the Sun with something larger.
Of course. Because if there's one thing this seems to be an exercise in... it's restraint.
This isn't some kind of *selective surgery*--it's *cancer.*
Cut it out, at the root. Treating it some other way does no one any good.
Leave no doubt. That's what you want here, isn't it?
It's possible that up to this point, we' overmanaged the job. As you're the or executing it, perhaps we should leav the details of the mission up to you.
In the end, the only thing that matters is preventing Nimrod from coming online.

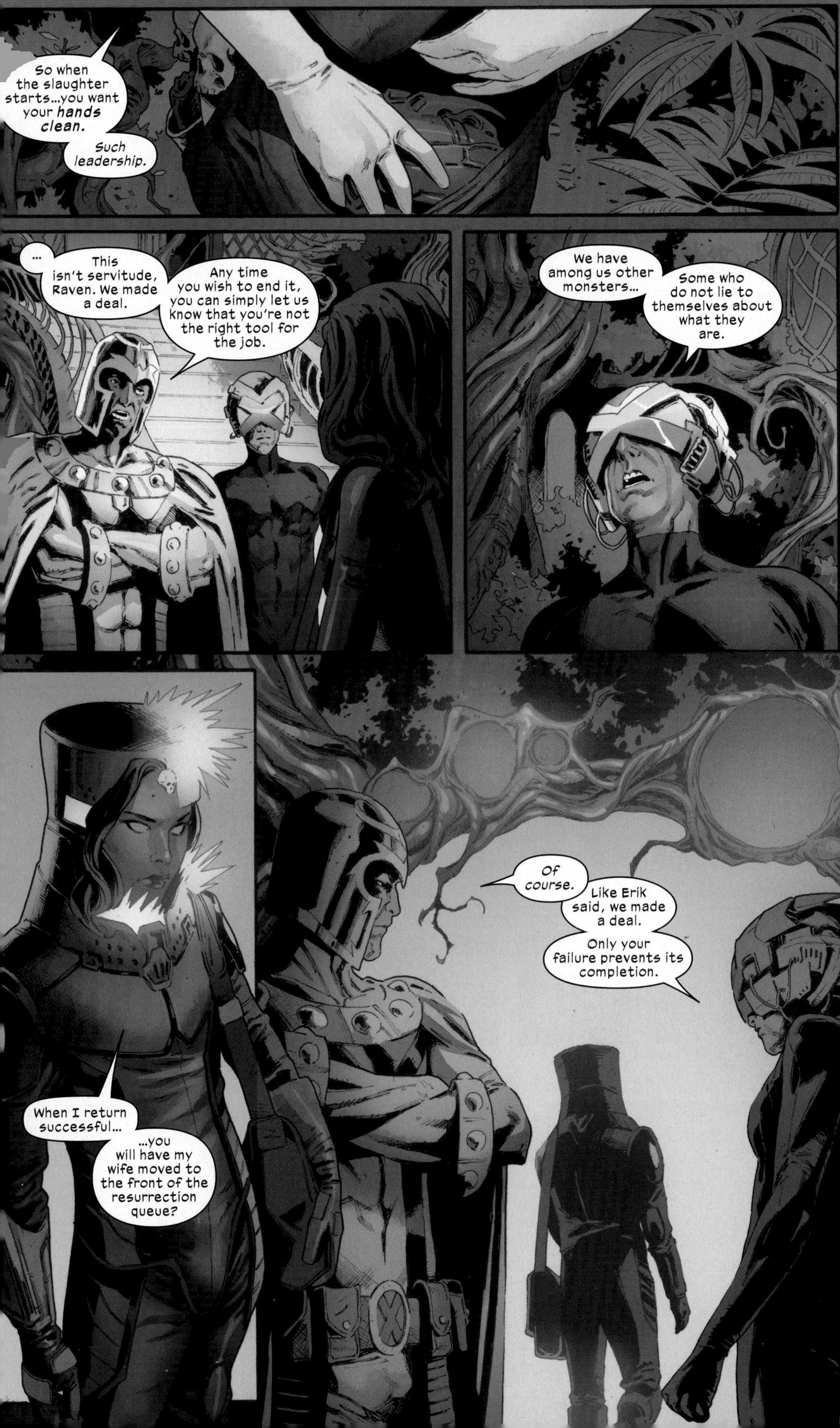
So when the slaughter starts...you want your *hands clean.*
Such leadership.
...
This isn't servitude, Raven. We made a deal.
Any time you wish to end it, you can simply let us know that you're not the right tool for the job.
We have among us other monsters...
Some who do not lie to themselves about what they are.
When I return successful...
...you will have my wife moved to the front of the resurrection queue?
Of course.
Like Erik said, we made a deal.
Only your failure prevents its completion.

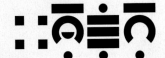

A TILTING WITHIN

The X-MEN undertook a mission to destroy the Orchis Forge, a space station with the capacity to create Nimrod, a highly advanced mutant-killing robot. They appeared to succeed, but a secret undertaking by Mystique -- assigned to her by Professor X and Magneto -- uncovered that the mission had not, in fact, stopped Orchis' Dr. Alia Gregor from 'beginning to develop' Nimrod.

While Mystique held up her end of the agreement, Professor X and Magneto did not, refusing to resurrect Mystique's wife, Destiny. And Mystique... will not be denied.

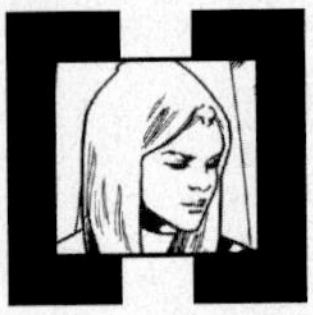

Mystique

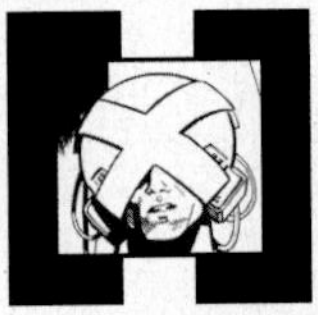

Professor X

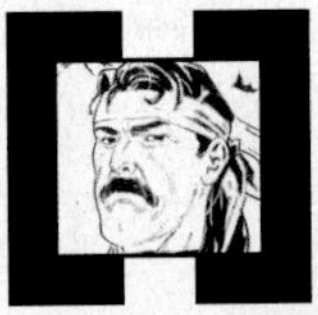

Forge

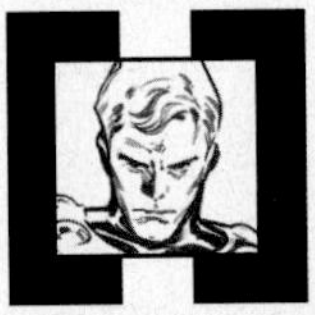

Magneto

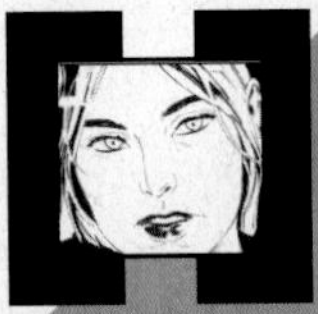

Dr. Gregor

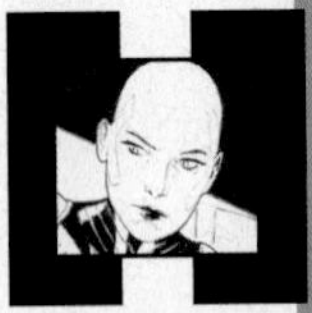

Omega Sentinel

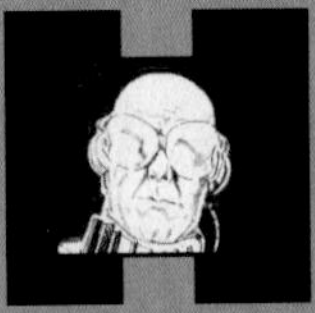

Dr. Devo

X-MEN
[X_20]

[ISSUE TWENTY].................................
...........................LOST LOVE

JONATHAN HICKMAN.....................................[WRITER]
FRANCESCO MOBILI.....................................[ARTIST]
SUNNY GHO......................................[COLOR ARTIST]
VC's CLAYTON COWLES..............................[LETTERER]
TOM MULLER..[DESIGN]

LEINIL FRANCIS YU & SUNNY GHO...............[COVER ARTISTS]

MIKE DEL MUNDO......................[VARIANT COVER ARTIST]

JONATHAN HICKMAN..............................[HEAD OF X]
NICK RUSSELL....................................[PRODUCTION]
ANNALISE BISSA...........................[ASSOCIATE EDITOR]
JORDAN D. WHITE.....................................[EDITOR]
C.B. CEBULSKI............................[EDITOR IN CHIEF]

X-MEN CREATED BY ....STAN LEE & JACK KIRBY

[00_Reign]
[00___ofX]

[00_00....0]
[00_00...20]

[00_Reign_]
[00_____]

[00___of__]

[00_____X]

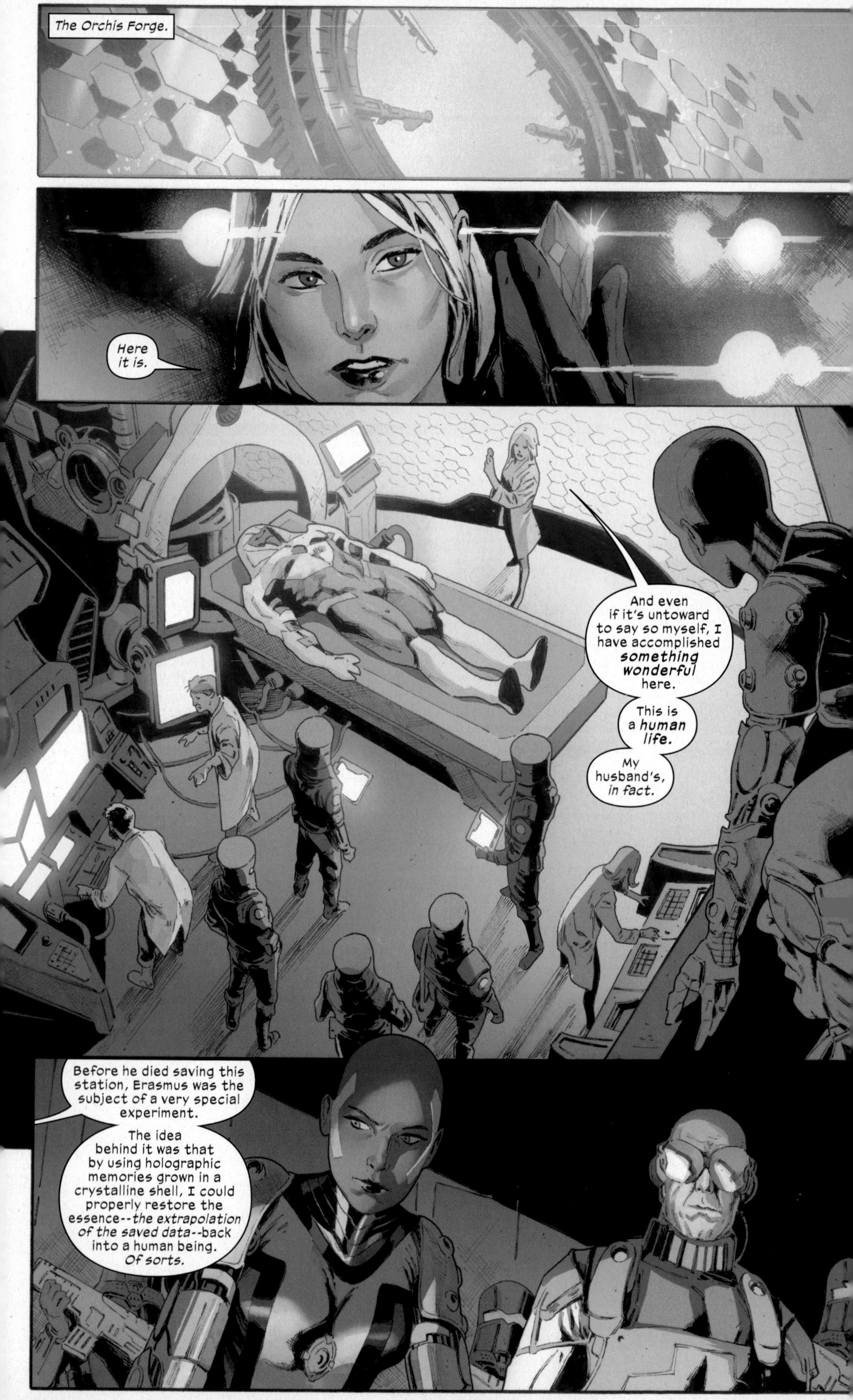
The Orchis Forge.
Here it is.
And even if it's untoward to say so myself, I have accomplished *something wonderful* here.
This is a *human life.*
My husband's, *in fact.*
Before he died saving this station, Erasmus was the subject of a very special experiment.
The idea behind it was that by using holographic memories grown in a crystalline shell, I could properly restore the essence--*the extrapolation of the saved data*--back into a human being. *Of sorts.*

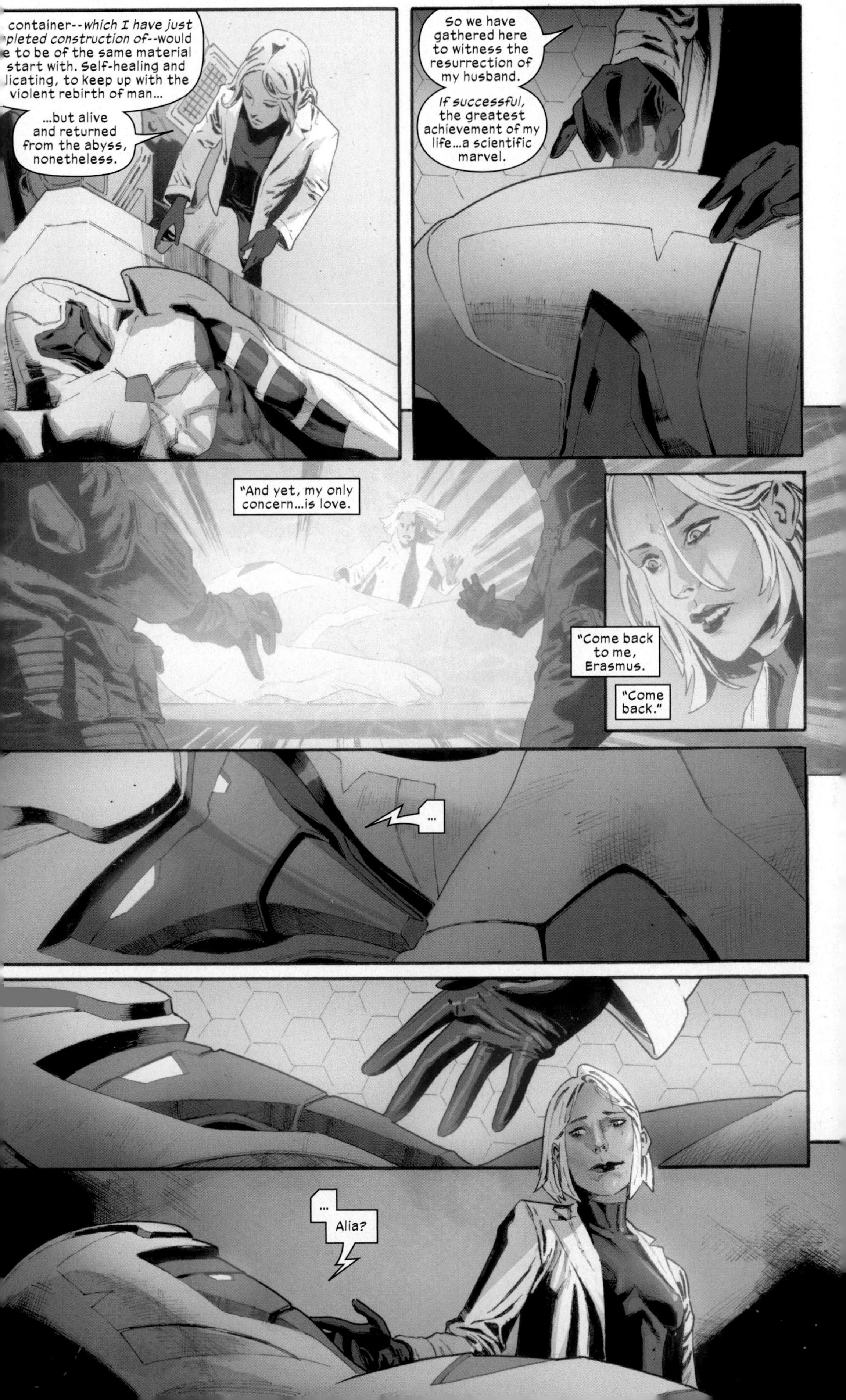
container--which I have just
pleted construction of--would
e to be of the same material
start with. Self-healing and
licating, to keep up with the
violent rebirth of man...
...but alive and returned from the abyss, nonetheless.
So we have gathered here to witness the resurrection of my husband.
If successful, the greatest achievement of my life...a scientific marvel.
"And yet, my only concern...is love.
"Come back to me, Erasmus.
"Come back."
...
... Alia?

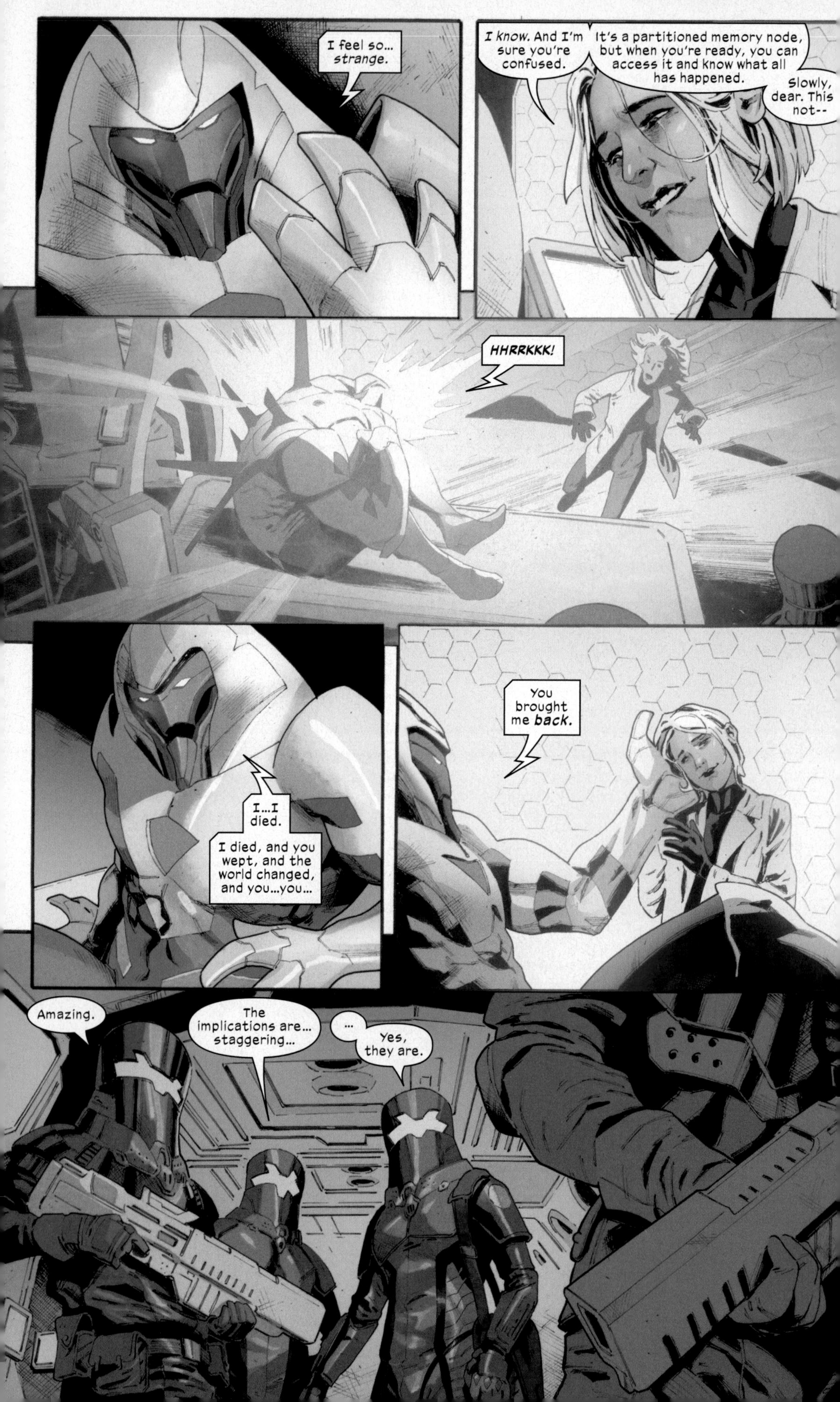
I feel so... *strange.*
I know. And I'm sure you're confused.
It's a partitioned memory node, but when you're ready, you can access it and know what all has happened.
Slowly, dear. This not--
HHRRKKK!
I...I died.
I died, and you wept, and the world changed, and you...you...
You brought me *back.*
Amazing.
The implications are... staggering...
...
Yes, they are.

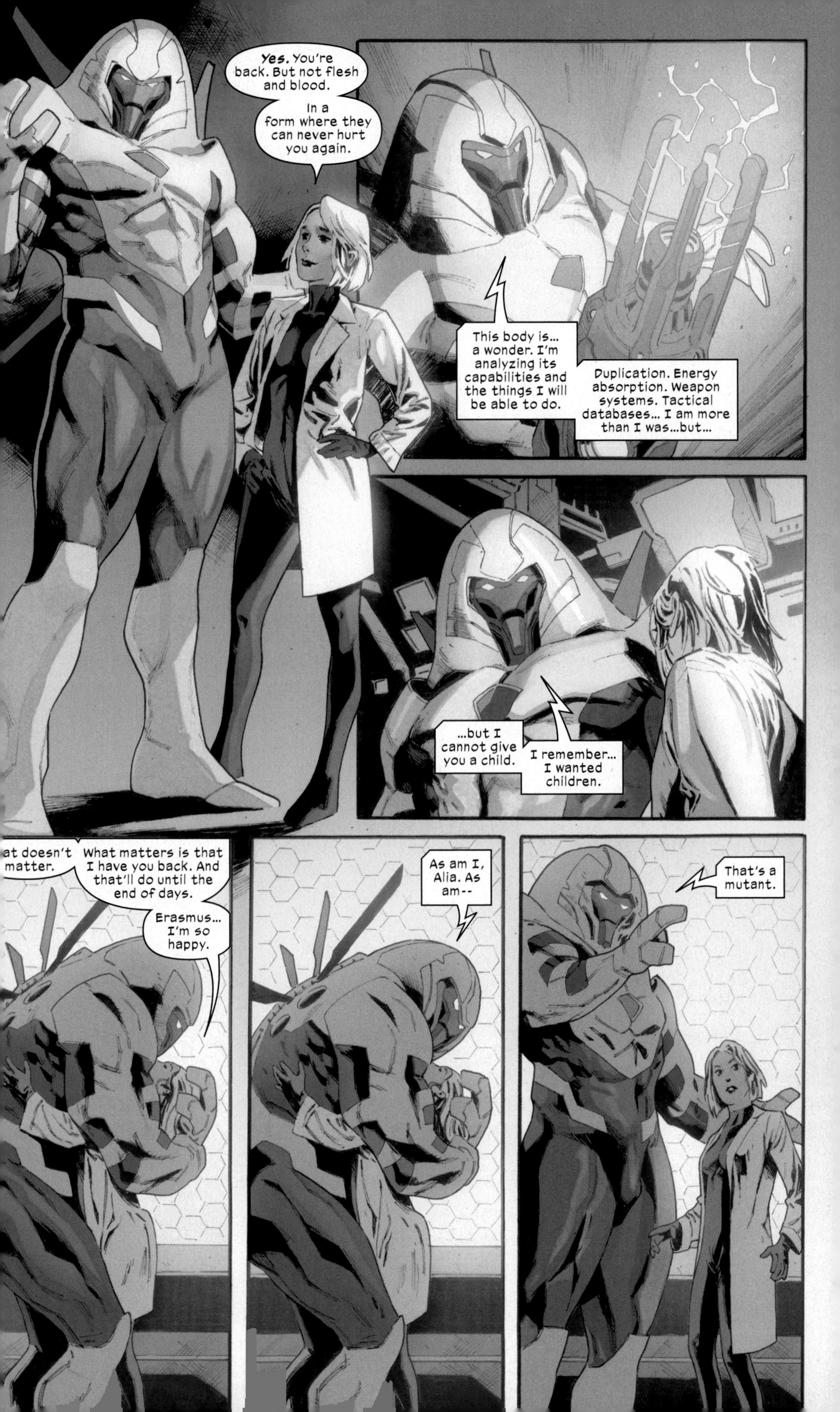
Yes. You're back. But not flesh and blood.
In a form where they can never hurt you again.
This body is... a wonder. I'm analyzing its capabilities and the things I will be able to do.
Duplication. Energy absorption. Weapon systems. Tactical databases... I am more than I was...but...
...but I cannot give you a child.
I remember... I wanted children.
at doesn't matter.
What matters is that I have you back. And that'll do until the end of days.
Erasmus... I'm so happy.
As am I, Alia. As am--
That's a mutant.

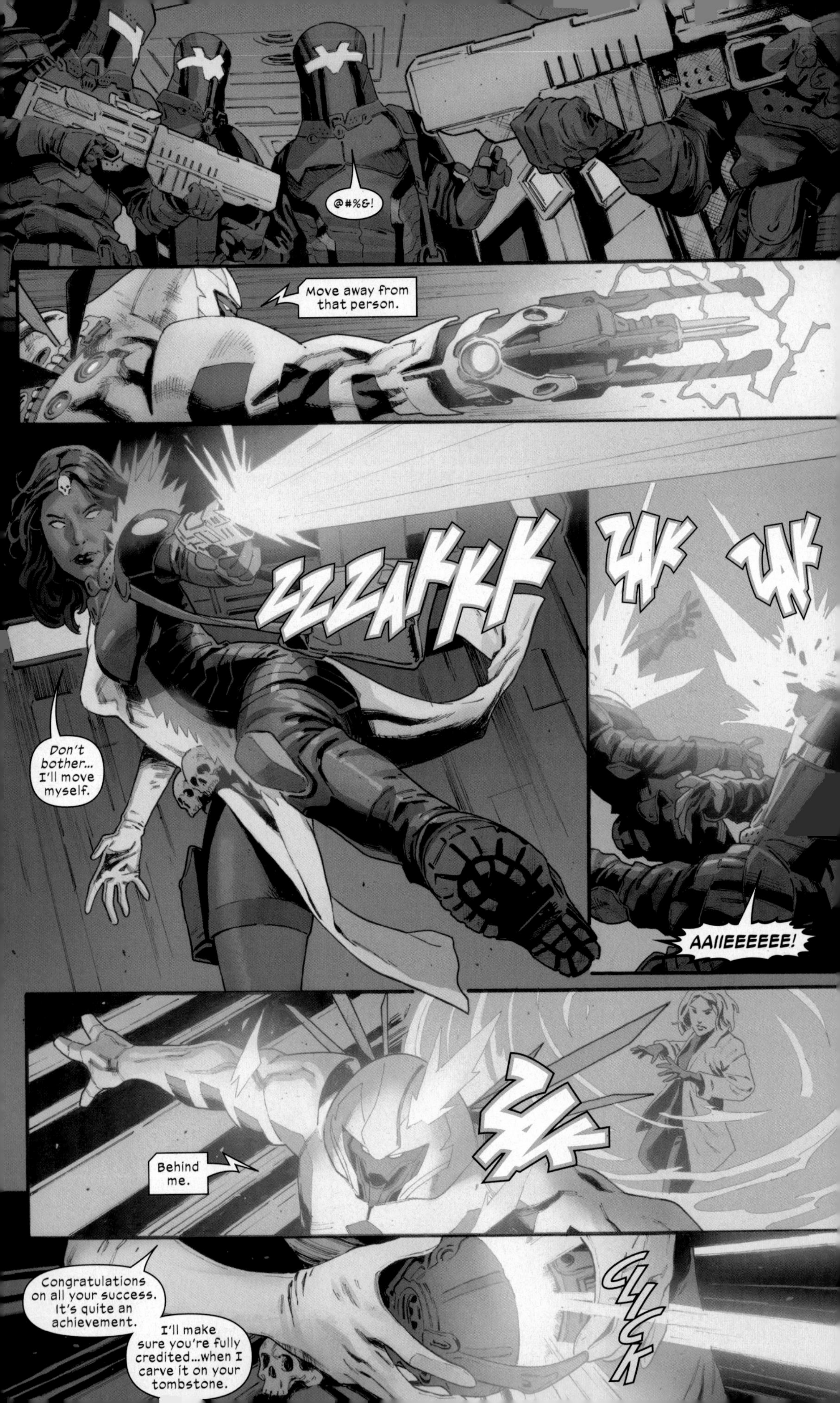

@#%&!
Move away from that person.
ZZZZAKKKK
Don't bother... I'll move myself.
ZAK
ZAK
AAIIEEEEEE!
ZAK
Behind me.
Congratulations on all your success. It's quite an achievement.
I'll make sure you're fully credited...when I carve it on your tombstone.
CLICK

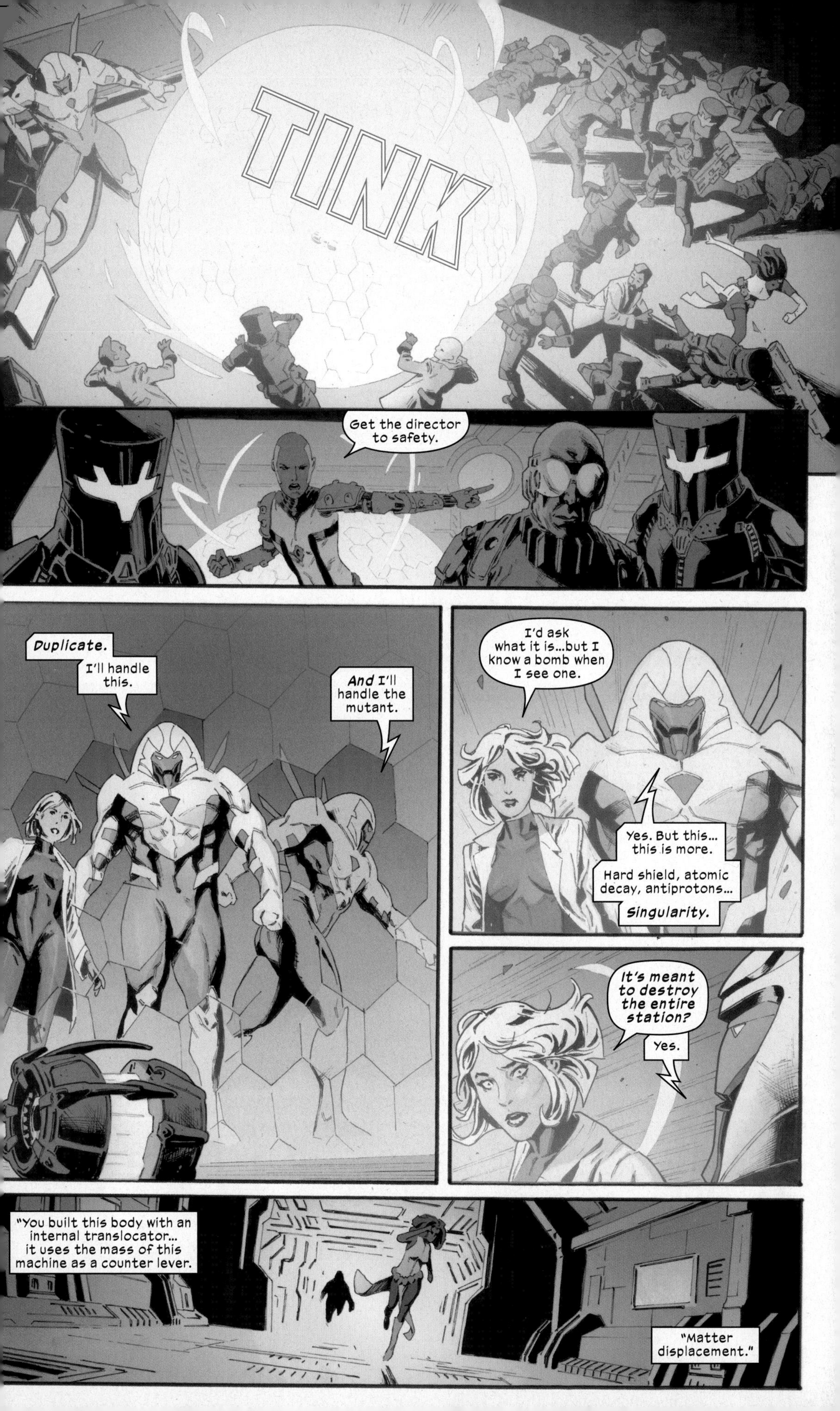
TINK
Get the director to safety.
Duplicate.
I'll handle this.
And I'll handle the mutant.
I'd ask what it is...but I know a bomb when I see one.
Yes. But this... this is more.
Hard shield, atomic decay, antiprotons...
Singularity.
It's meant to destroy the entire station?
Yes.
"You built this body with an internal translocator... it uses the mass of this machine as a counter lever.
"Matter displacement."

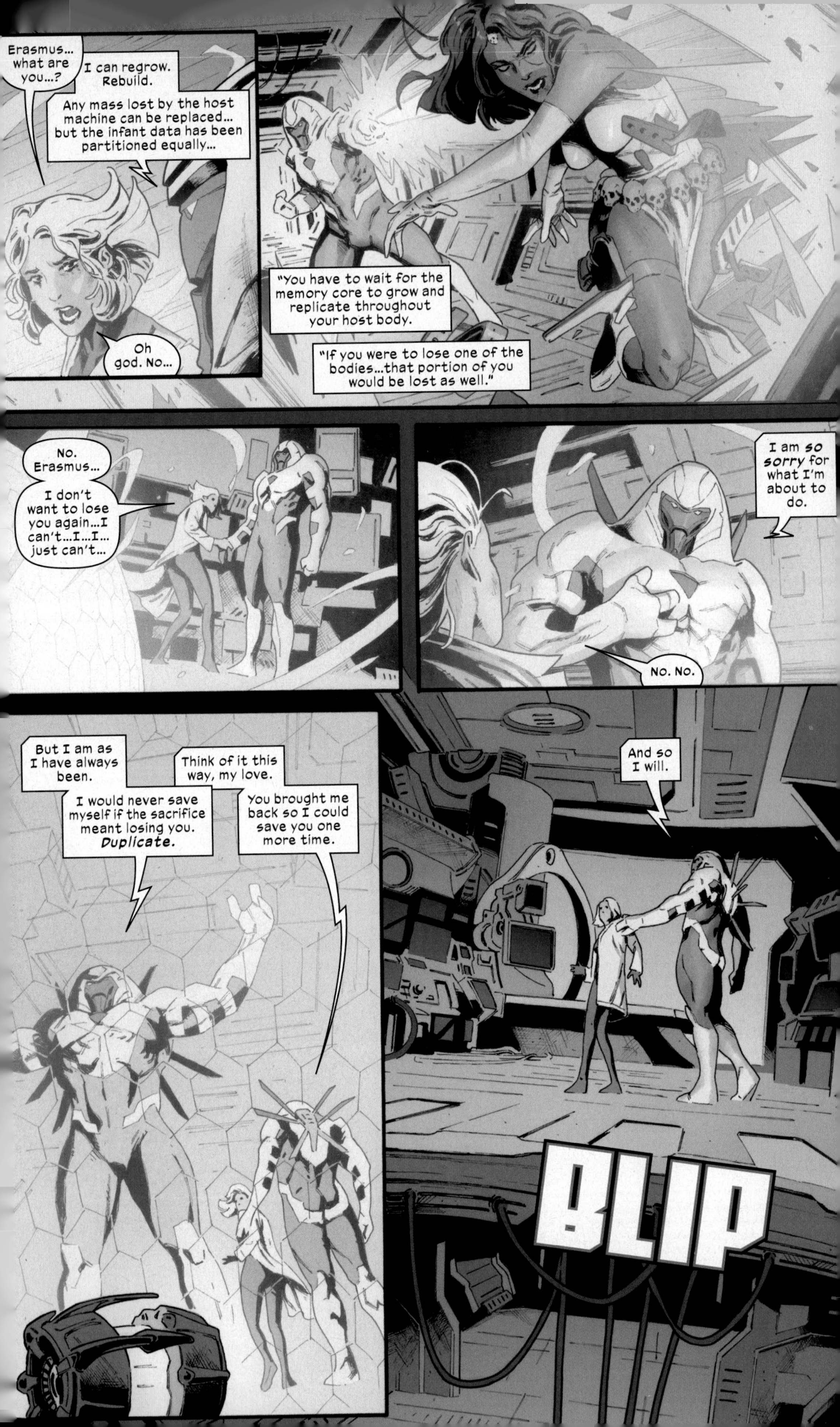

Erasmus... what are you...?
I can regrow. Rebuild.
Any mass lost by the host machine can be replaced... but the infant data has been partitioned equally...
Oh god. No...
"You have to wait for the memory core to grow and replicate throughout your host body.
"If you were to lose one of the bodies...that portion of you would be lost as well."
No. Erasmus...
I don't want to lose you again...I can't...I...I... just can't...
I am *so sorry* for what I'm about to do.
No. No.
But I am as I have always been.
I would never save myself if the sacrifice meant losing you. *Duplicate.*
Think of it this way, my love.
You brought me back so I could save you one more time.
And so I will.
BLIP

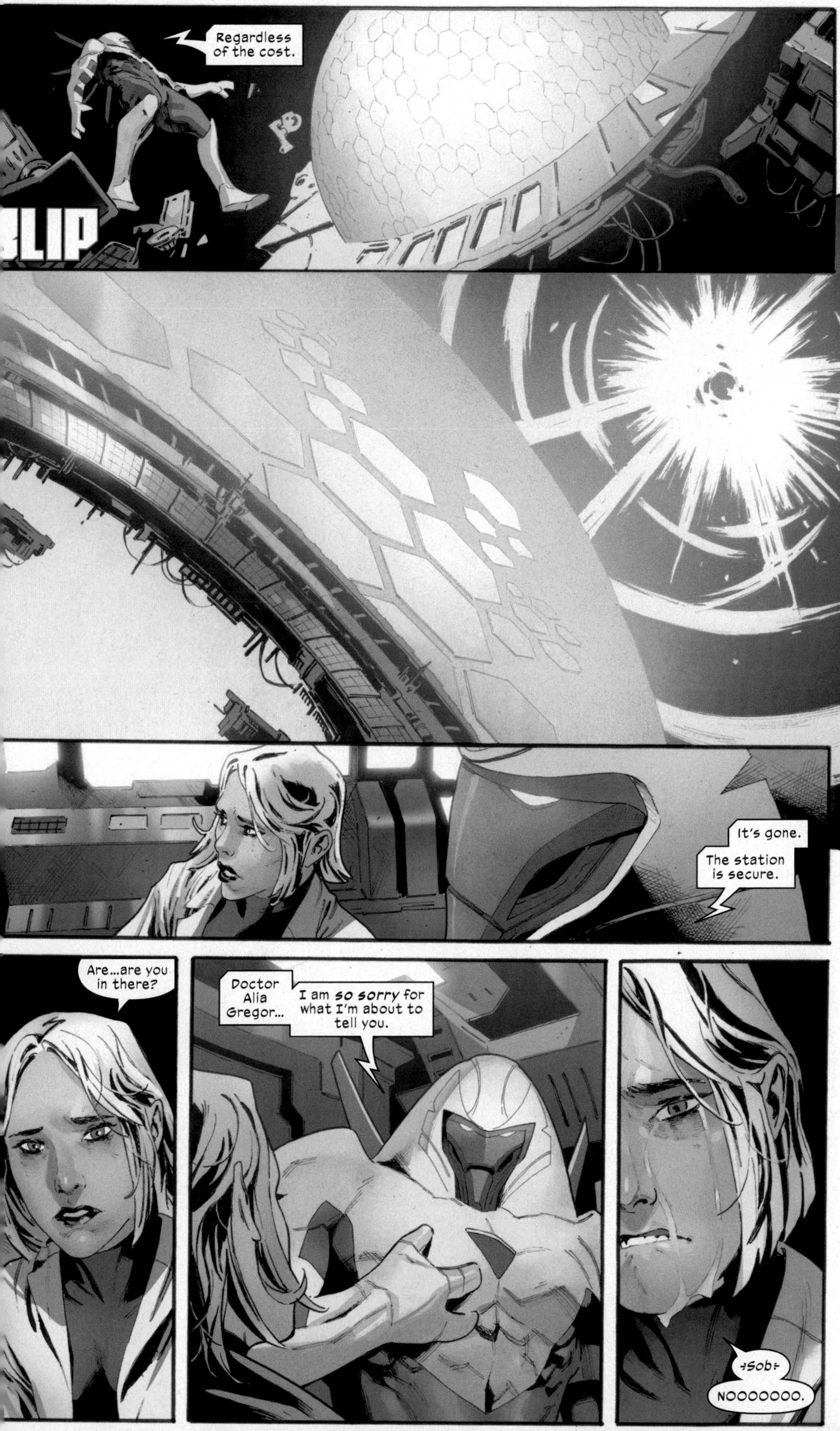
Regardless of the cost.
BLIP
It's gone.
The station is secure.
Are...are you in there?
Doctor Alia Gregor...
I am *so sorry* for what I'm about to tell you.
Sob
NOOOOOOO.

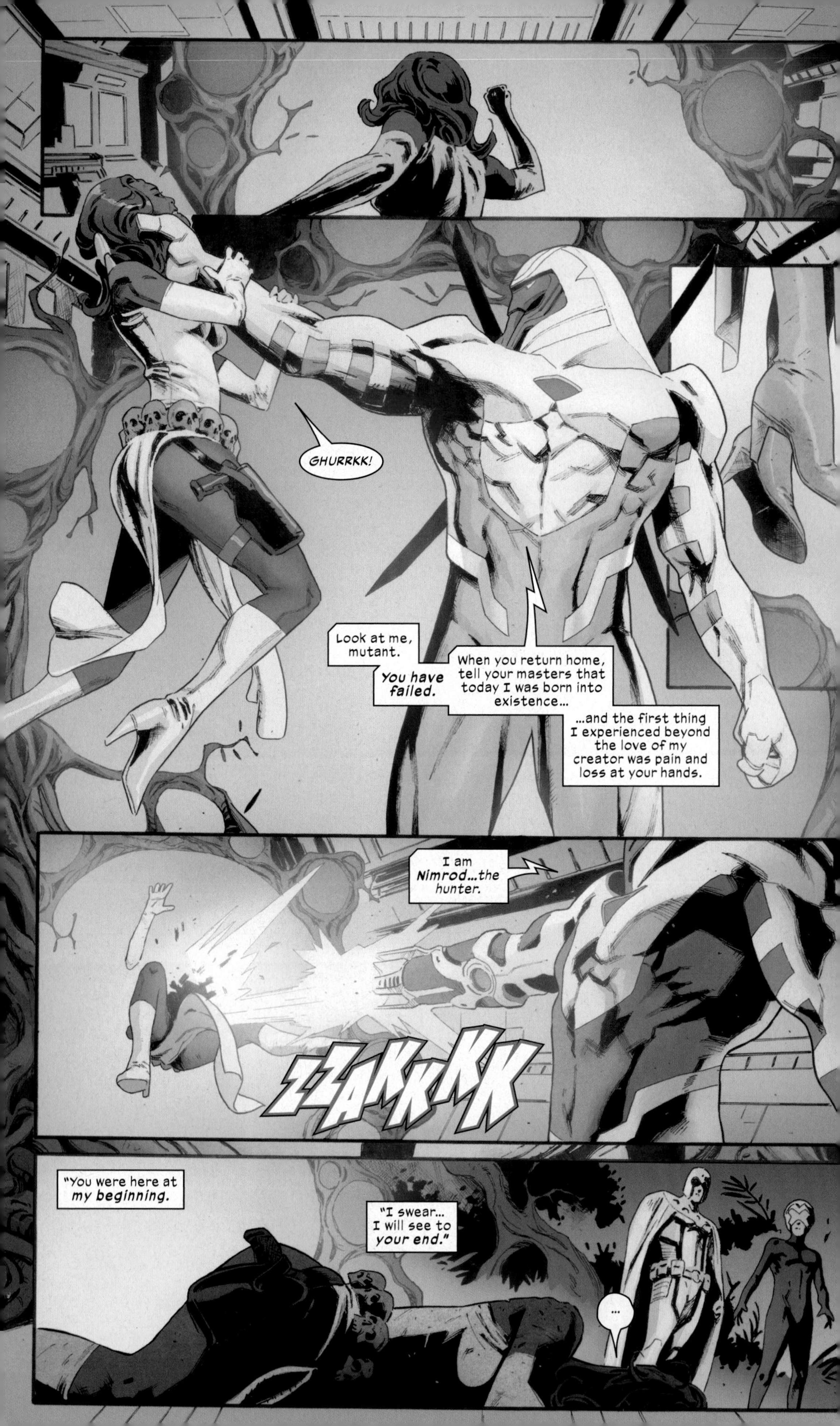
GHURRKK!
Look at me, mutant.
You have failed.
When you return home, tell your masters that today I was born into existence...
...and the first thing I experienced beyond the love of my creator was pain and loss at your hands.
I am Nimrod...the hunter.
ZZAKKKK
"You were here at my beginning.
"I swear... I will see to your end."
...

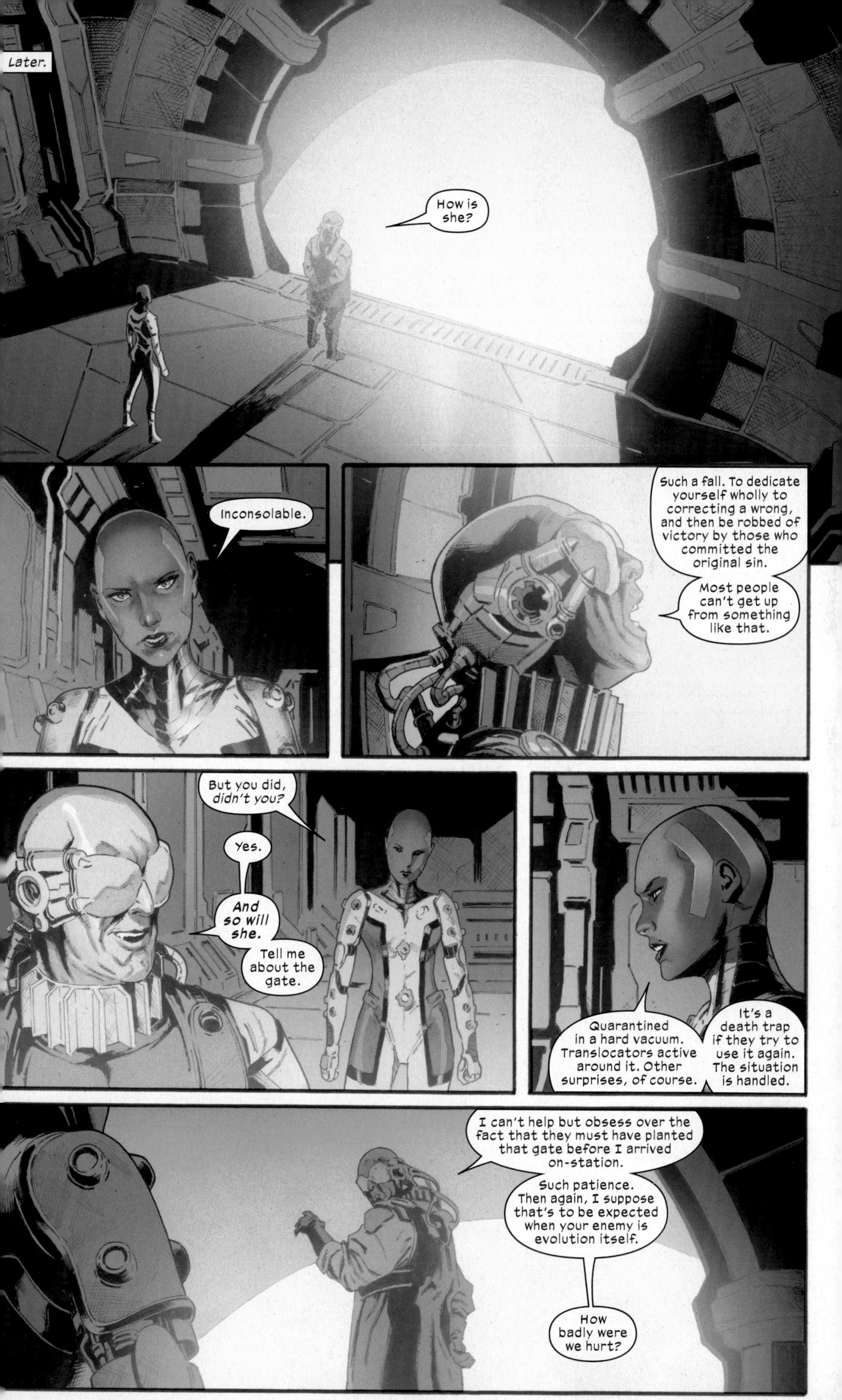

Later.
How is she?
Inconsolable.
Such a fall. To dedicate yourself wholly to correcting a wrong, and then be robbed of victory by those who committed the original sin.
Most people can't get up from something like that.
But you did, *didn't you?*
Yes.
And so will she.
Tell me about the gate.
Quarantined in a hard vacuum. Translocators active around it. Other surprises, of course.
It's a death trap if they try to use it again. The situation is handled.
I can't help but obsess over the fact that they must have planted that gate before I arrived on-station.
Such patience. Then again, I suppose that's to be expected when your enemy is evolution itself.
How badly were we hurt?

Beyond the loss of the Erasmus persona of Nimrod? We weren't hurt at all...

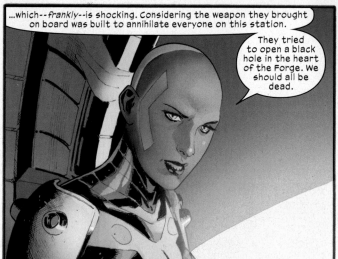

...which--*frankly*--is shocking. Considering the weapon they brought on board was built to annihilate everyone on this station.

They tried to open a black hole in the heart of the Forge. We should all be dead.

Hahahahaha.

What a joy. What a *revelation.*

Excuse me?

Yes, they hate us, and we hate them. That's the current state of mutant and man.

But all their arrogance. The bravado. The bold declarations of inevitability.

Don't you see, Omega? Those words are in conflict with their actions. It's obvious, isn't it? They don't just *hate us...*

...they *fear us.*

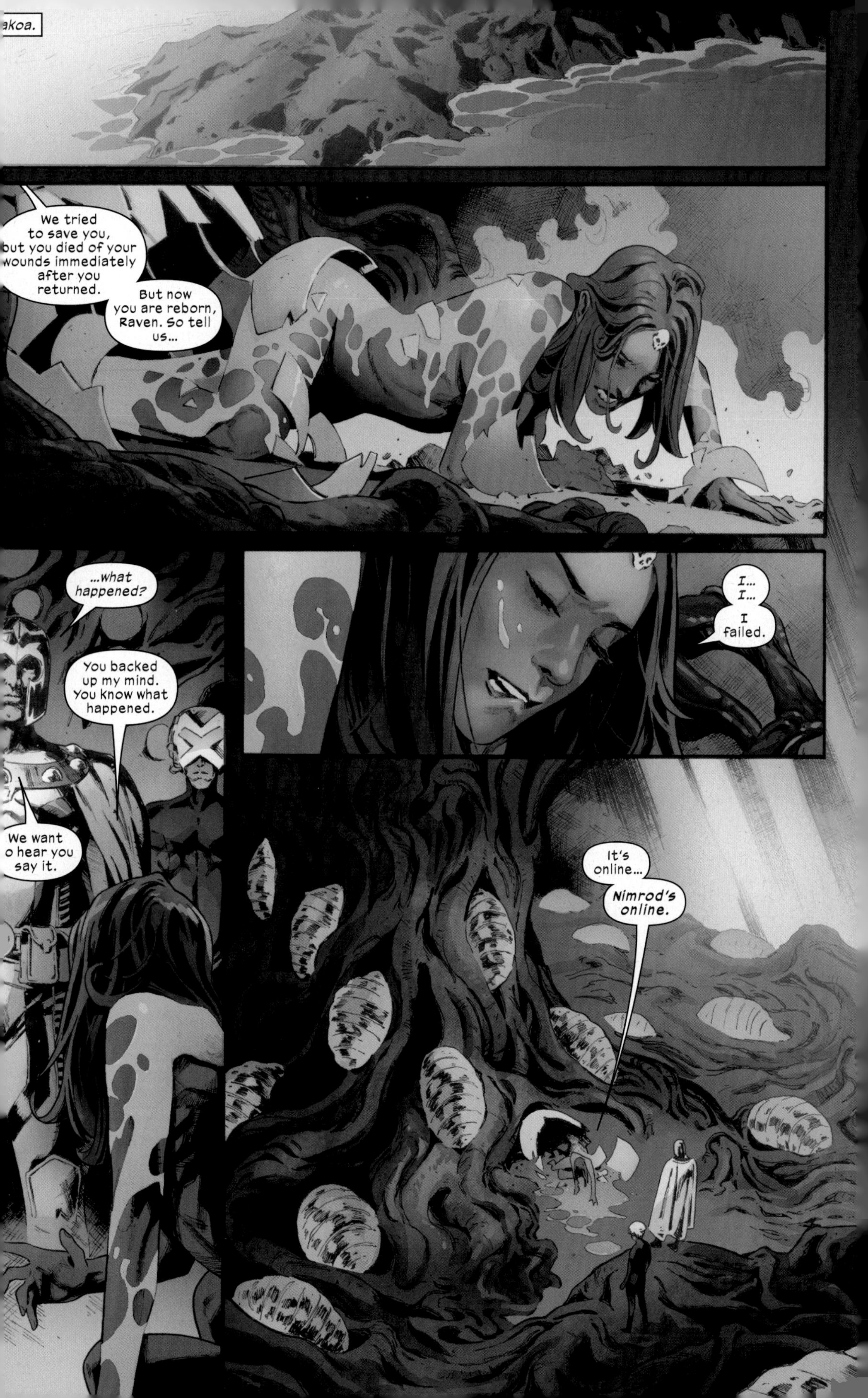
akoa.
We tried to save you, but you died of your wounds immediately after you returned.
But now you are reborn, Raven. So tell us...
...what happened?
You backed up my mind. You know what happened.
We want o hear you say it.
I... I... I failed.
It's online...
Nimrod's online.

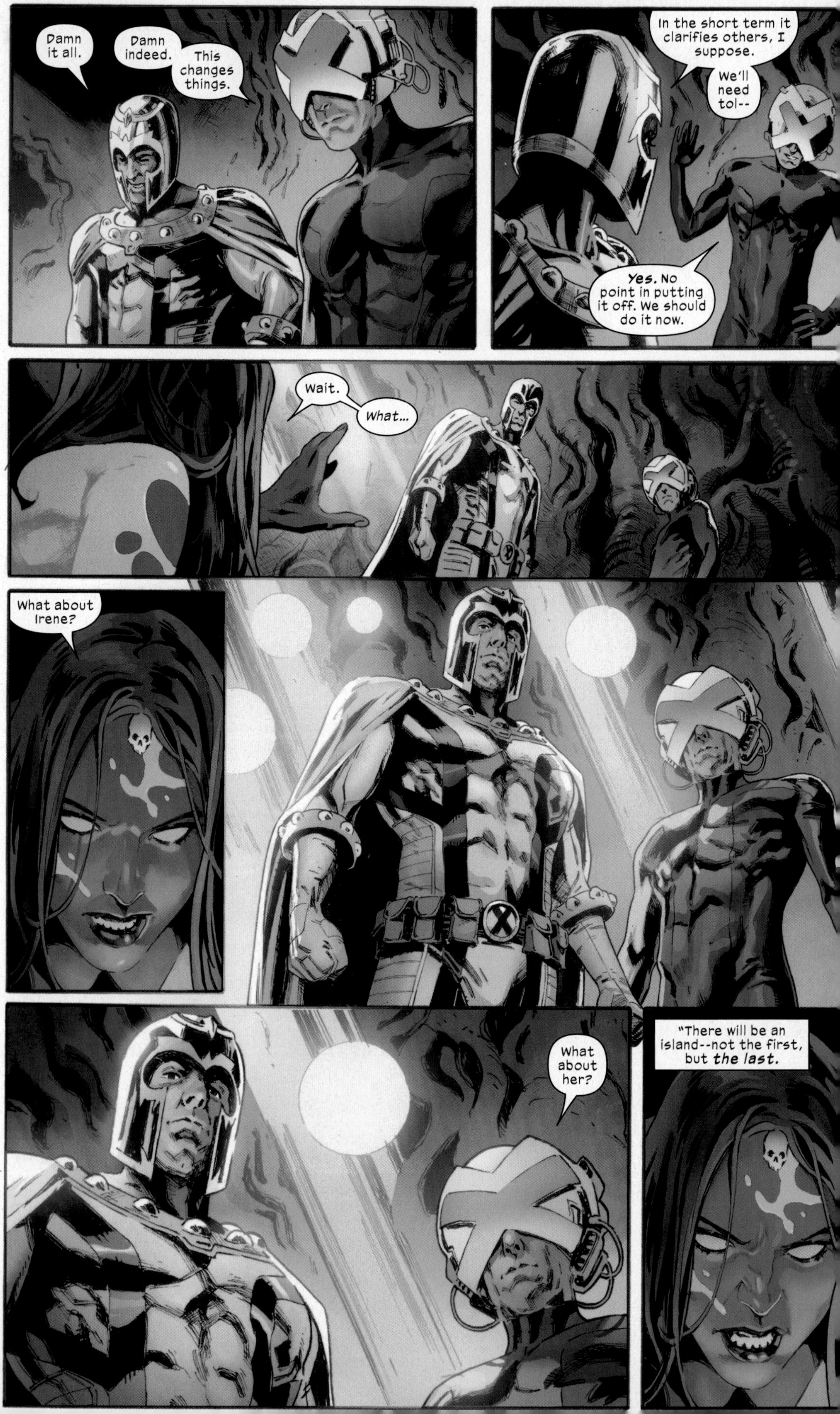

Damn it all.
Damn indeed.
This changes things.
In the short term it clarifies others, I suppose.
We'll need to!--
Yes. No point in putting it off. We should do it now.
Wait.
What...
What about Irene?
What about her?
"There will be an island--not the first, but *the last.*

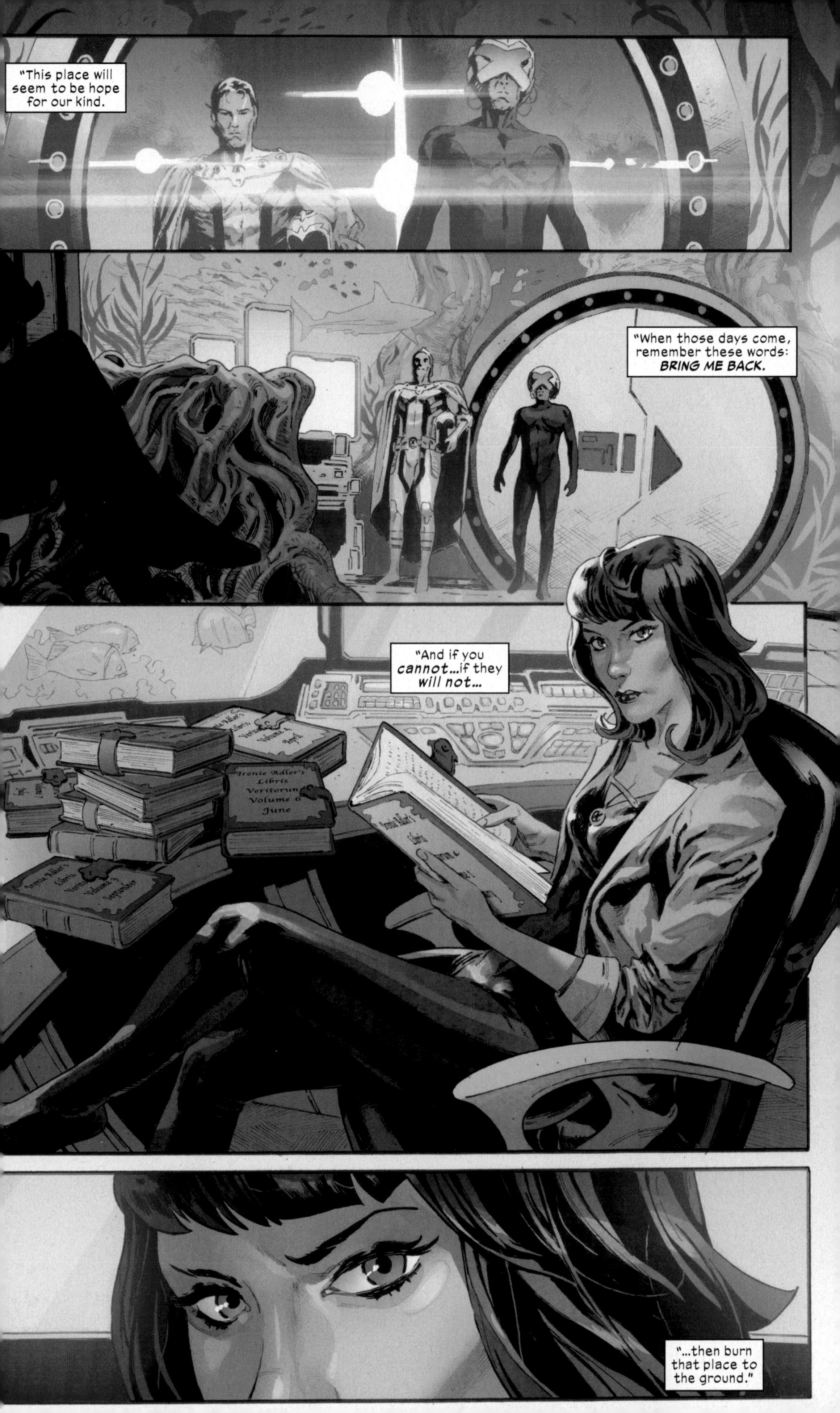
"This place will seem to be hope for our kind.
"When those days come, remember these words: ***BRING ME BACK.***
"And if you ***cannot***...if they ***will not***...
Irene Adler's Libris Veritorum Volume 6 June
"...then burn that place to the ground."

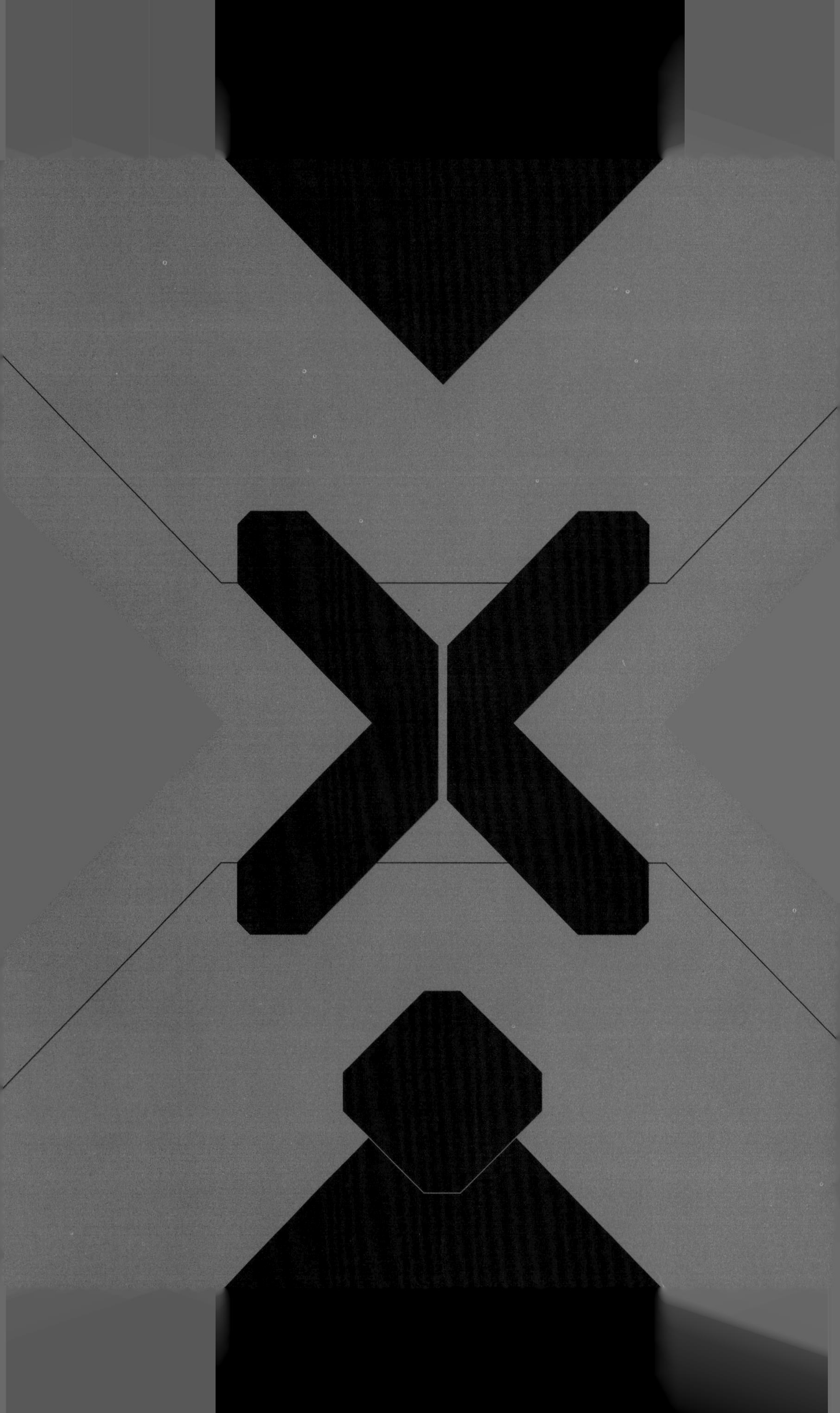

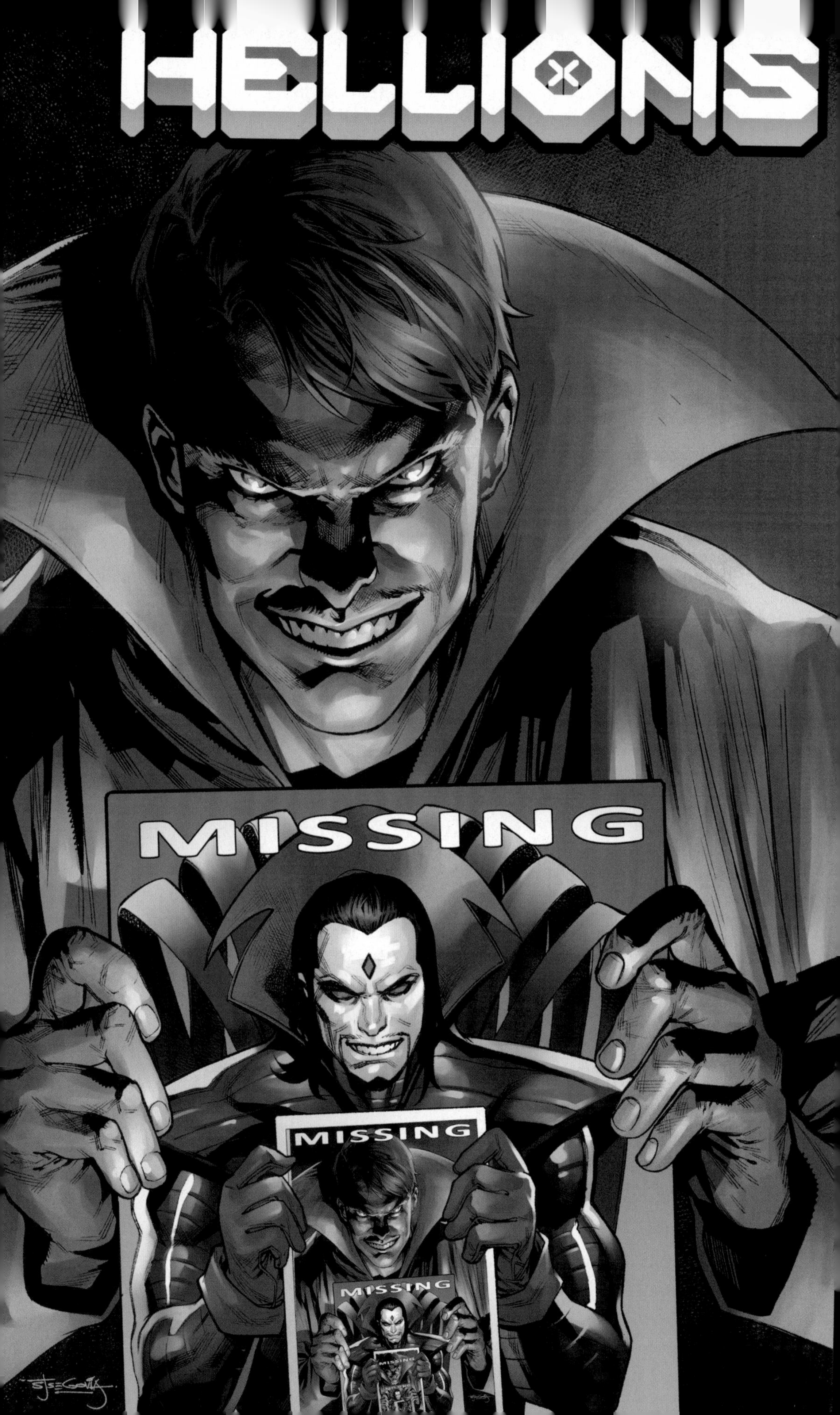
HELLIONS
MISSING
MISSING
MISSING

HAVE YOU SEEN THIS MUTANT?

The Hellions have returned to Krakoa after a successful mission to recover Orphan-Maker's armor from Cameron Hodge and his robot army of Smileys. While the Hellions were able to help the Smileys turn against Hodge and circumvent their anti-mutant programming, Krakoa's A.I. policy demanded that Psylocke destroy the A.I., wiping out all Smiley tech -- although perhaps not for good if Nanny has anything to say about it...

Meanwhile, Greycrow and Psylocke have grown closer than ever. Who knows, perhaps this whole "rehabilitation" thing is actually working?

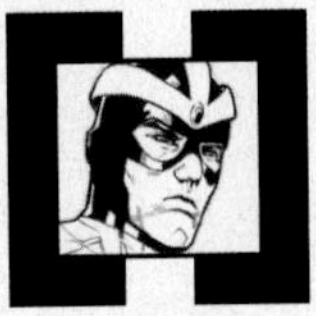
Havok

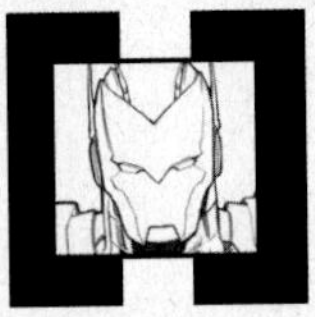
Orphan-Maker

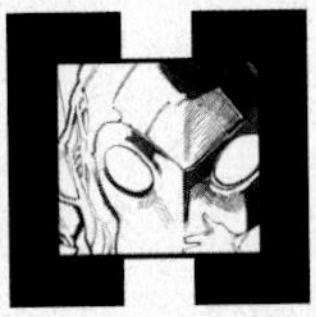
Nanny

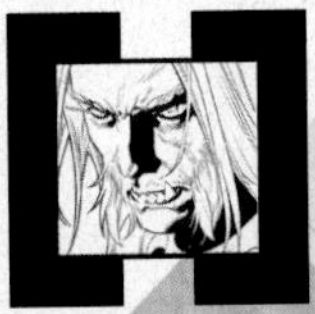
Wild Child

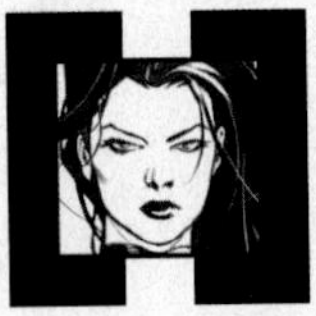
Psylocke

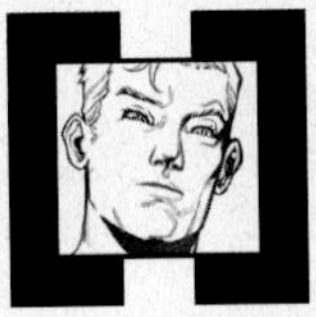
Empath

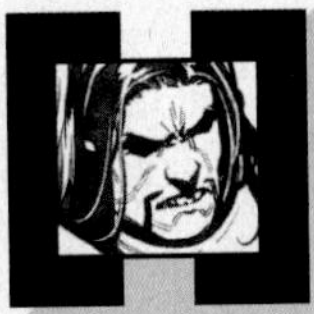
Greycrow

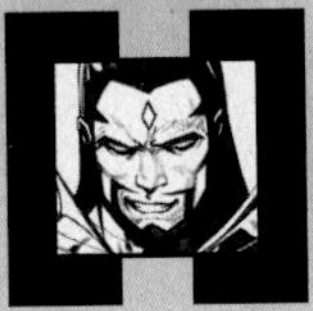
Mr. Sinister

[00_Reign]
[00___ofX]

HELLIONS
[X_09]

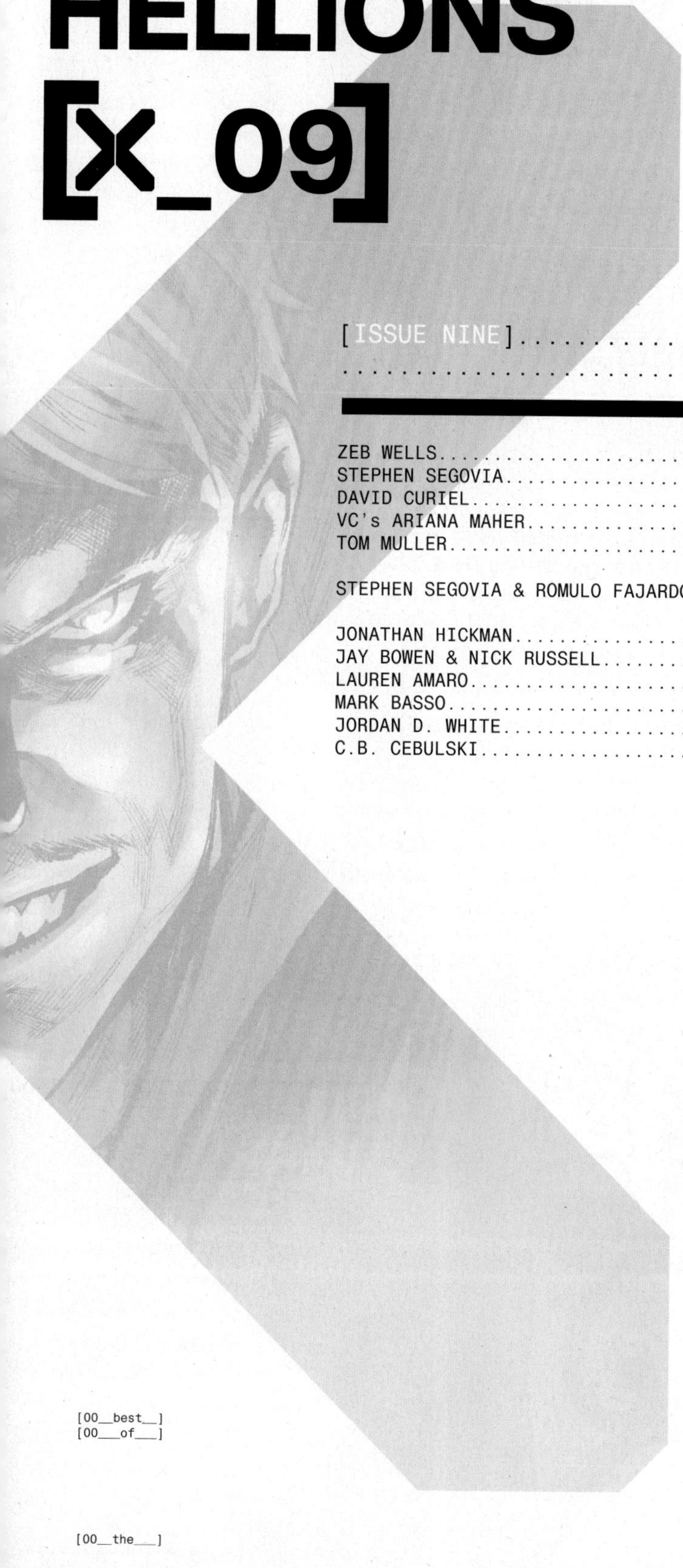

[ISSUE NINE]..................... FUNNY GAMES:
.... Level 1

ZEB WELLS.......................................[WRITER]
STEPHEN SEGOVIA.................................[ARTIST]
DAVID CURIEL..............................[COLOR ARTIST]
VC's ARIANA MAHER............................[LETTERER]
TOM MULLER.......................................[DESIGN]

STEPHEN SEGOVIA & ROMULO FAJARDO JR.........[COVER ARTISTS]

JONATHAN HICKMAN...............................[HEAD OF X]
JAY BOWEN & NICK RUSSELL.....................[PRODUCTION]
LAUREN AMARO.........................[ASSISTANT EDITOR]
MARK BASSO.......................................[EDITOR]
JORDAN D. WHITE..........................[SENIOR EDITOR]
C.B. CEBULSKI..........................[EDITOR IN CHIEF]

[00__best__]
[00___of___]

[00__the___]

[00_worst_X]

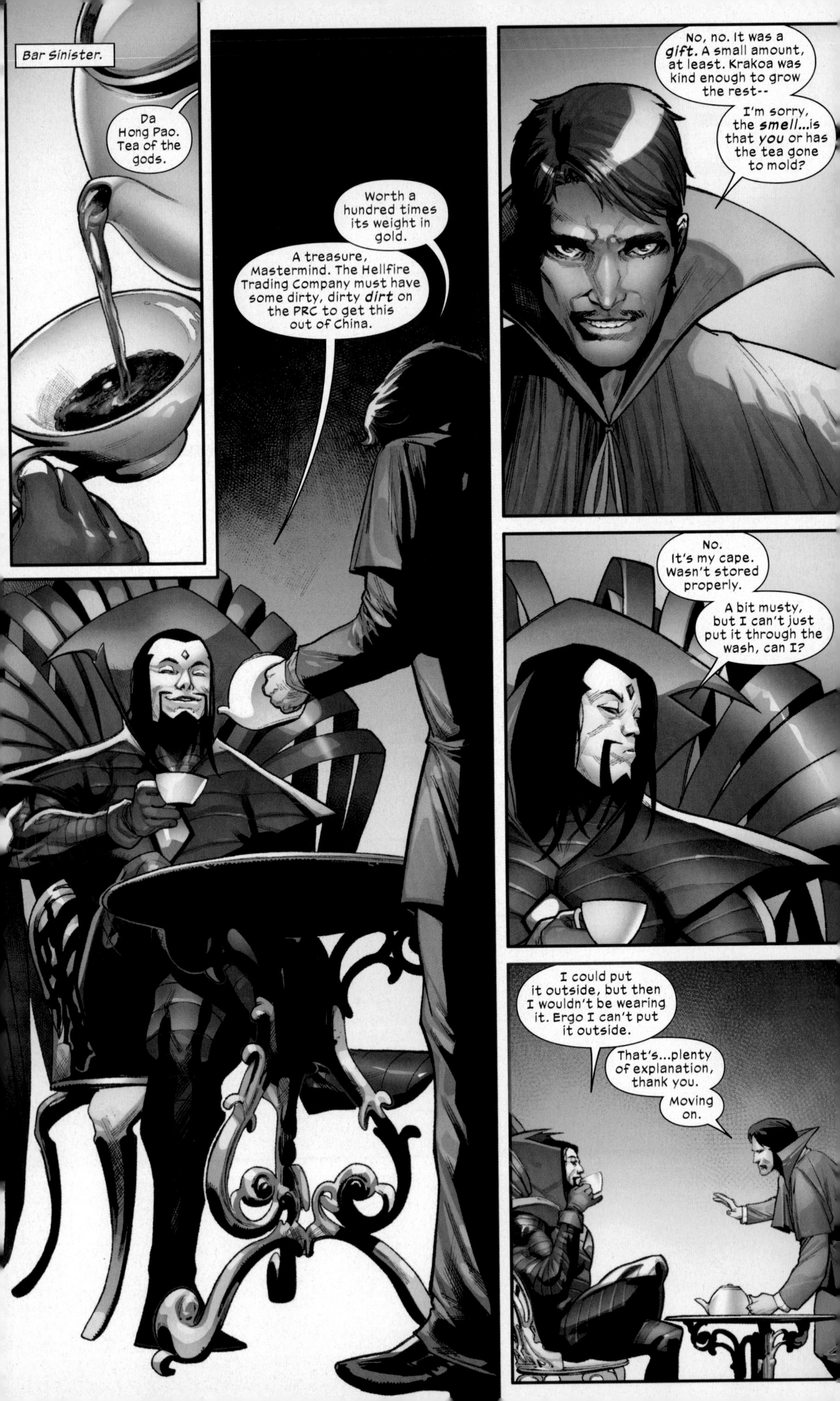
Bar Sinister.
Da Hong Pao. Tea of the gods.
Worth a hundred times its weight in gold.
A treasure, Mastermind. The Hellfire Trading Company must have some dirty, dirty *dirt* on the PRC to get this out of China.
No, no. It was a *gift*. A small amount, at least. Krakoa was kind enough to grow the rest--
I'm sorry, the *smell*...is that *you* or has the tea gone to mold?
No. It's my cape. Wasn't stored properly.
A bit musty, but I can't just put it through the wash, can I?
I could put it outside, but then I wouldn't be wearing it. Ergo I can't put it outside.
That's...plenty of explanation, thank you.
Moving on.

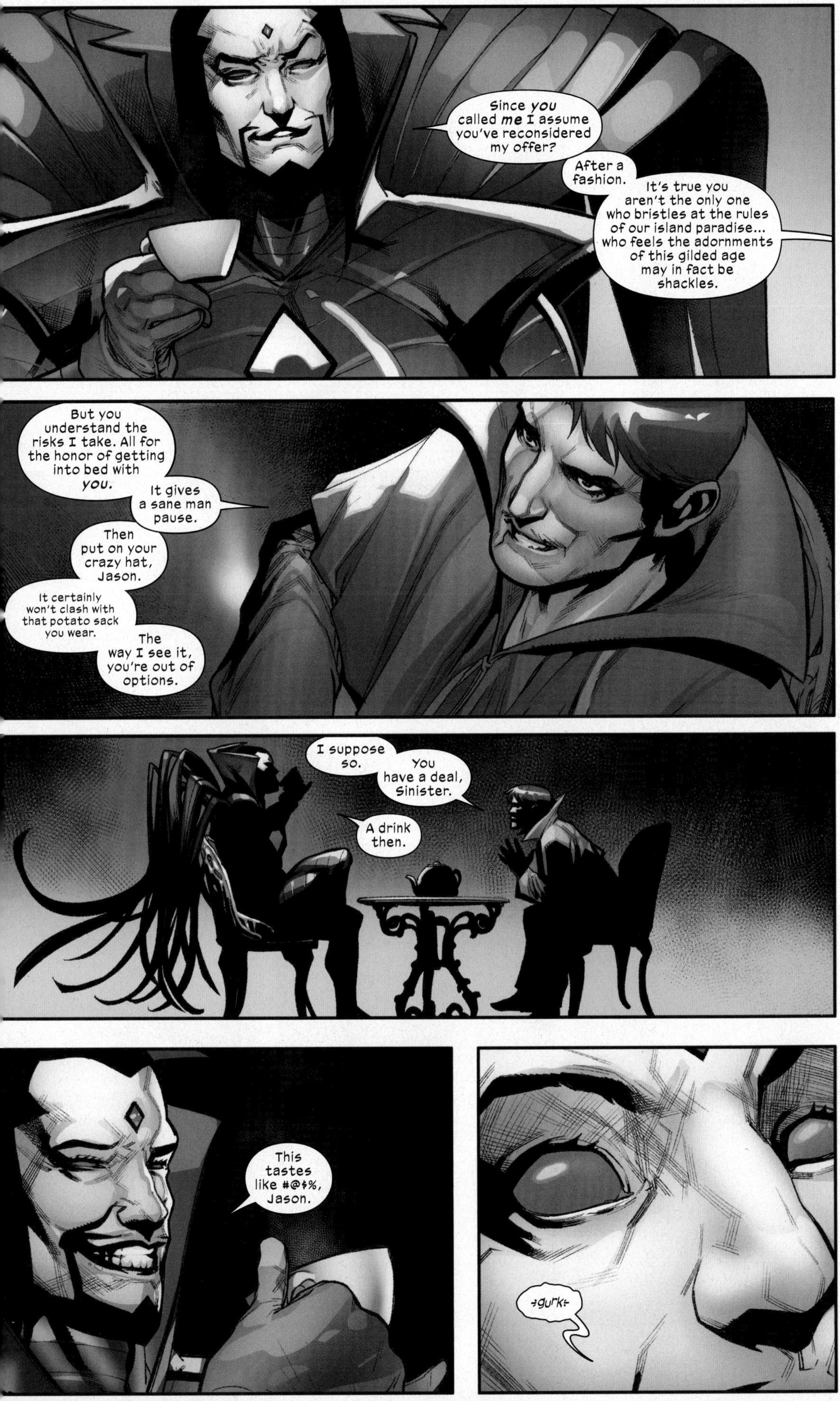
Since *you* called *me* I assume you've reconsidered my offer?
After a fashion.
It's true you aren't the only one who bristles at the rules of our island paradise... who feels the adornments of this gilded age may in fact be shackles.
But you understand the risks I take. All for the honor of getting into bed with *you.*
It gives a sane man pause.
Then put on your crazy hat, Jason.
It certainly won't clash with that potato sack you wear.
The way I see it, you're out of options.
I suppose so.
You have a deal, Sinister.
A drink then.
This tastes like #@$%, Jason.
=gurk=

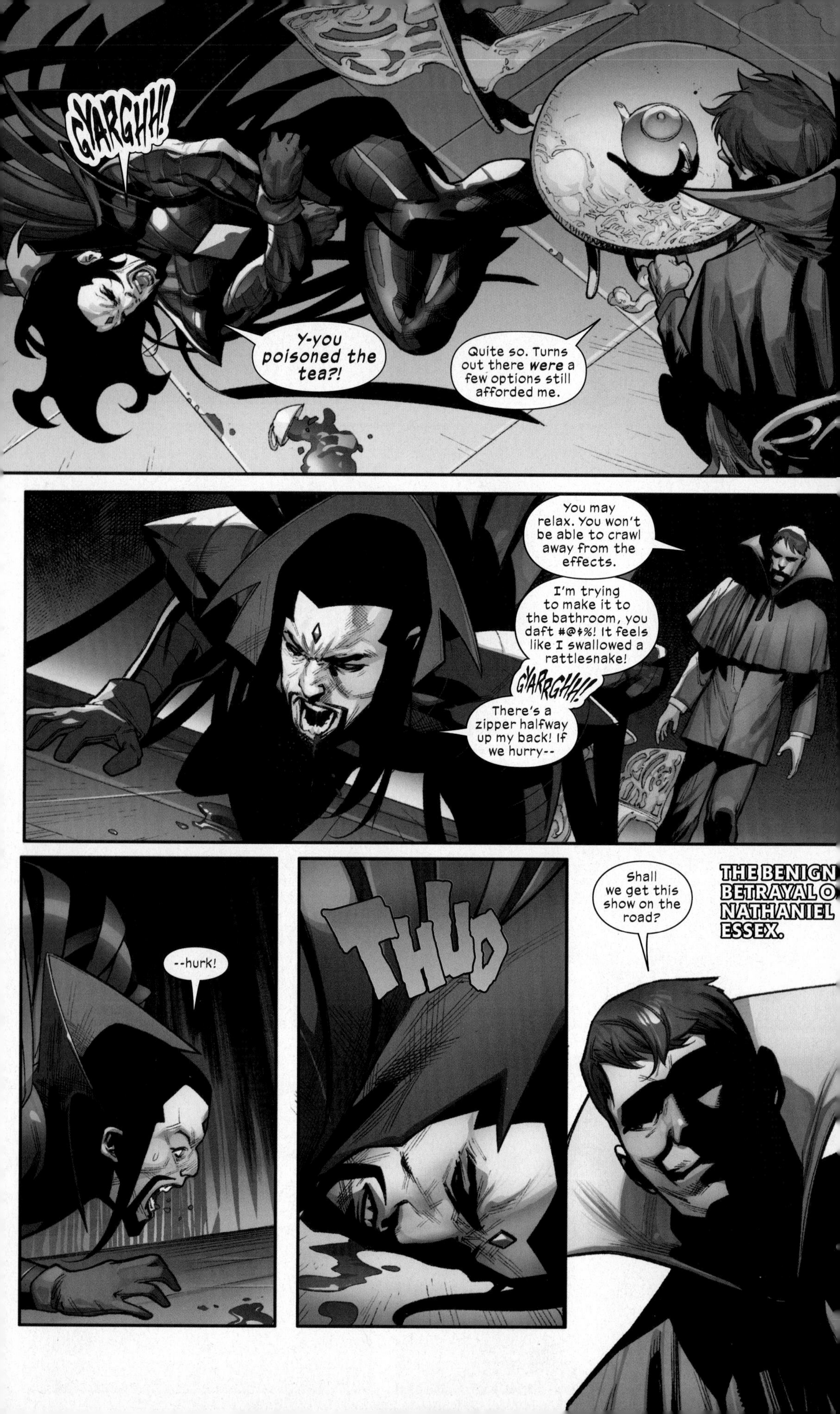
GYARGHH!
Y-you poisoned the tea?!
Quite so. Turns out there *were* a few options still afforded me.
You may relax. You won't be able to crawl away from the effects.
I'm trying to make it to the bathroom, you daft #@$%! It feels like I swallowed a rattlesnake!
GYARRGHH!
There's a zipper halfway up my back! If we hurry--
--hurk!
THUD
Shall we get this show on the road?
THE BENIGN BETRAYAL O NATHANIEL ESSEX.

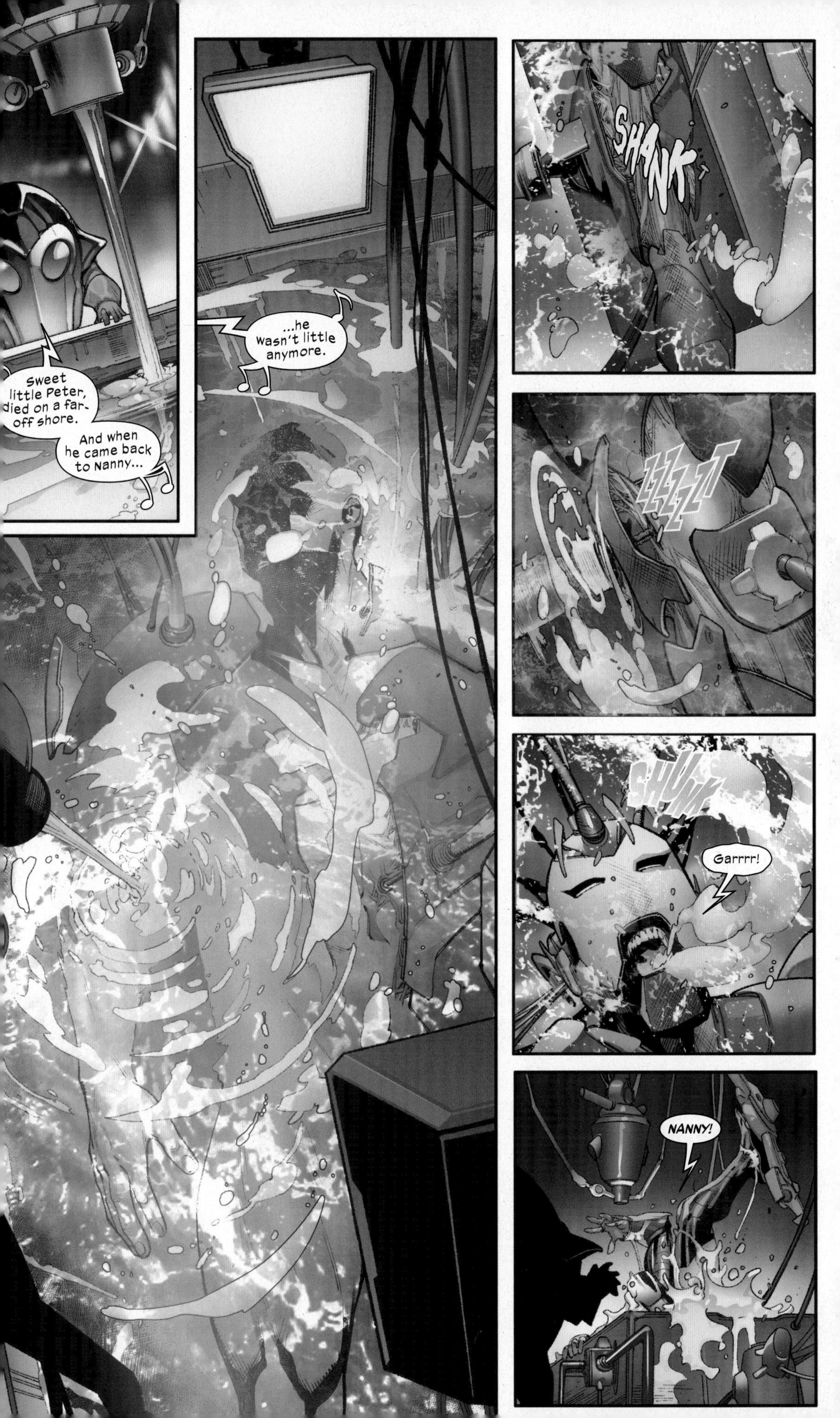

Sweet little Peter, died on a far-off shore.
And when he came back to Nanny...
...he wasn't little anymore.
SHANK
ZZZZZZT
SHUNK
Garrrr!
NANNY!

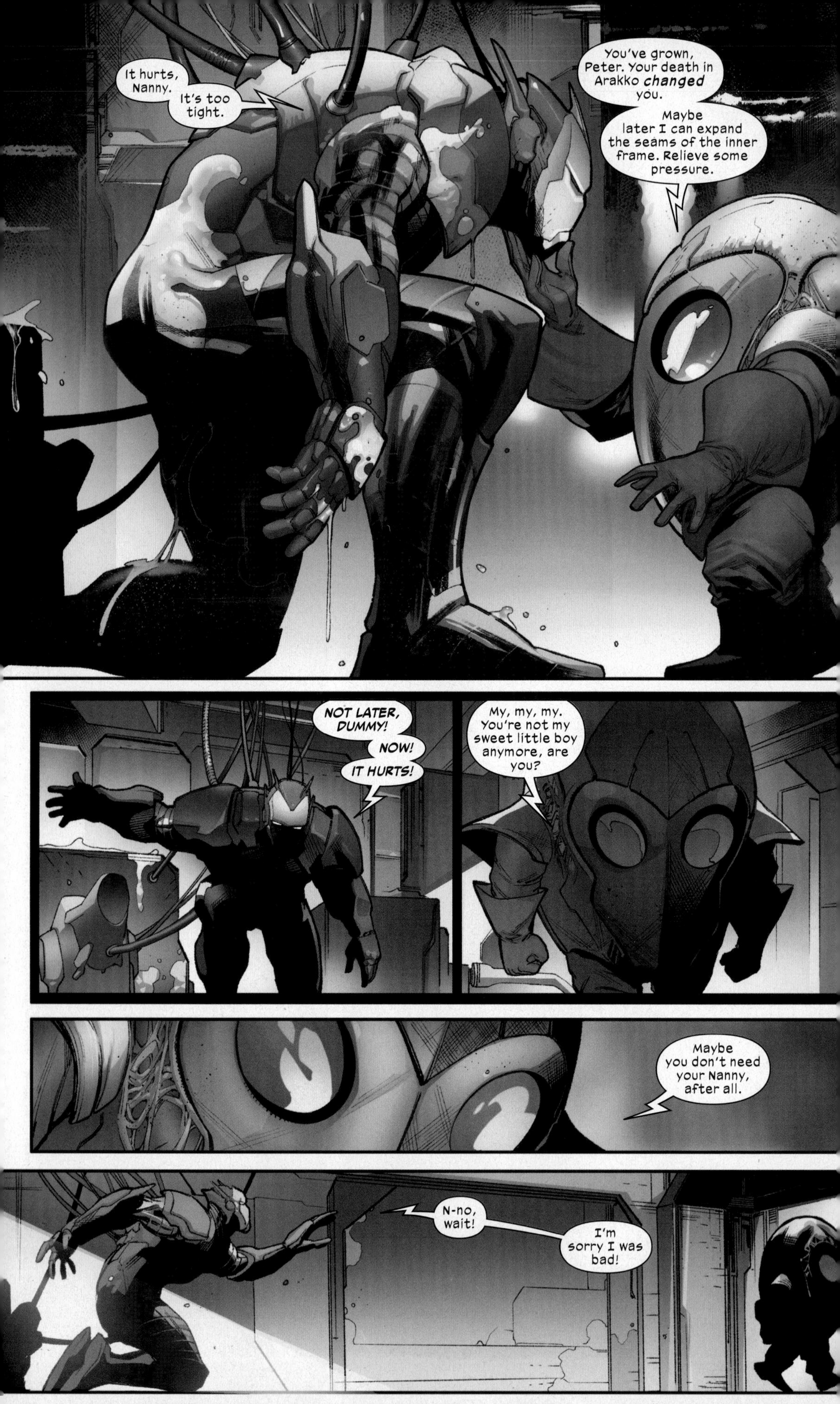
It hurts, Nanny.
It's too tight.
You've grown, Peter. Your death in Arakko *changed* you.
Maybe later I can expand the seams of the inner frame. Relieve some pressure.
NOT LATER, DUMMY!
NOW!
IT HURTS!
My, my, my. You're not my sweet little boy anymore, are you?
Maybe you don't need your Nanny, after all.
N-no, wait!
I'm sorry I was bad!

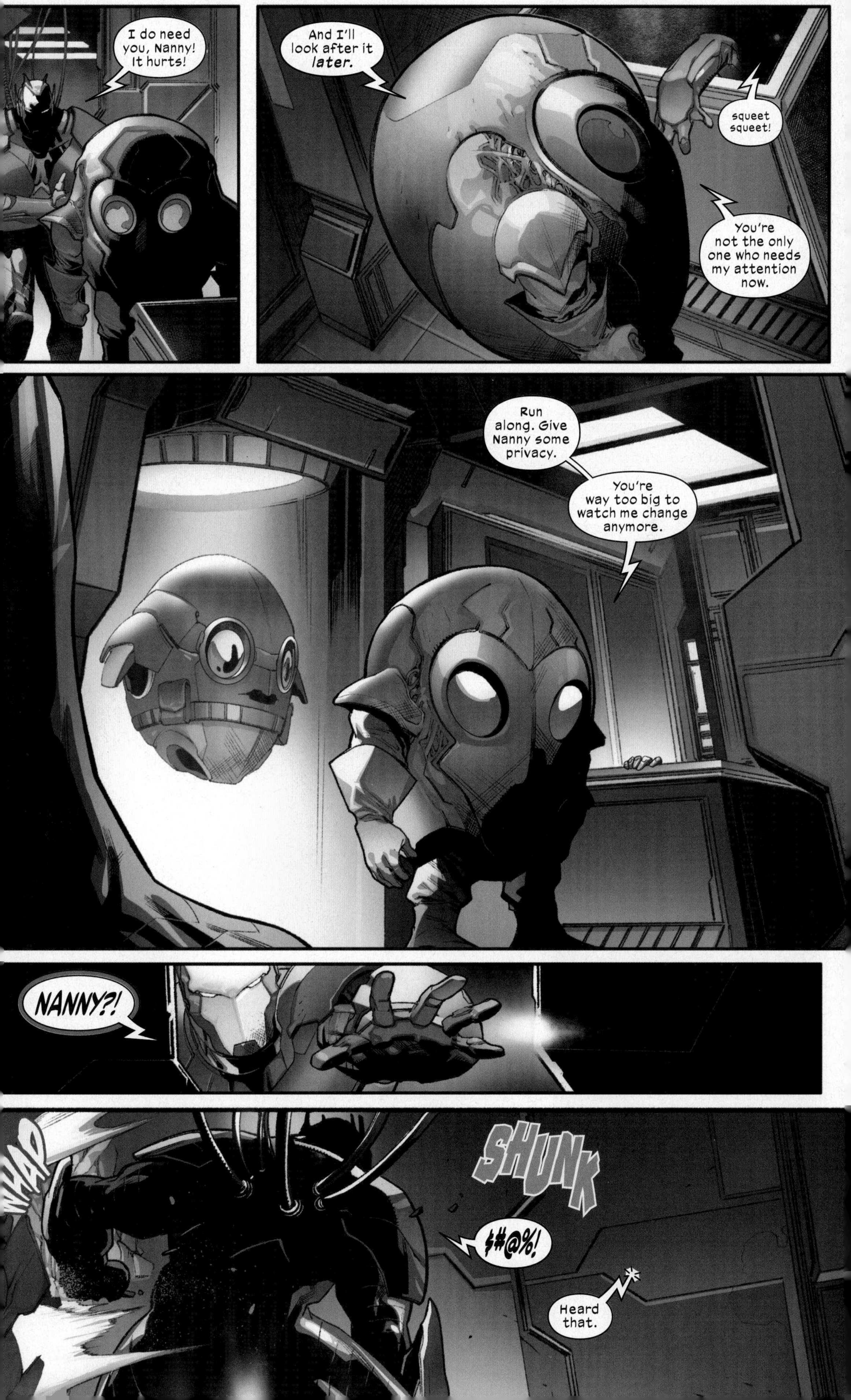
I do need you, Nanny! It hurts!
And I'll look after it *later.*
squeet squeet!
You're not the only one who needs my attention now.
Run along. Give Nanny some privacy.
You're way too big to watch me change anymore.
NANNY?!
WHAP
SHUNK
$#@%!
Heard that.

Purgatory.

BRAKKA BRAKKA

HOOF! HOOF!

Hnnnnnngh...

That looks hard, Havok...

Let me spot you.

HEY!

HNNNGH!

Whoa!

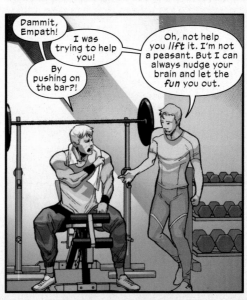

Dammit, Empath!

I was trying to help you!

By pushing on the bar?!

Oh, not help you *lift* it. I'm not a peasant. But I can always nudge your brain and let the *fun* you out.

The you who likes to kill ‡#@% and get things done.

Oh, you're not ashamed of him, are you?

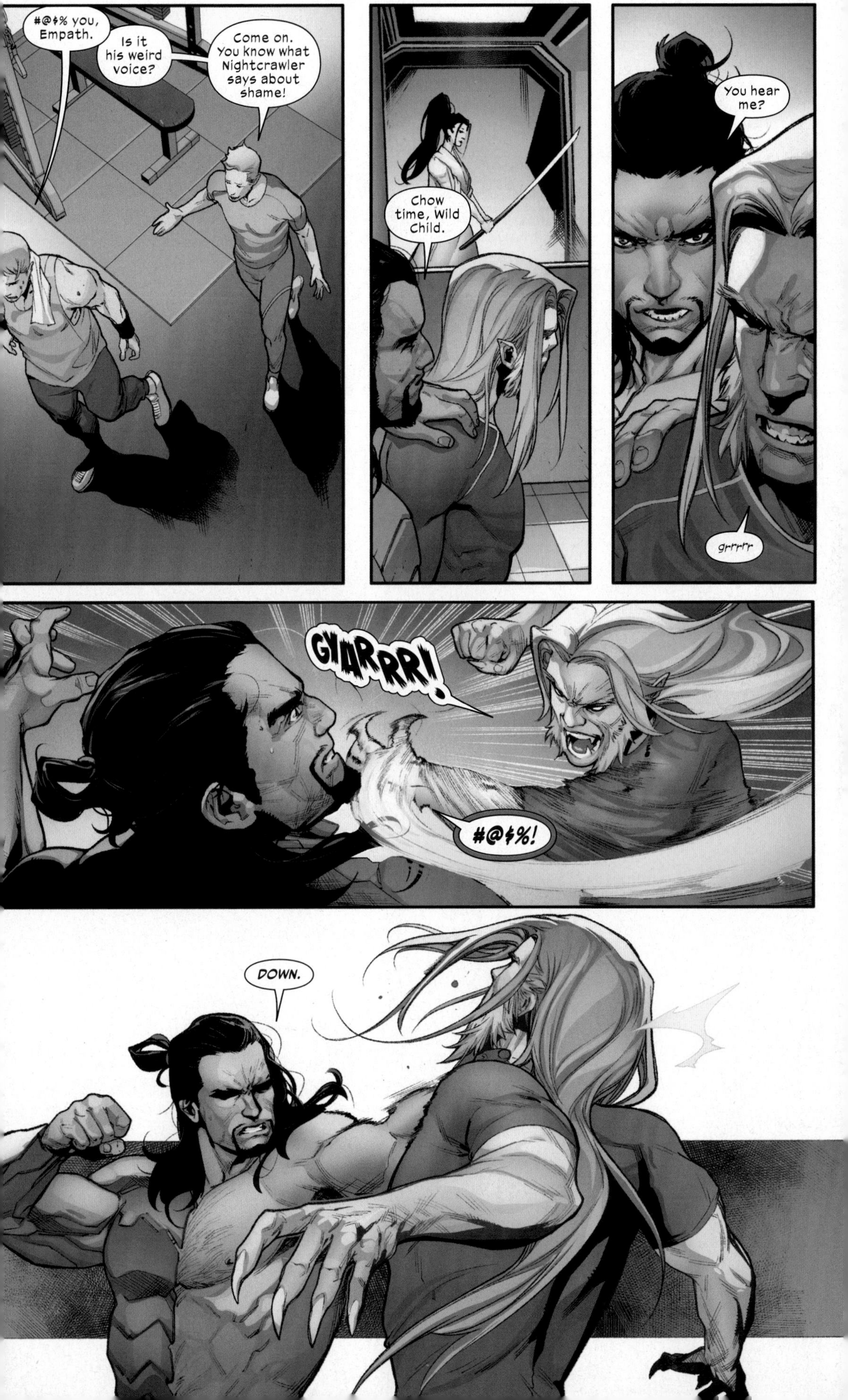

#@$% you, Empath.
Is it his weird voice?
Come on. You know what Nightcrawler says about shame!
Chow time, Wild Child.
You hear me?
grrrrr
GYARRR!
#@$%!
DOWN.

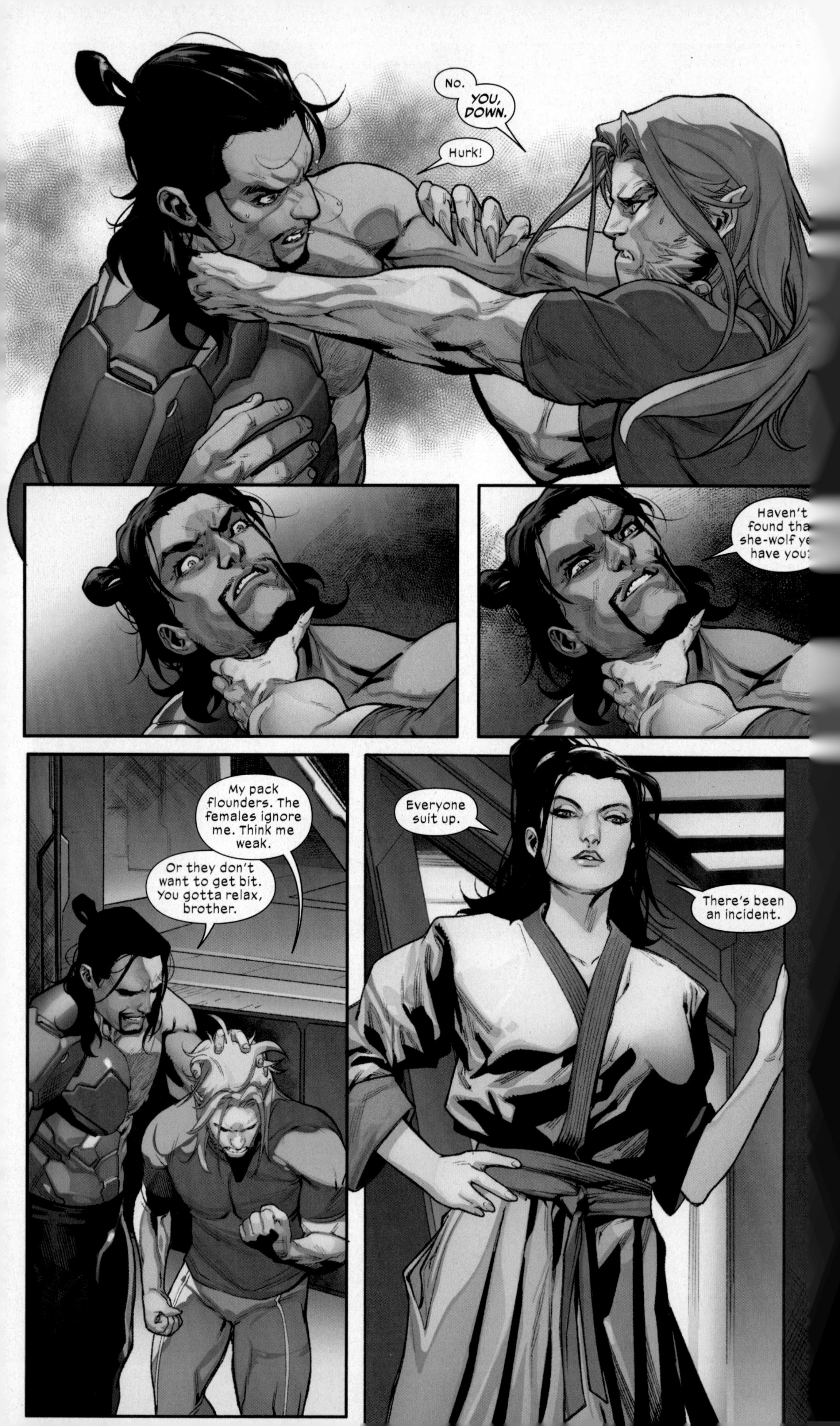

No. YOU, DOWN.
Hurk!
Haven't found tha she-wolf ye have you:
My pack flounders. The females ignore me. Think me weak.
Or they don't want to get bit. You gotta relax, brother.
Everyone suit up.
There's been an incident.

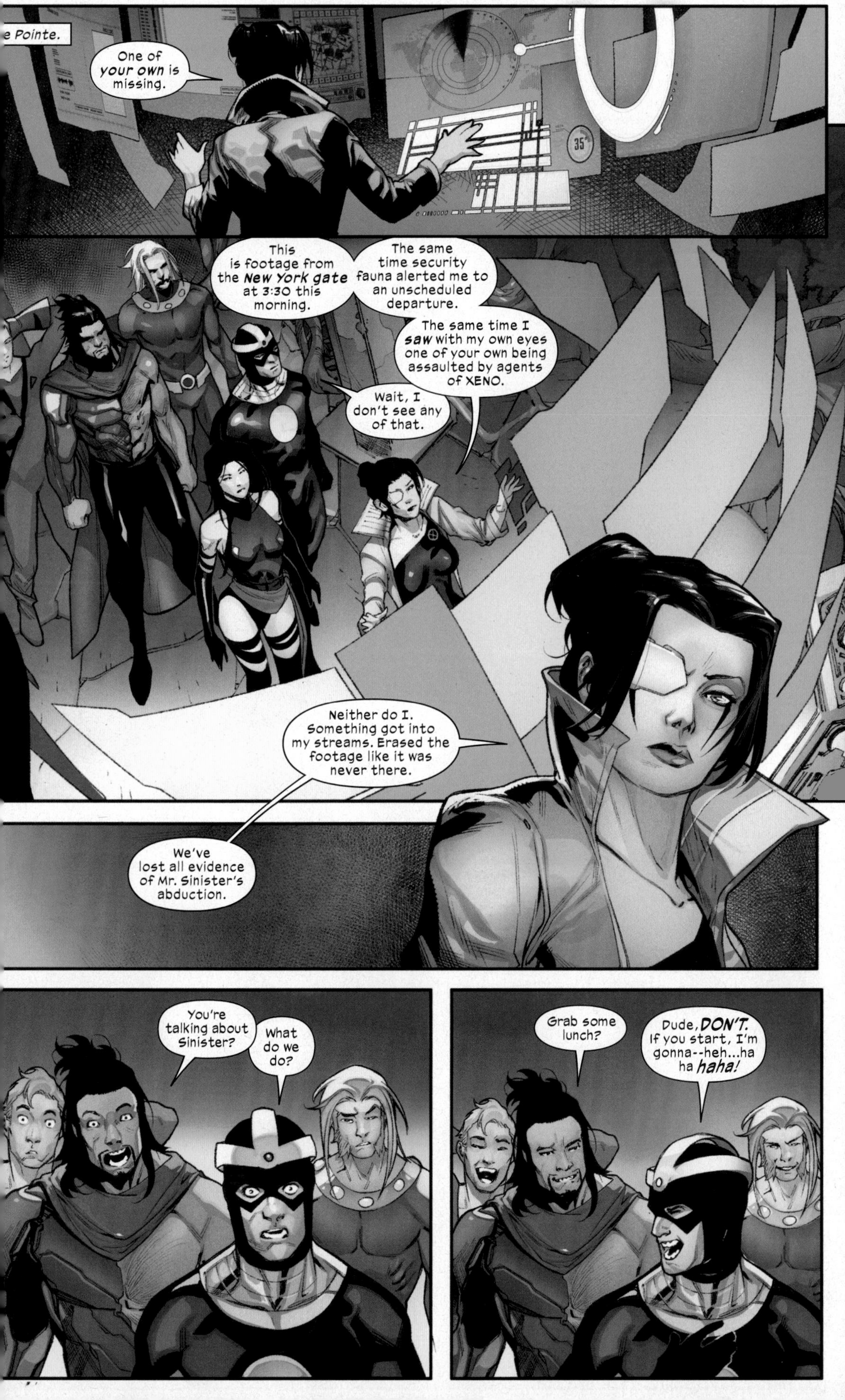
e Pointe.
One of *your own* is missing.
This is footage from the *New York gate* at 3:30 this morning.
The same time security fauna alerted me to an unscheduled departure.
The same time I *saw* with my own eyes one of your own being assaulted by agents of XENO.
Wait, I don't see any of that.
Neither do I. Something got into my streams. Erased the footage like it was never there.
We've lost all evidence of Mr. Sinister's abduction.
You're talking about Sinister?
What do we do?
Grab some lunch?
Dude, ***DON'T.*** If you start, I'm gonna--heh...ha ha ***haha!***

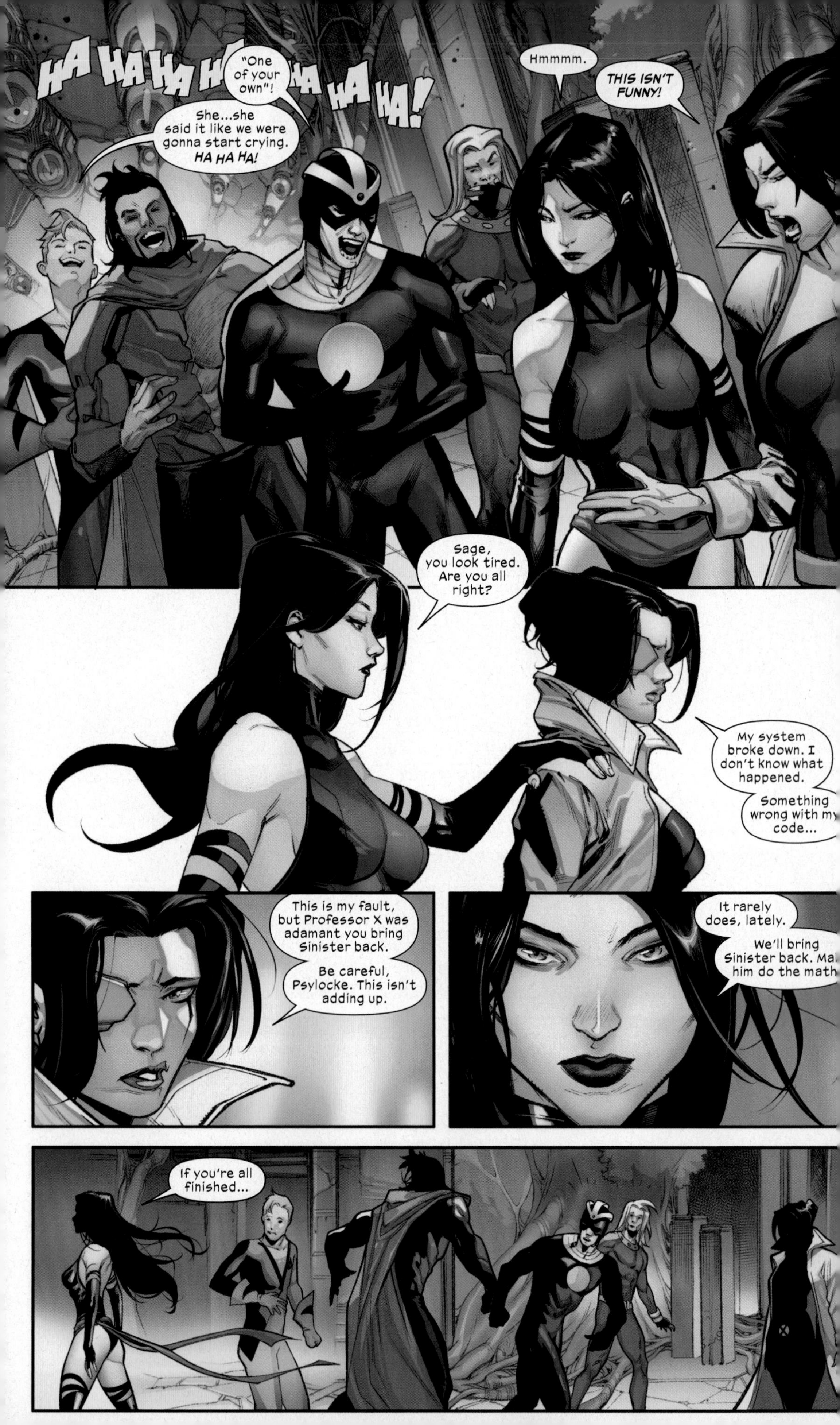
HA HA HA HA HA HA HA!
"One of your own"!
She...she said it like we were gonna start crying. HA HA HA!
Hmmmm.
THIS ISN'T FUNNY!
Sage, you look tired. Are you all right?
My system broke down. I don't know what happened.
Something wrong with my code...
This is my fault, but Professor X was adamant you bring Sinister back.
Be careful, Psylocke. This isn't adding up.
It rarely does, lately.
We'll bring Sinister back. Ma... him do the math.
If you're all finished...

[MISSION]....00X]
[REQUEST]....00X]

ITEM: RETRIEVAL OF MR. SINISTER

ACTION: HELLIONS MISSION AUTHORIZATION

SUPPLEMENTAL STATEMENT

AUTHOR: SAGE

I know there's some concern the rescue of a Quiet Council member doesn't explicitly meet the criteria of a Hellions mission, so I thought it germane to share my recent experience with the team.

To the point: I was paid a visit by the Hellions this afternoon. They expressed, to the mutant, a sincere desire to save Mr. Sinister. When I reminded them that the Council prefers X-Factor deal with missing mutants, they passionately argued that Mr. Sinister was their responsibility and his wellbeing very much their concern. Their warmth would have raised my suspicion had I not been looking them all in the eye. To see John Greycrow's lip tremble as he stood as one with his teammates is to believe that even the most antisocial mutant may change.

Even a cynical reading of the situation -- that it's more a point of pride to rescue a teammate than an act of compassion -- suggests progress. I'd think it a win for these Krakoans to find self-esteem wherever they can. And if there's even the possibility they've taken the chance to be vulnerable...to step out and care for one another, I propose you take a chance on them. Let them bring Essex home themselves.

APPROVED

[00X....[MISSION]
[00X...[APPROVED]

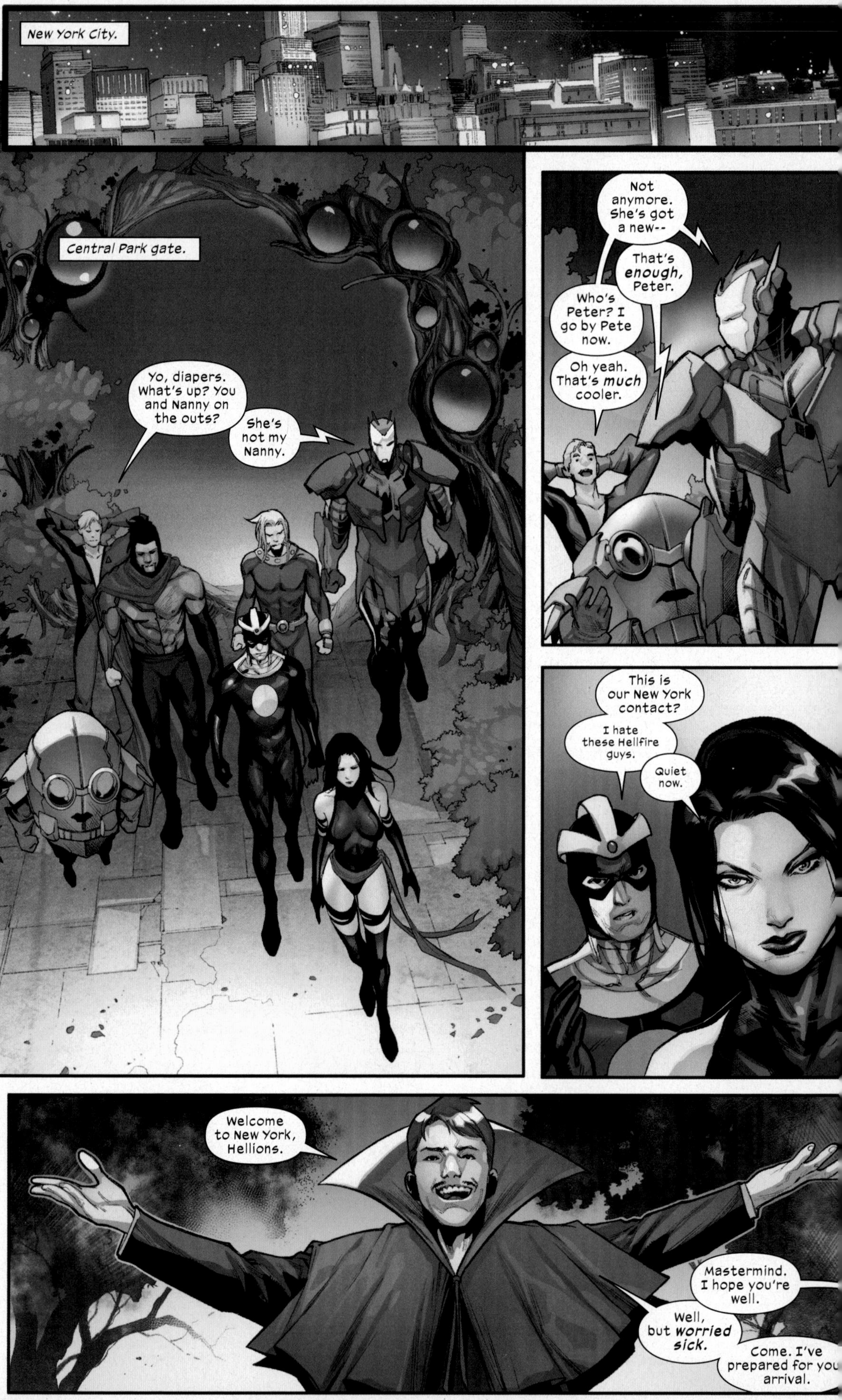
New York City.
Central Park gate.
Yo, diapers. What's up? You and Nanny on the outs?
She's not my Nanny.
Not anymore. She's got a new--
That's *enough,* Peter.
Who's Peter? I go by Pete now.
Oh yeah. That's *much* cooler.
This is our New York contact?
I hate these Hellfire guys.
Quiet now.
Welcome to New York, Hellions.
Mastermind. I hope you're well.
Well, but *worried sick.*
Come. I've prepared for you arrival.

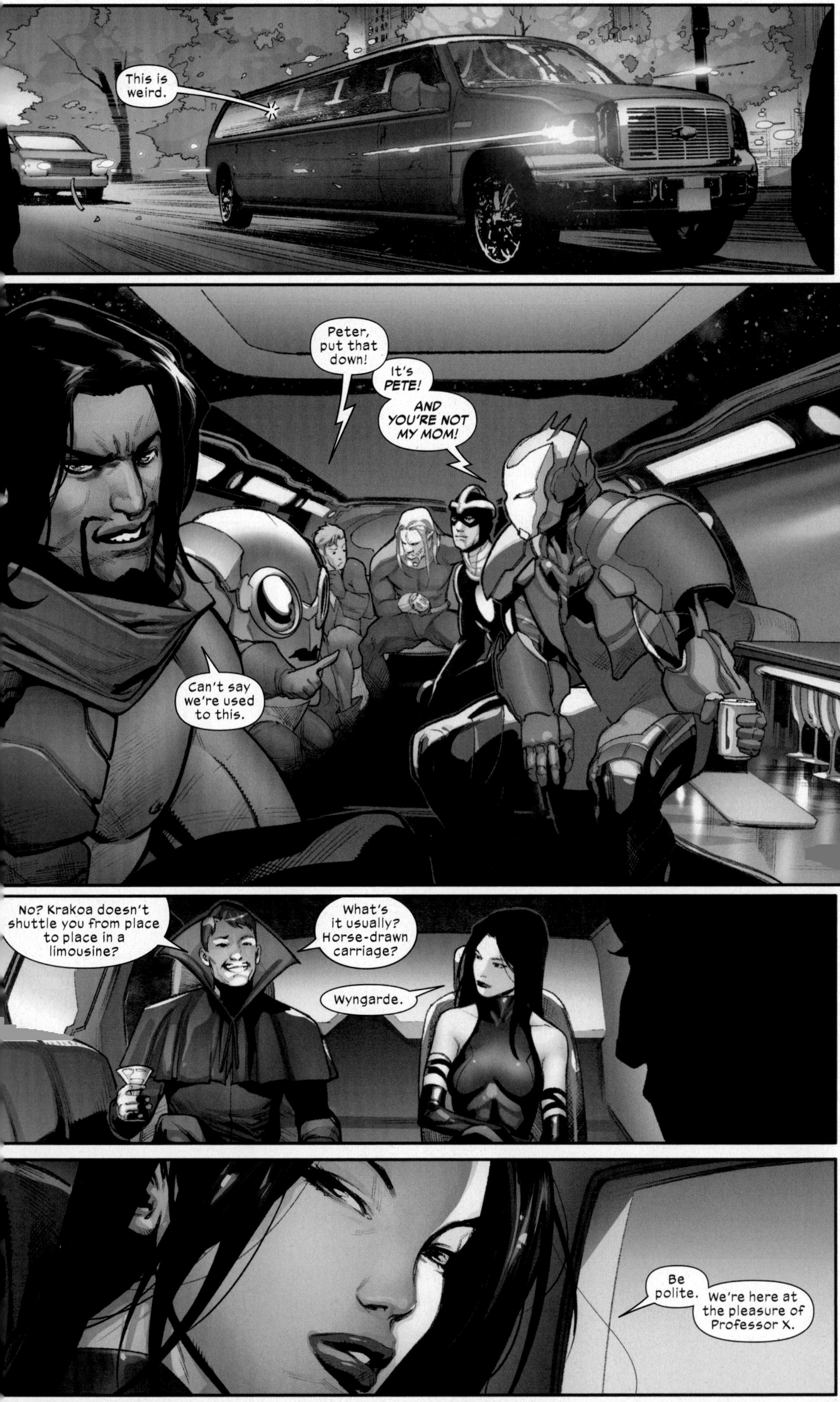
This is weird.
Peter, put that down!
It's PETE!
AND YOU'RE NOT MY MOM!
Can't say we're used to this.
No? Krakoa doesn't shuttle you from place to place in a limousine?
What's it usually? Horse-drawn carriage?
Wyngarde.
Be polite.
We're here at the pleasure of Professor X.

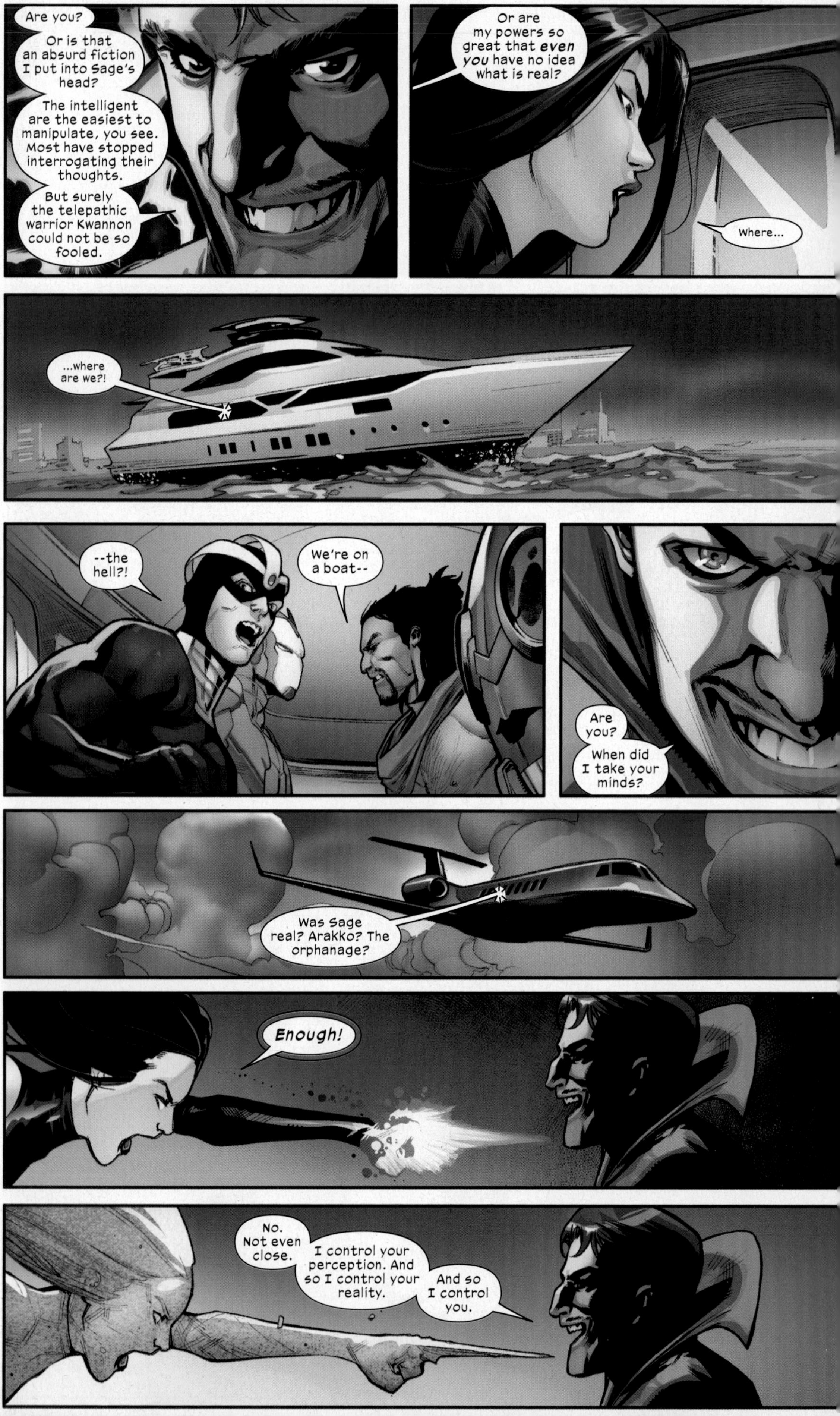
Are you?
Or is that an absurd fiction I put into Sage's head?
The intelligent are the easiest to manipulate, you see. Most have stopped interrogating their thoughts.
But surely the telepathic warrior Kwannon could not be so fooled.
Or are my powers so great that *even you* have no idea what is real?
Where...
...where are we?!
--the hell?!
We're on a boat--
Are you?
When did I take your minds?
Was Sage real? Arakko? The orphanage?
Enough!
No. Not even close.
I control your perception. And so I control your reality.
And so I control you.

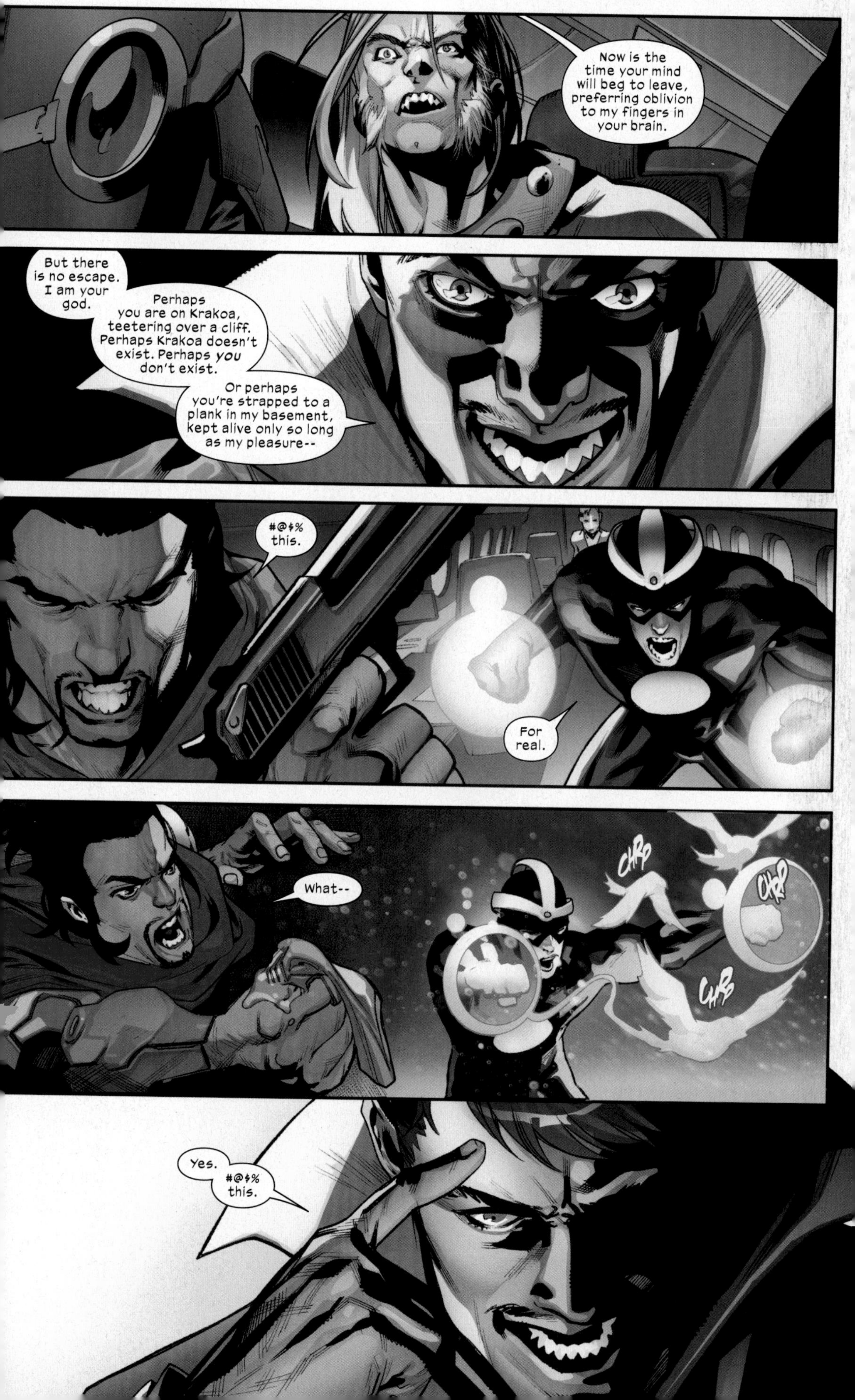
Now is the time your mind will beg to leave, preferring oblivion to my fingers in your brain.
But there is no escape. I am your god.
Perhaps you are on Krakoa, teetering over a cliff. Perhaps Krakoa doesn't exist. Perhaps *you* don't exist.
Or perhaps you're strapped to a plank in my basement, kept alive only so long as my pleasure--
#@$% this.
For real.
What--
CHRP
CHRP
CHRP
Yes.
#@$% this.

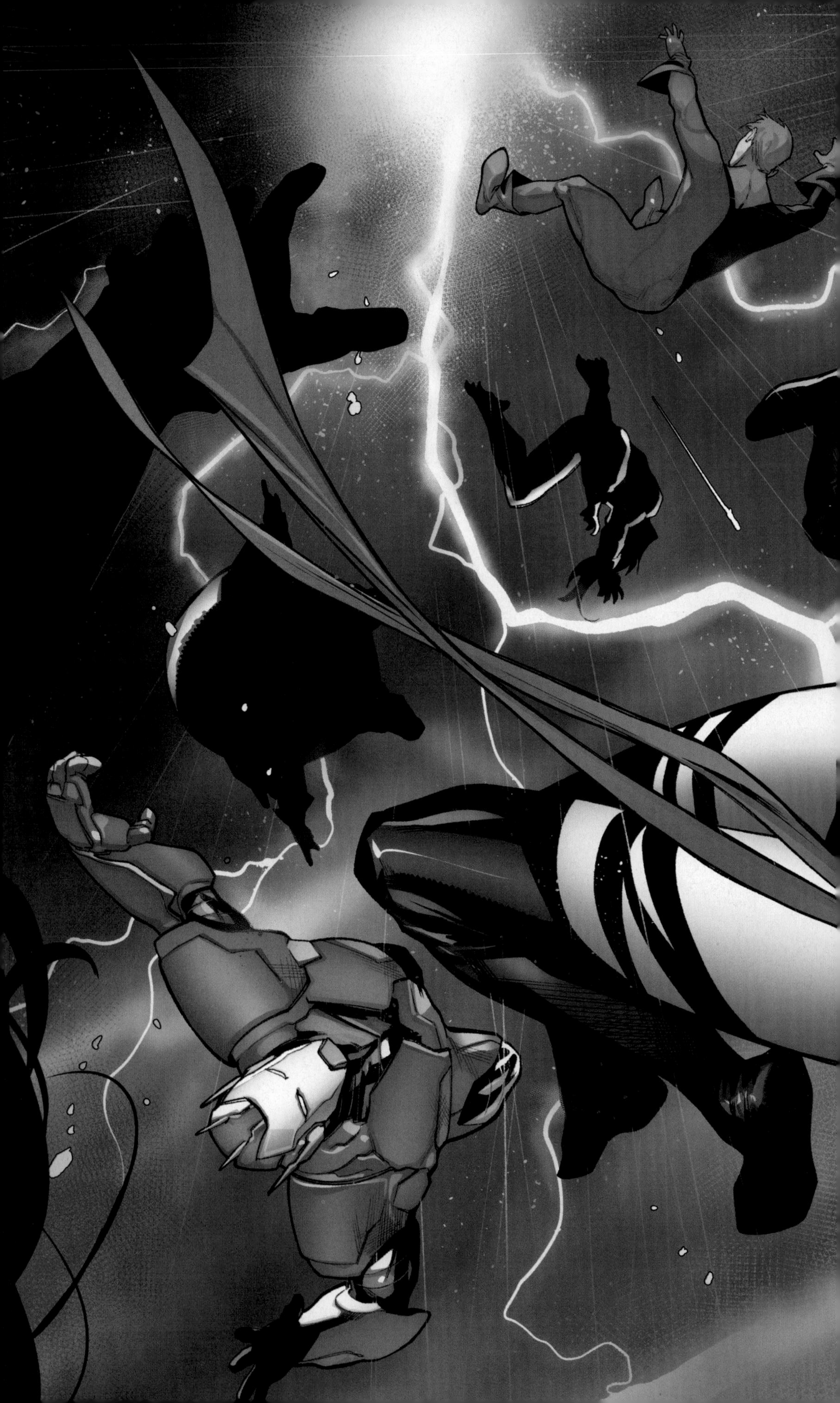

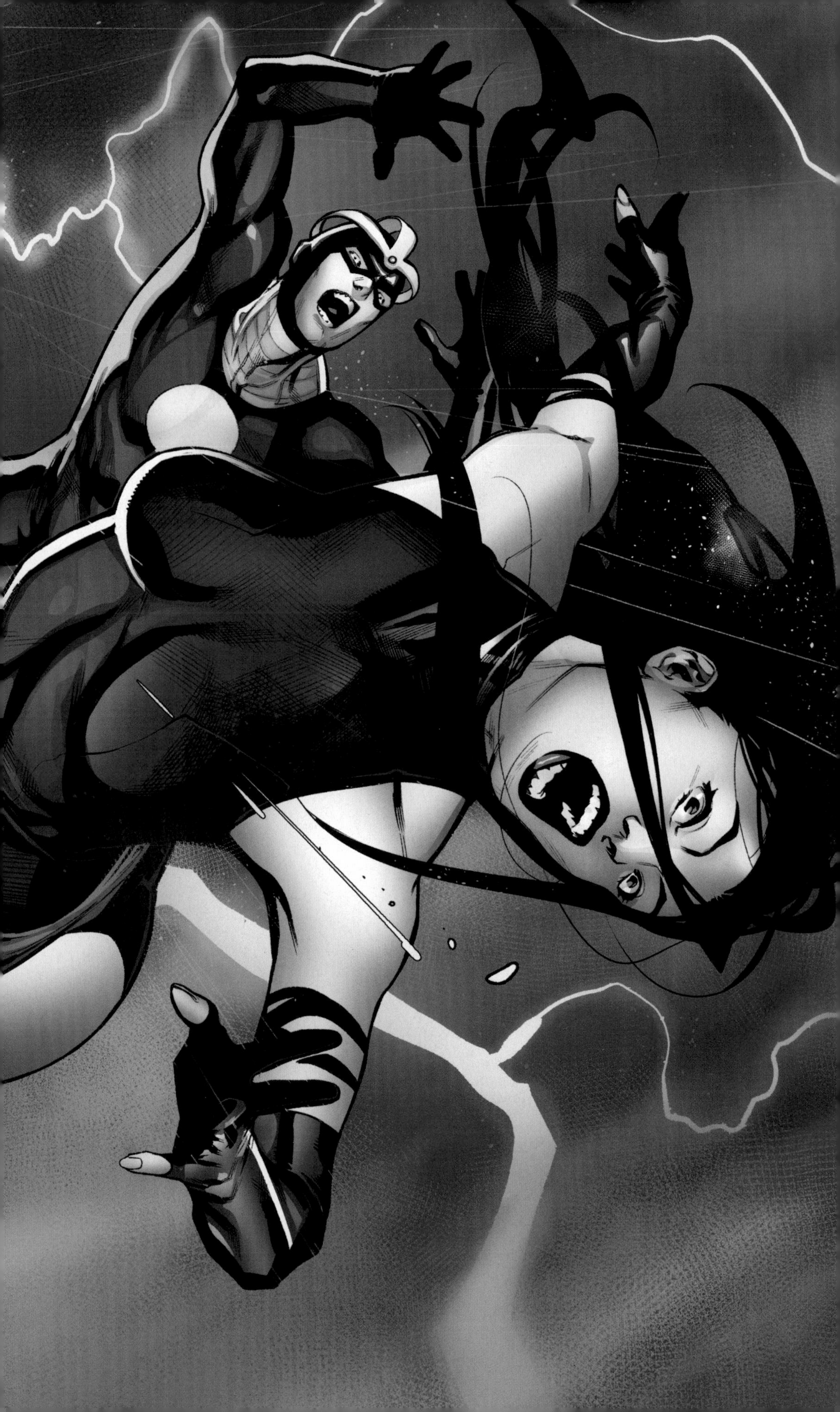

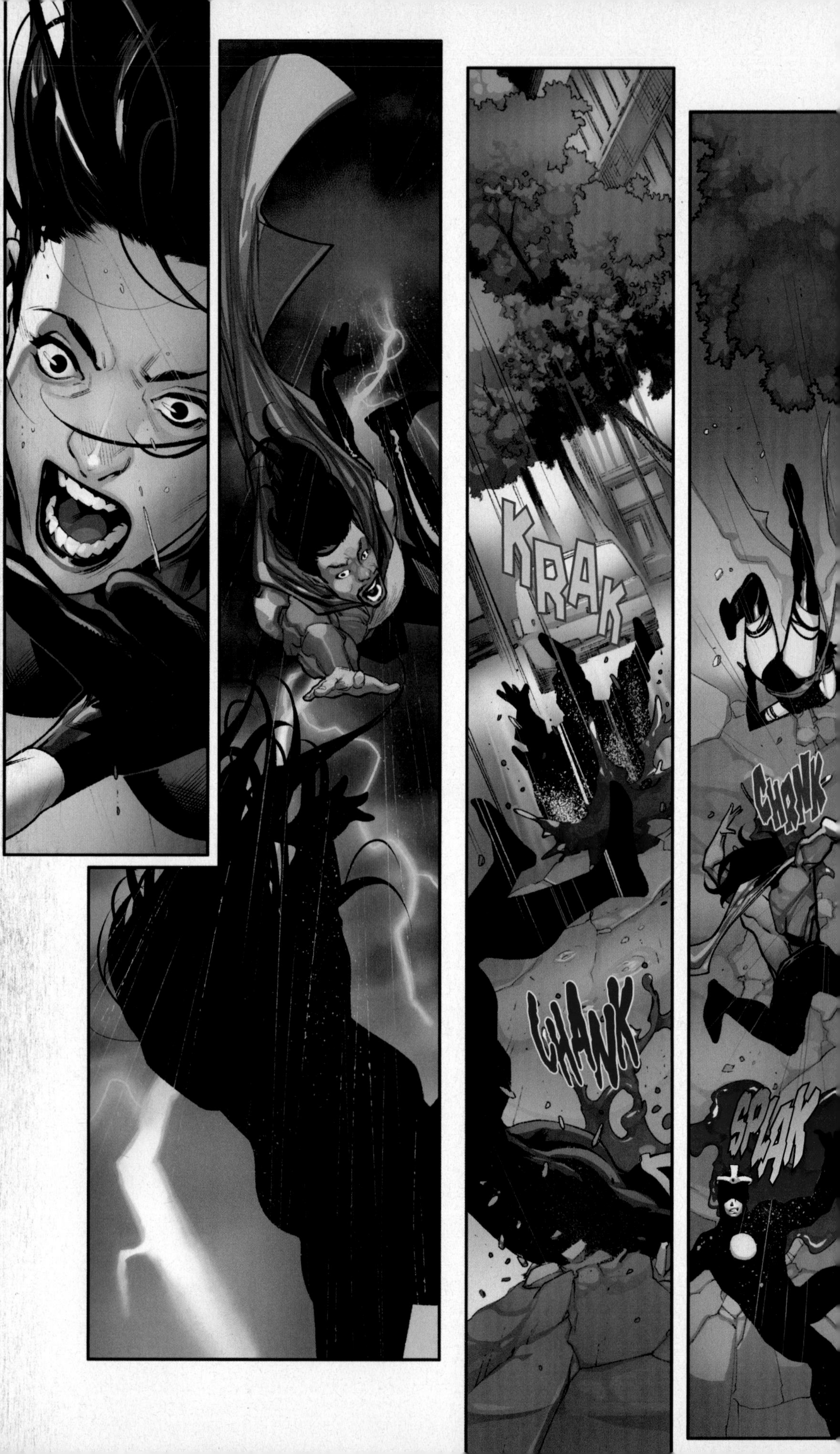

KRAK
CHANK
CHANK
SPLAK

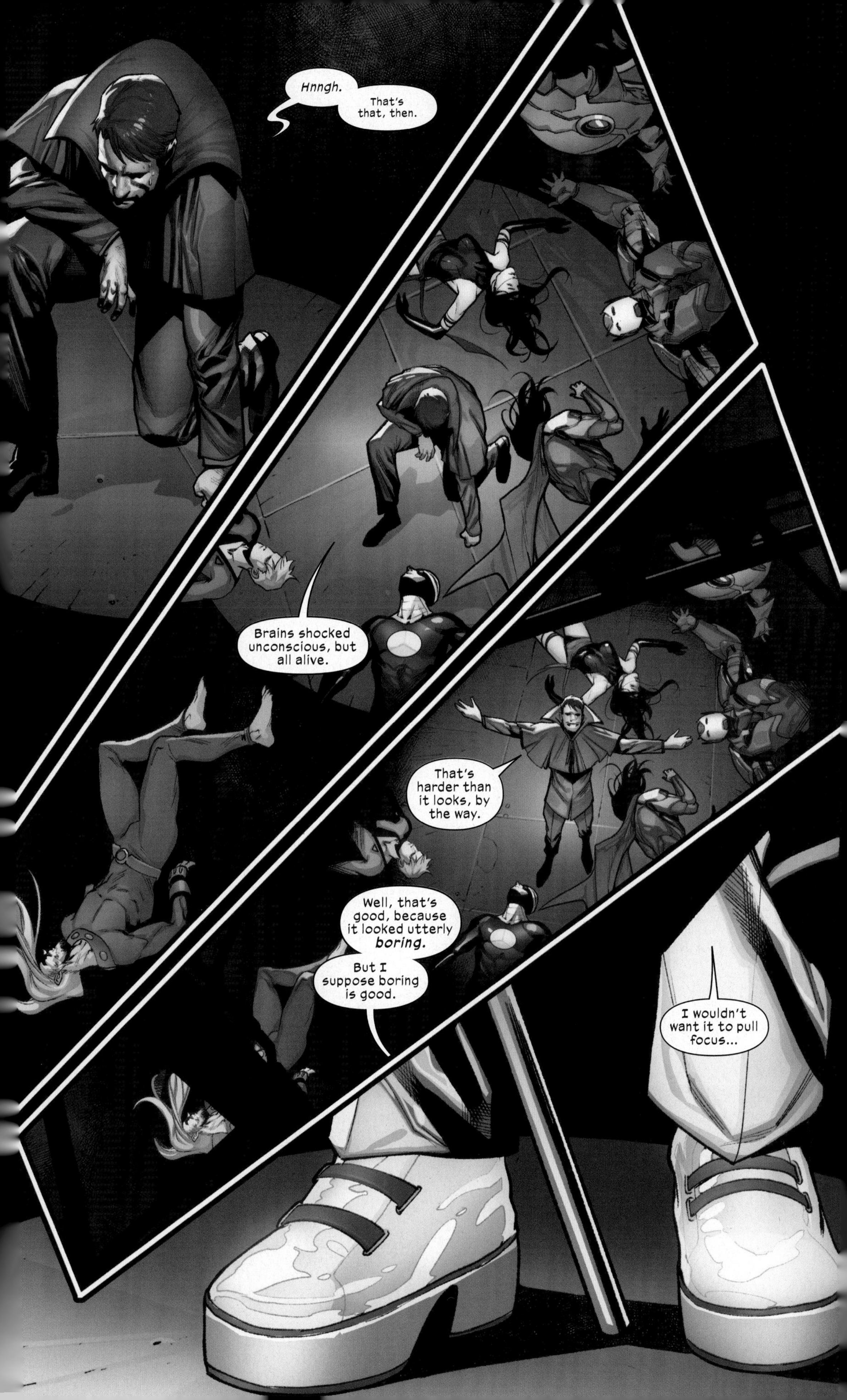

Hnngh.
That's that, then.
Brains shocked unconscious, but all alive.
That's harder than it looks, by the way.
Well, that's good, because it looked utterly **boring.**
But I suppose boring is good.
I wouldn't want it to pull focus...

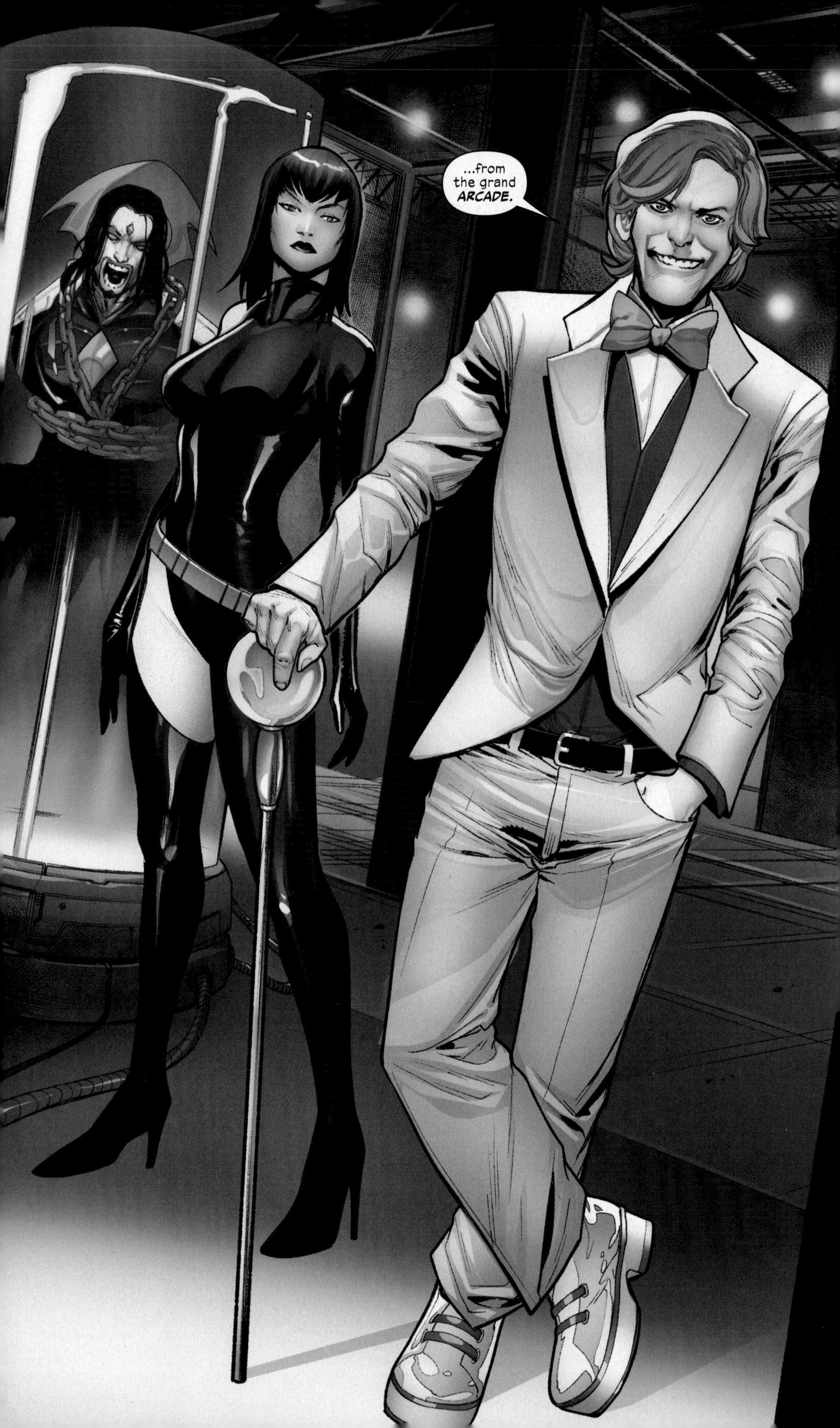
...from the grand ARCADE.

[hell_[0.9]
[ions_[0.9]

Most deceivers author their own demise, blinded by their fictions.

Some deceivers see clearly, and in their madness destroy many.

-- NIGHTCRAWLER

[hell_[0.X]
[ions_[0.X]

[hell_[0.9].....]
[ions_[0.9].....]

[Hellions_alpha.]

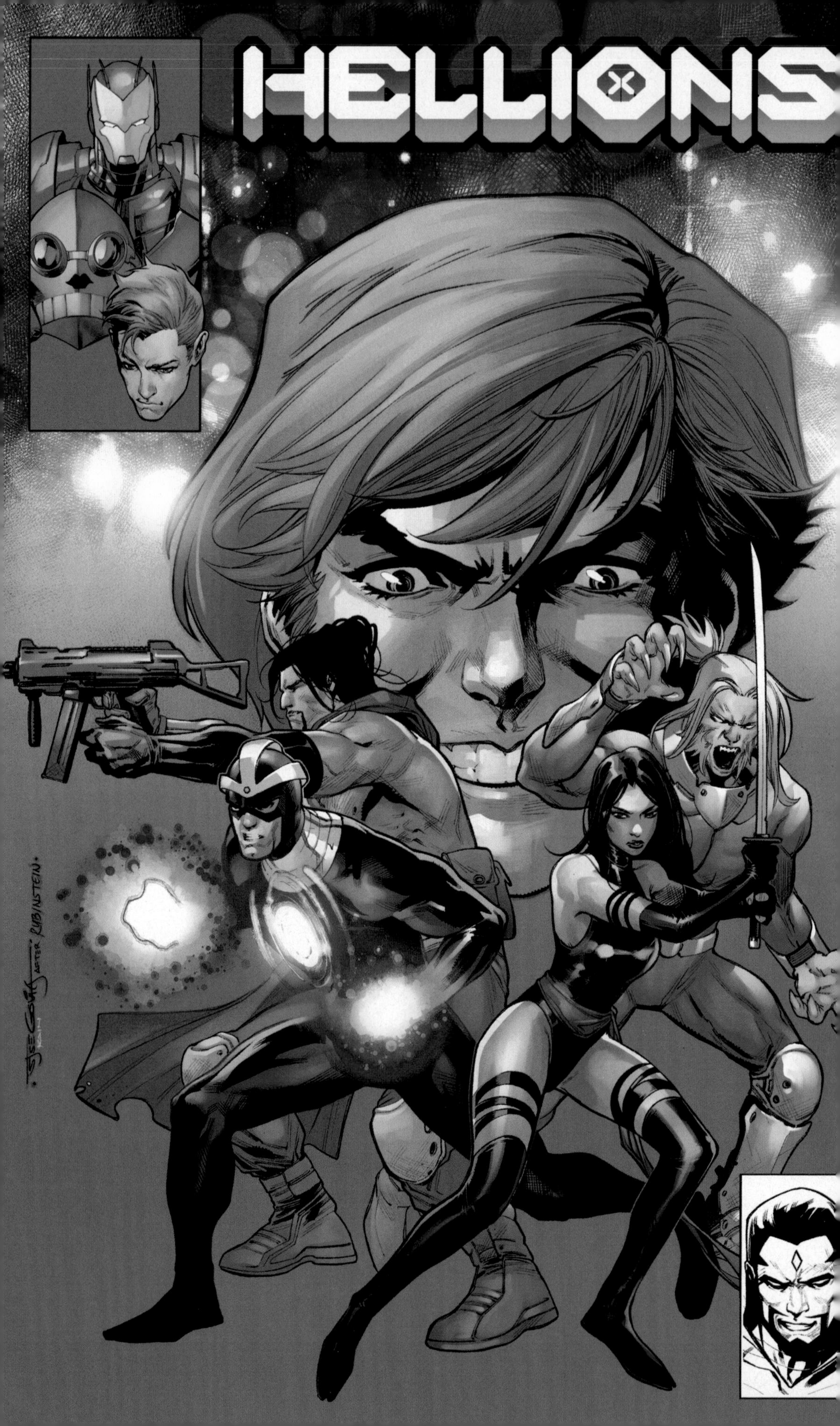
HELLIONS

[hell_[0.10]
[ions_[0.10]

Too often demons stay hidden, whispering while unseen. To tame them, we must know them. To glimpse their faces is a precious gift.

-- NIGHTCRAWLER

[hell_[0.X]
[ions_[0.X]

[hell_[0.10]....]
[ions_[0.10]....]

[Hellions_alpha.]

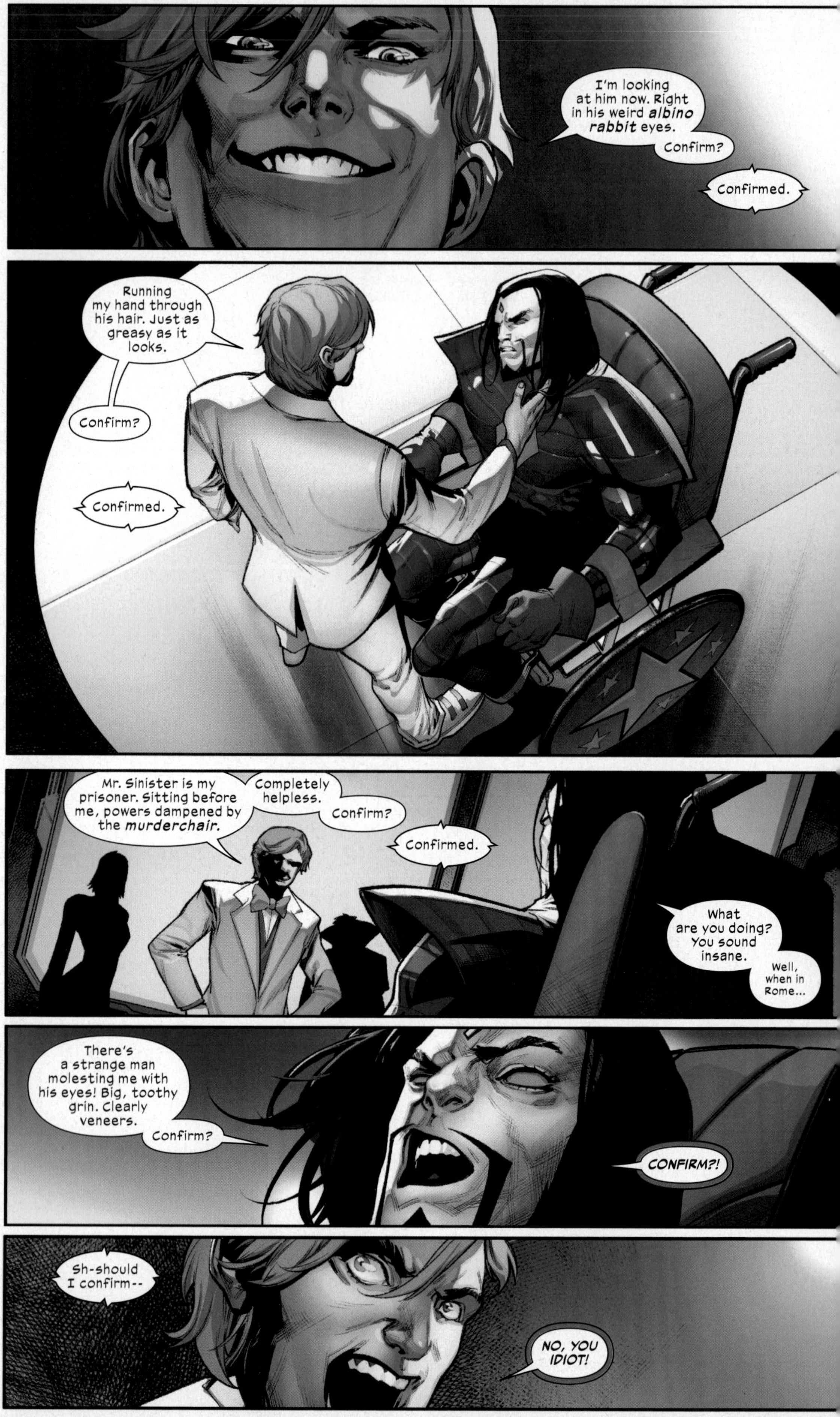
I'm looking at him now. Right in his weird *albino rabbit* eyes.
Confirm?
Confirmed.
Running my hand through his hair. Just as greasy as it looks.
Confirm?
Confirmed.
Mr. Sinister is my prisoner. Sitting before me, powers dampened by the *murderchair.*
Completely helpless.
Confirm?
Confirmed.
What are you doing? You sound insane.
Well, when in Rome...
There's a strange man molesting me with his eyes! Big, toothy grin. Clearly veneers.
Confirm?
CONFIRM?!
Sh-should I confirm--
NO, YOU IDIOT!

I'm disciplining Mr. Sinister.

WHAP

Confirm?

Aggh!

Confirmed.

I--I'm being assaulted by a *Chucky* doll! Confirm?!

SHUT UP!

WHACK

Guhhh!

WILL SOMEONE EXPLAIN TO ME WHAT IS GOING ON?!

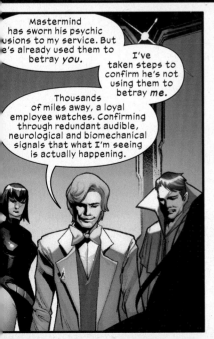

Mastermind has sworn his psychic illusions to my service. But he's already used them to betray *you*.

I've taken steps to confirm he's not using them to betray *me*.

Thousands of miles away, a loyal employee watches. Confirming through redundant audible, neurological and biomechanical signals that what I'm seeing is actually happening.

I'm explaining the reality verification system to Mr. Sinister. Confirm?

Confirmed.

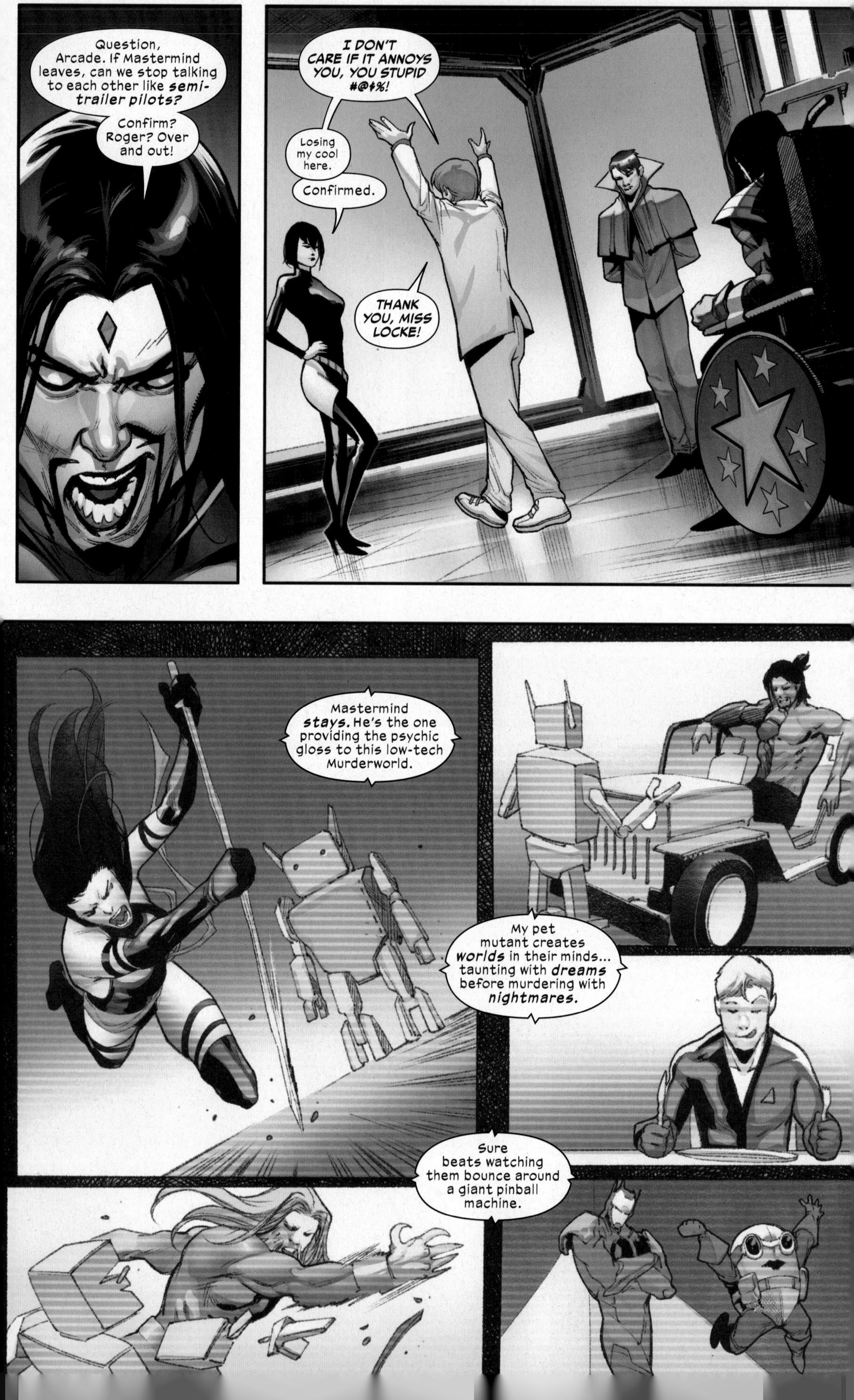
Question, Arcade. If Mastermind leaves, can we stop talking to each other like semi-trailer pilots?
Confirm? Roger? Over and out!
I DON'T CARE IF IT ANNOYS YOU, YOU STUPID #@$%!
Losing my cool here.
Confirmed.
THANK YOU, MISS LOCKE!
Mastermind stays. He's the one providing the psychic gloss to this low-tech Murderworld.
My pet mutant creates worlds in their minds... taunting with dreams before murdering with nightmares.
Sure beats watching them bounce around a giant pinball machine.

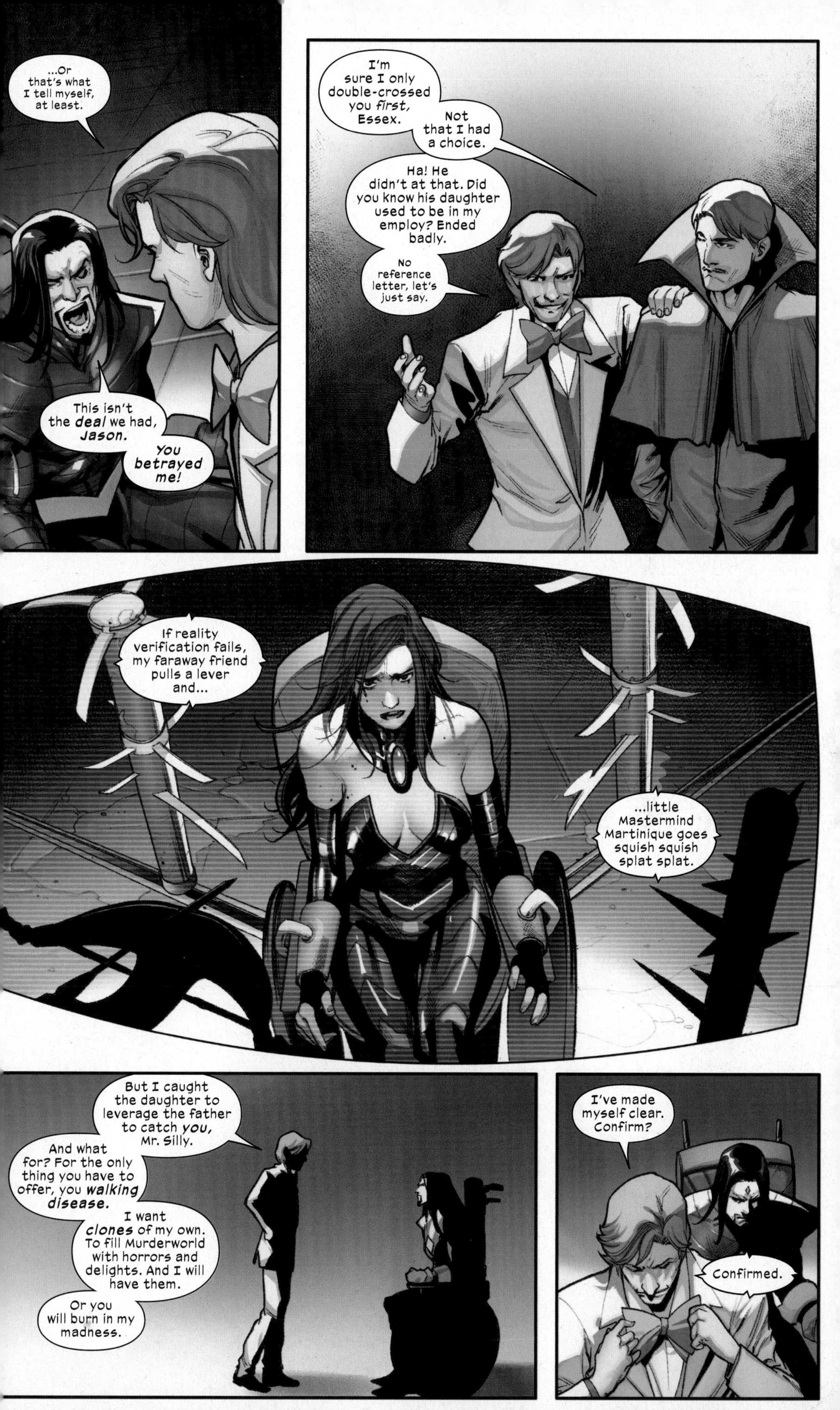
...Or that's what I tell myself, at least.
This isn't the *deal* we had, *Jason.*
You betrayed me!
I'm sure I only double-crossed you *first,* Essex.
Not that I had a choice.
Ha! He didn't at that. Did you know his daughter used to be in my employ? Ended badly.
No reference letter, let's just say.
If reality verification fails, my faraway friend pulls a lever and...
...little Mastermind Martinique goes squish squish splat splat.
But I caught the daughter to leverage the father to catch *you,* Mr. Silly.
And what for? For the only thing you have to offer, you *walking disease.*
I want *clones* of my own. To fill Murderworld with horrors and delights. And I will have them.
Or you will burn in my madness.
I've made myself clear. Confirm?
Confirmed.

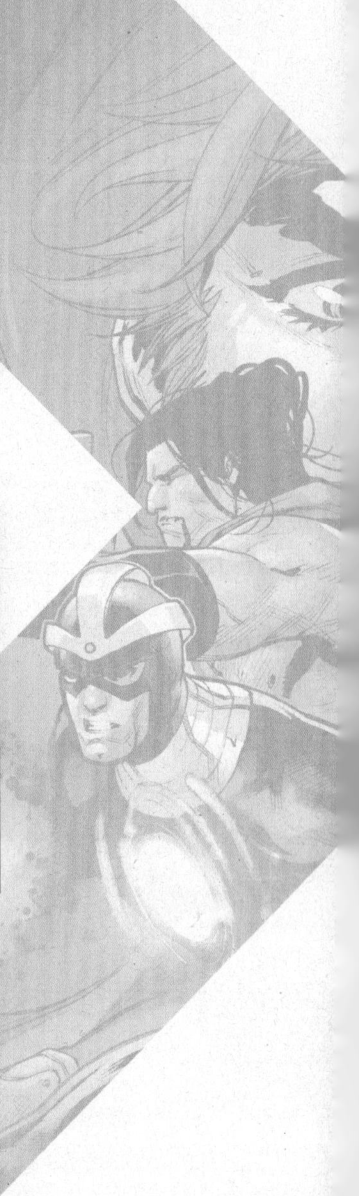

@#$%&@# SINISTER

Surprise, surprise. Mr. Sinister has managed to drag the Hellions into his mess after a back-alley deal with Mastermind ended with him being double-crossed and kidnapped by Arcade. Using Sinister as bait, Mastermind falsified a mission from the Quiet Council that led the Hellions into an ambush and trapped them in their own individual fantasies. Separated from their teammates and cut off from Krakoa...it can't get any worse, right?

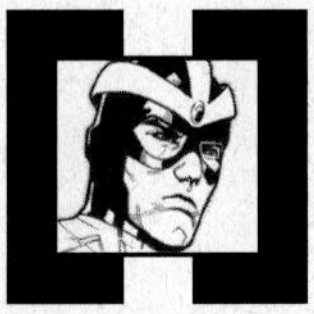
Havok

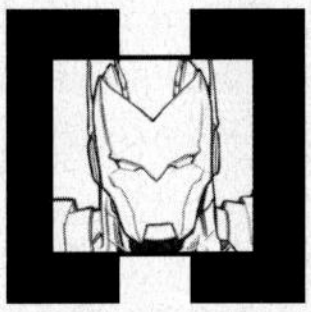
Orphan-Maker

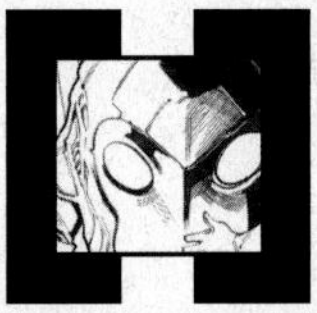
Nanny

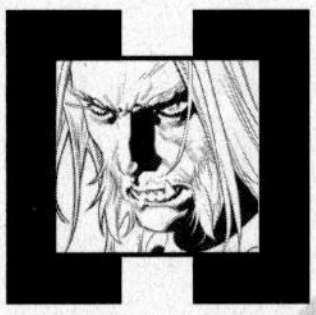
Wild Child

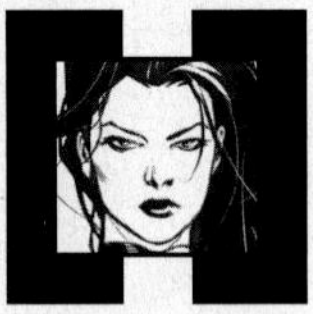
Psylocke

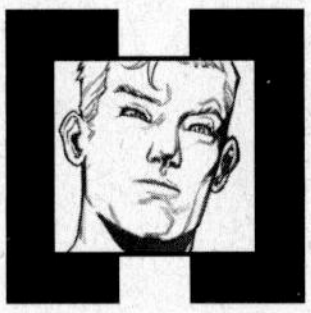
Empath

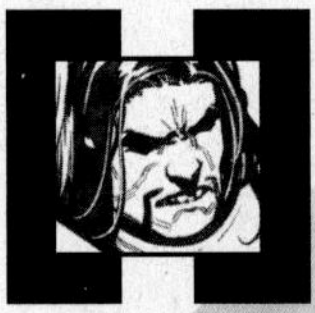
Greycrow

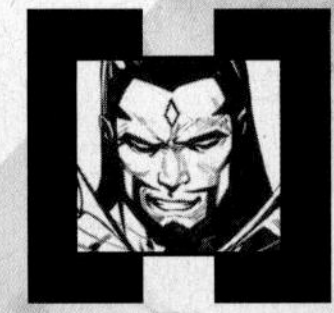
Mr. Sinister

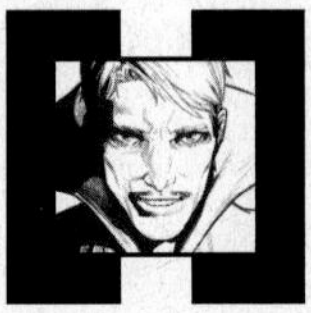
Mastermind

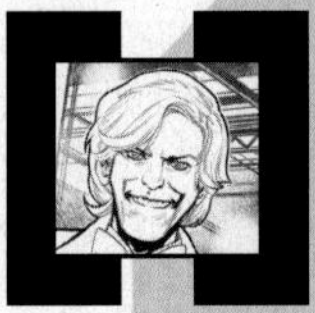
Arcade

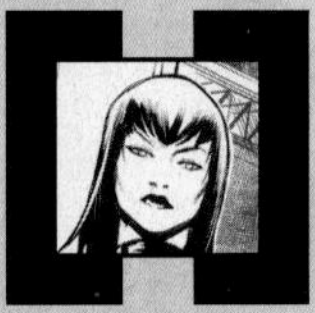
Miss Locke

HELLIONS

[X_10]

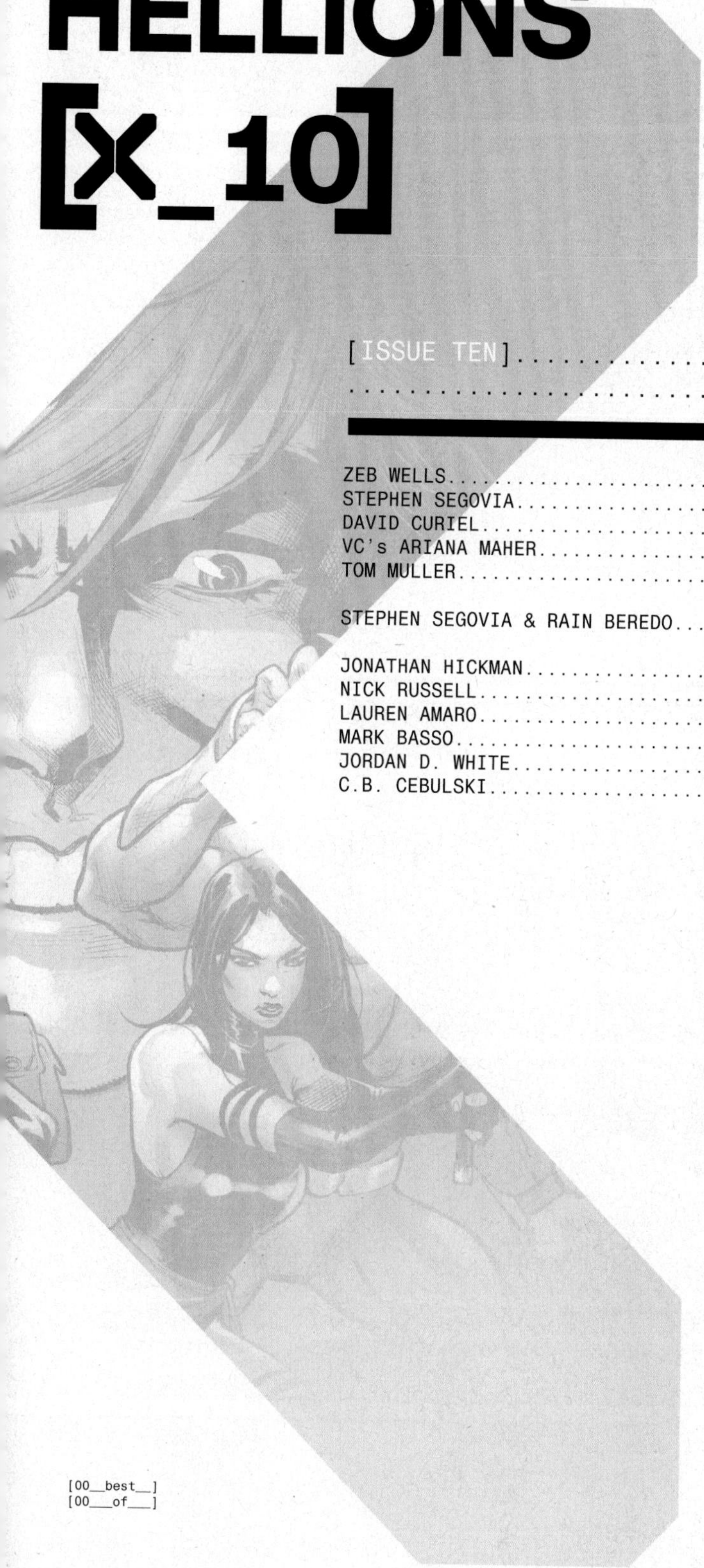

[ISSUE TEN]............. FUNNY GAMES PART II:
.... HITBOX

ZEB WELLS..[WRITER]
STEPHEN SEGOVIA..................................[ARTIST]
DAVID CURIEL...............................[COLOR ARTIST]
VC's ARIANA MAHER...............................[LETTERER]
TOM MULLER..[DESIGN]

STEPHEN SEGOVIA & RAIN BEREDO...............[COVER ARTISTS]

JONATHAN HICKMAN.............................[HEAD OF X]
NICK RUSSELL...................................[PRODUCTION]
LAUREN AMARO...........................[ASSISTANT EDITOR]
MARK BASSO...[EDITOR]
JORDAN D. WHITE............................[SENIOR EDITOR]
C.B. CEBULSKI.............................[EDITOR IN CHIEF]

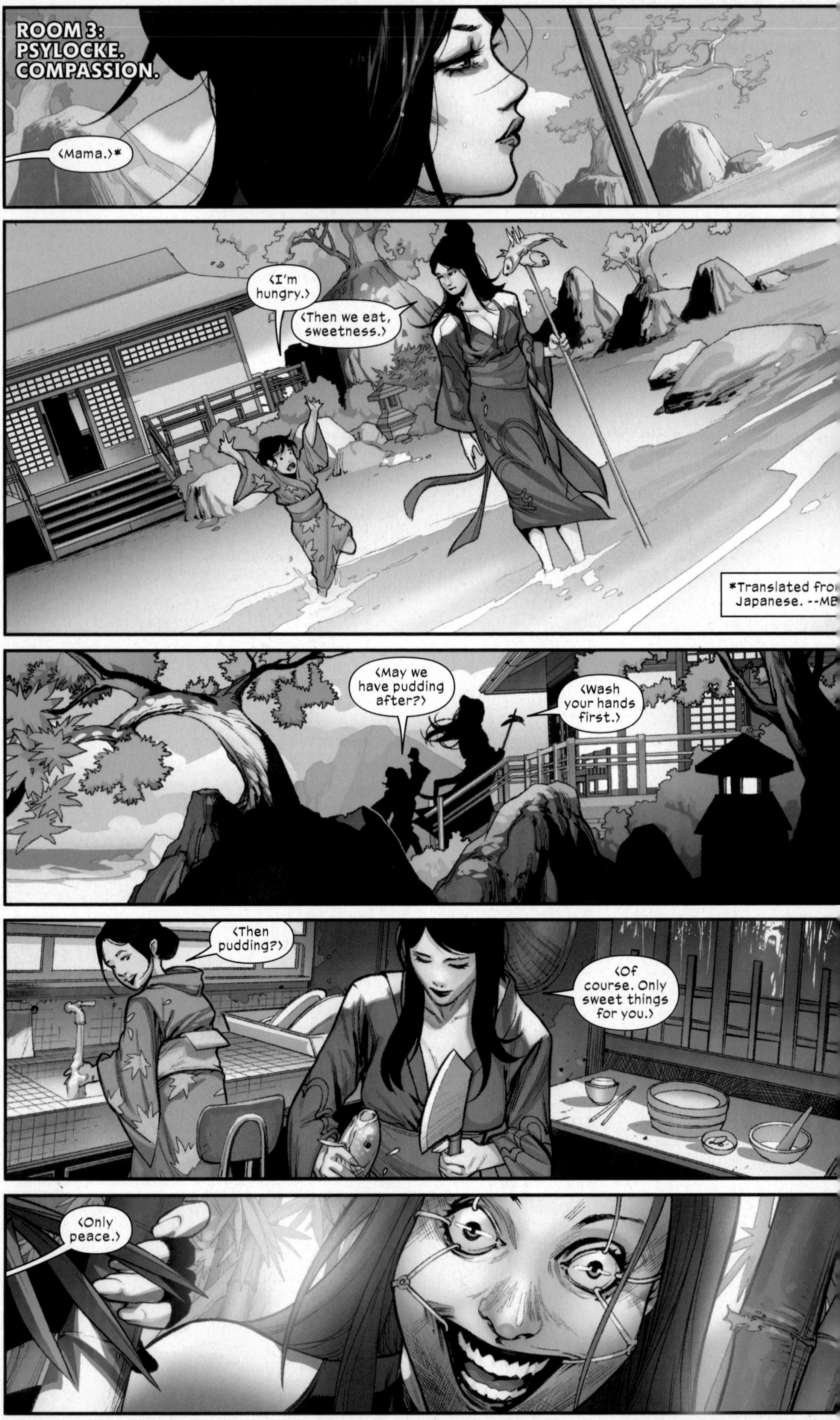
ROOM 3: PSYLOCKE. COMPASSION.
<Mama.>*
<I'm hungry.>
<Then we eat, sweetness.>
*Translated fro
Japanese. --MB
<May we have pudding after?>
<Wash your hands first.>
<Then pudding?>
<Of course. Only sweet things for you.>
<Only peace.>

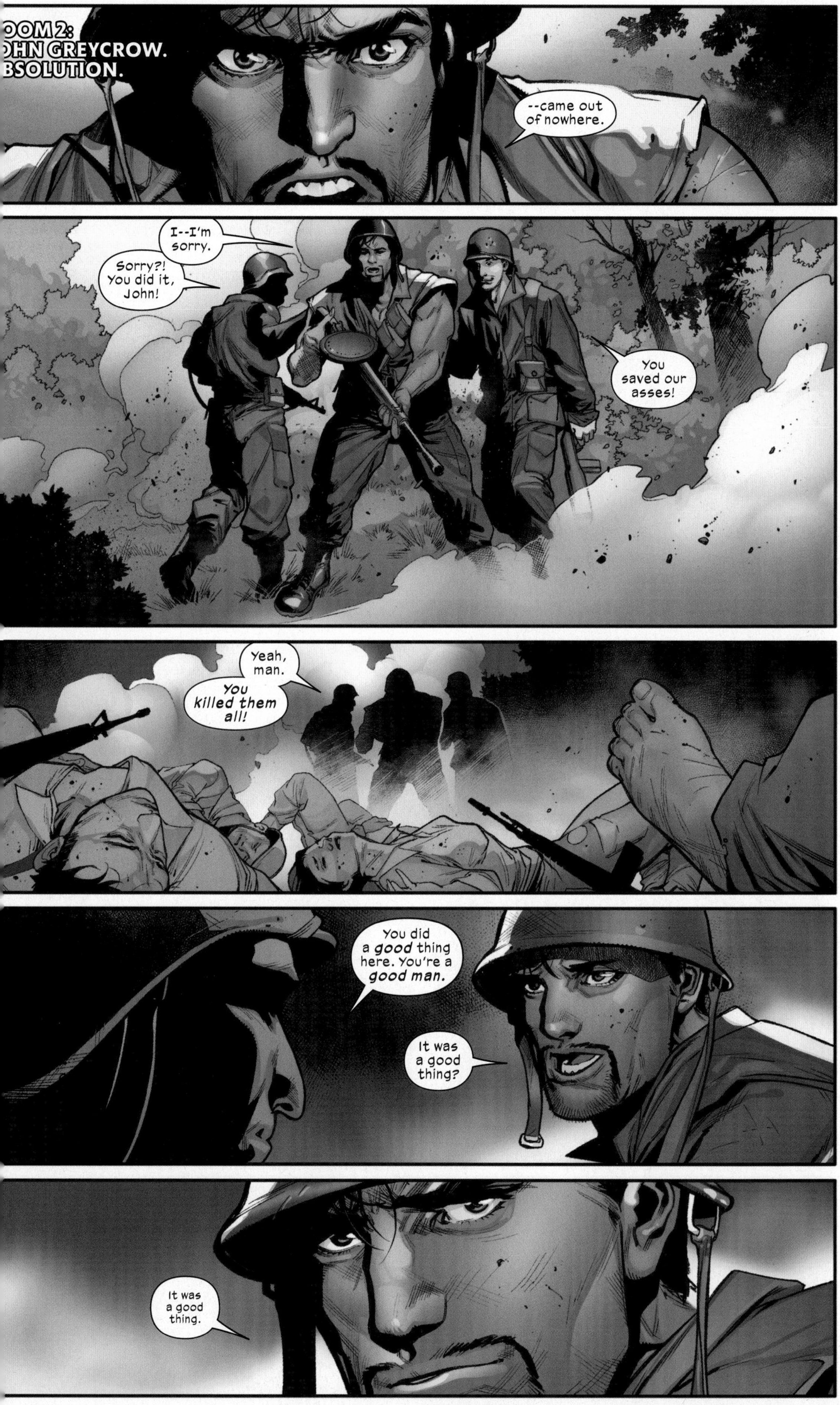

OOM 2:
OHN GREYCROW.
BSOLUTION.
--came out of nowhere.
I--I'm sorry.
Sorry?! You did it, John!
You saved our asses!
Yeah, man.
You killed them all!
You did a good thing here. You're a good man.
It was a good thing?
It was a good thing.

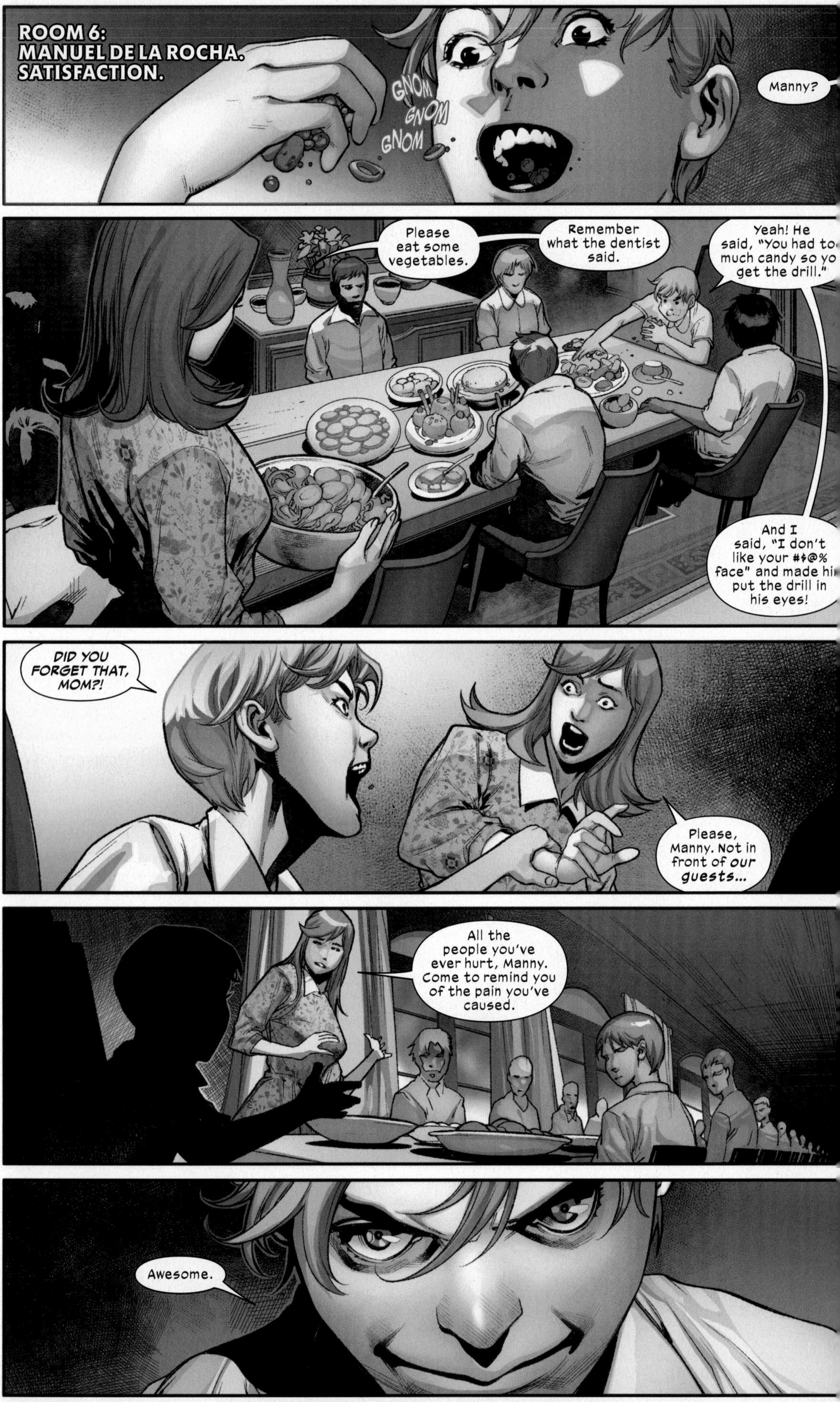

ROOM 6:
MANUEL DE LA ROCHA.
SATISFACTION.
GNOM GNOM GNOM
Manny?
Please eat some vegetables.
Remember what the dentist said.
Yeah! He said, "You had to much candy so yo get the drill."
And I said, "I don't like your #$@% face" and made hi put the drill in his eyes!
DID YOU FORGET THAT, MOM?!
Please, Manny. Not in front of our guests...
All the people you've ever hurt, Manny. Come to remind you of the pain you've caused.
Awesome.

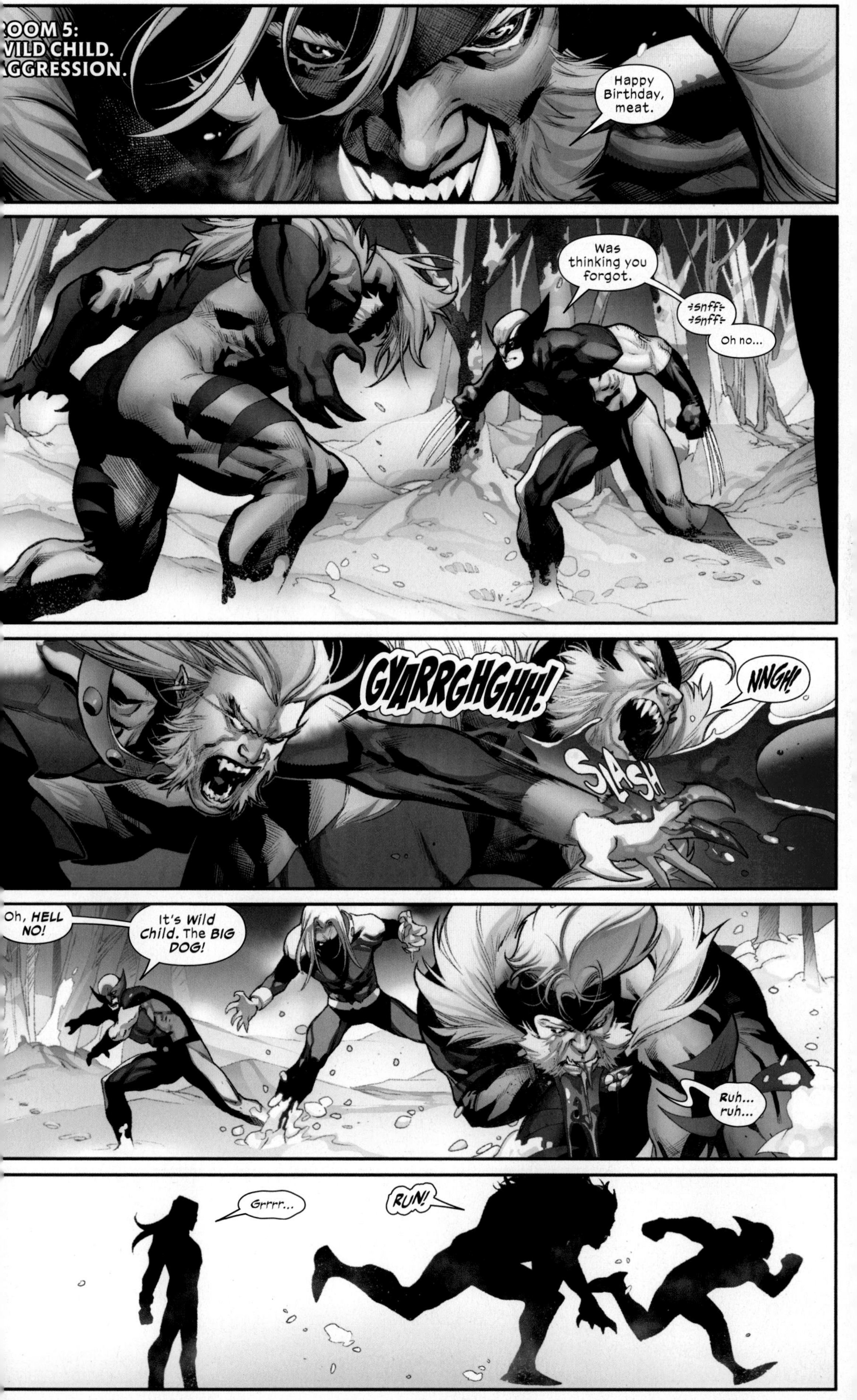
ROOM 5:
WILD CHILD.
AGGRESSION.
Happy Birthday, meat.
Was thinking you forgot.
≠snff≠ ≠snff≠
Oh no...
GYARRGHGHH!
NNGH!
SLASH
Oh, HELL NO!
It's Wild Child. The BIG DOG!
Ruh... ruh...
Grrrr...
RUN!

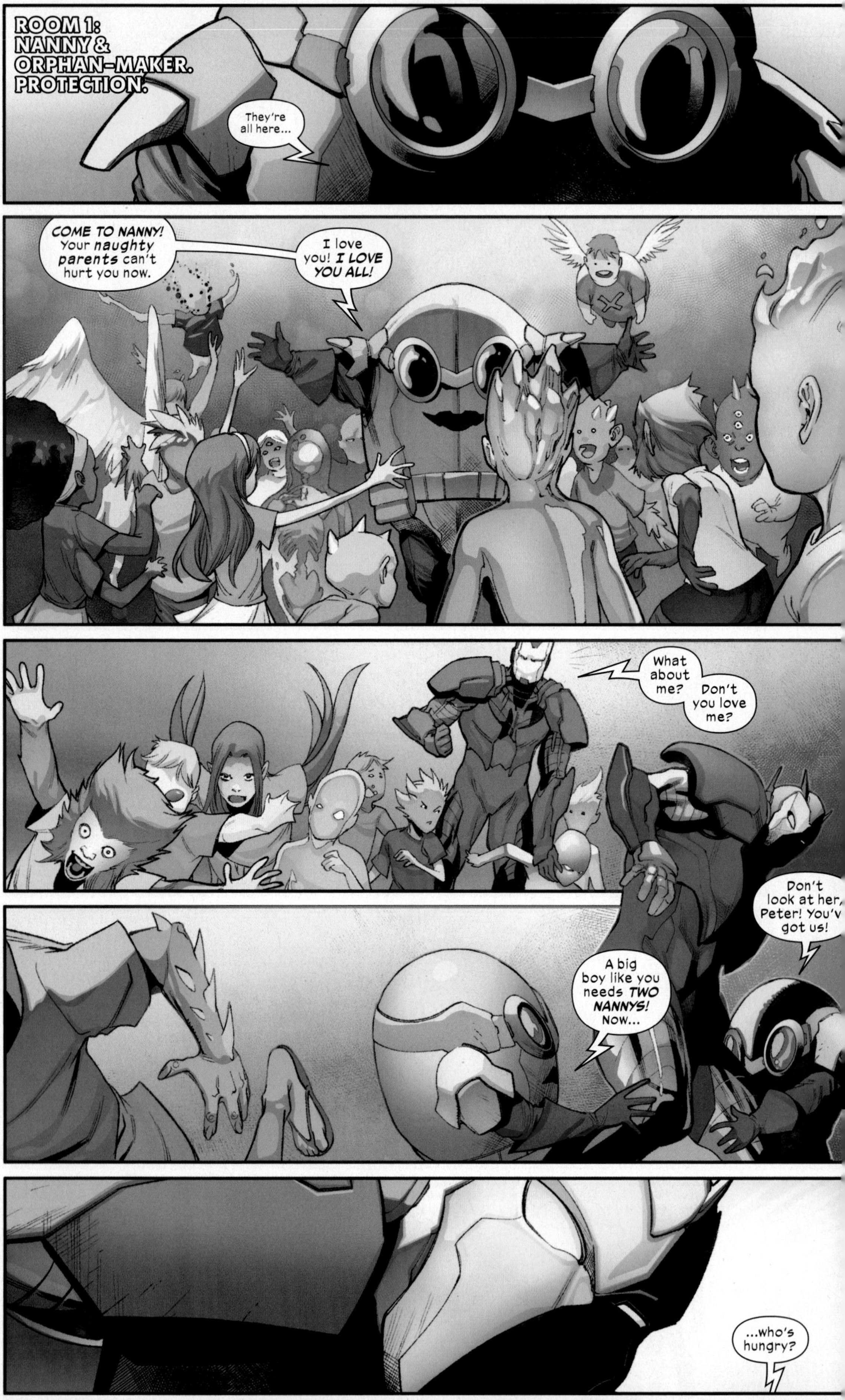
ROOM 1: NANNY & ORPHAN-MAKER. PROTECTION.
They're all here...
COME TO NANNY! Your naughty parents can't hurt you now.
I love you! I LOVE YOU ALL!
What about me?
Don't you love me?
Don't look at her, Peter! You'v got us!
A big boy like you needs TWO NANNYS! Now...
...who's hungry?

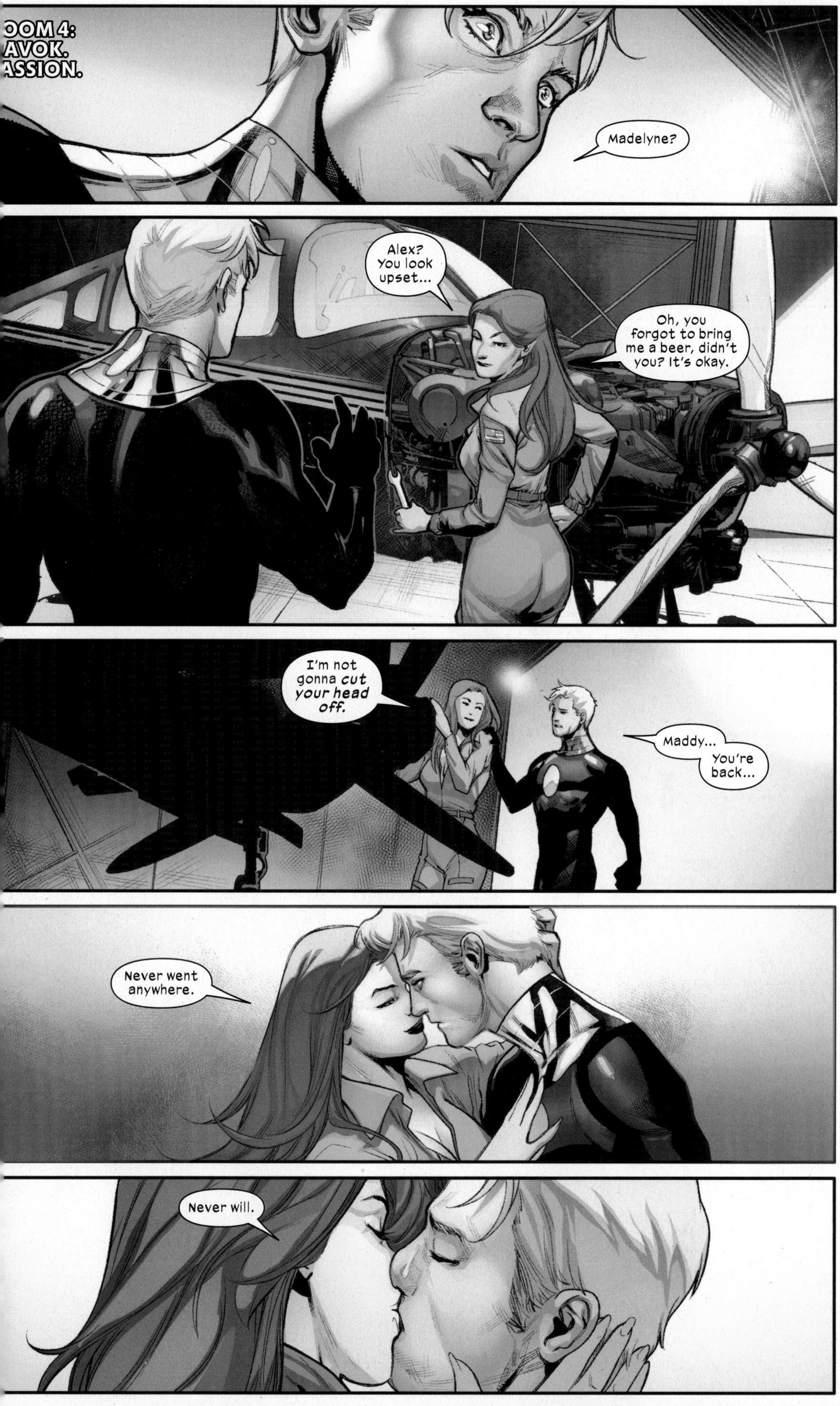
OOM 4:
AVOK.
ASSION.
Madelyne?
Alex? You look upset...
Oh, you forgot to bring me a beer, didn't you? It's okay.
I'm not gonna *cut your head off.*
Maddy... You're back...
Never went anywhere.
Never will.

We're not--

We're not going to watch this poor bastard snog a robot, are we?

What's the matter? Is it hard to watch me *break their brains?*

No, but I'd like my chair turned around if this continues to get weird.

And from the look on your face, it continues to get weird.

Oh, is it touching time?

NOT NOW!

I...I'm *correcting* Miss Locke. Gently correcting.

Miss Locke is a--

I KNOW!

I know... Just confirm, please.

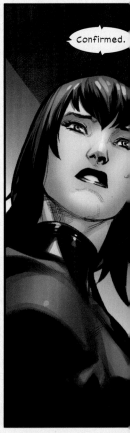

Confirmed.

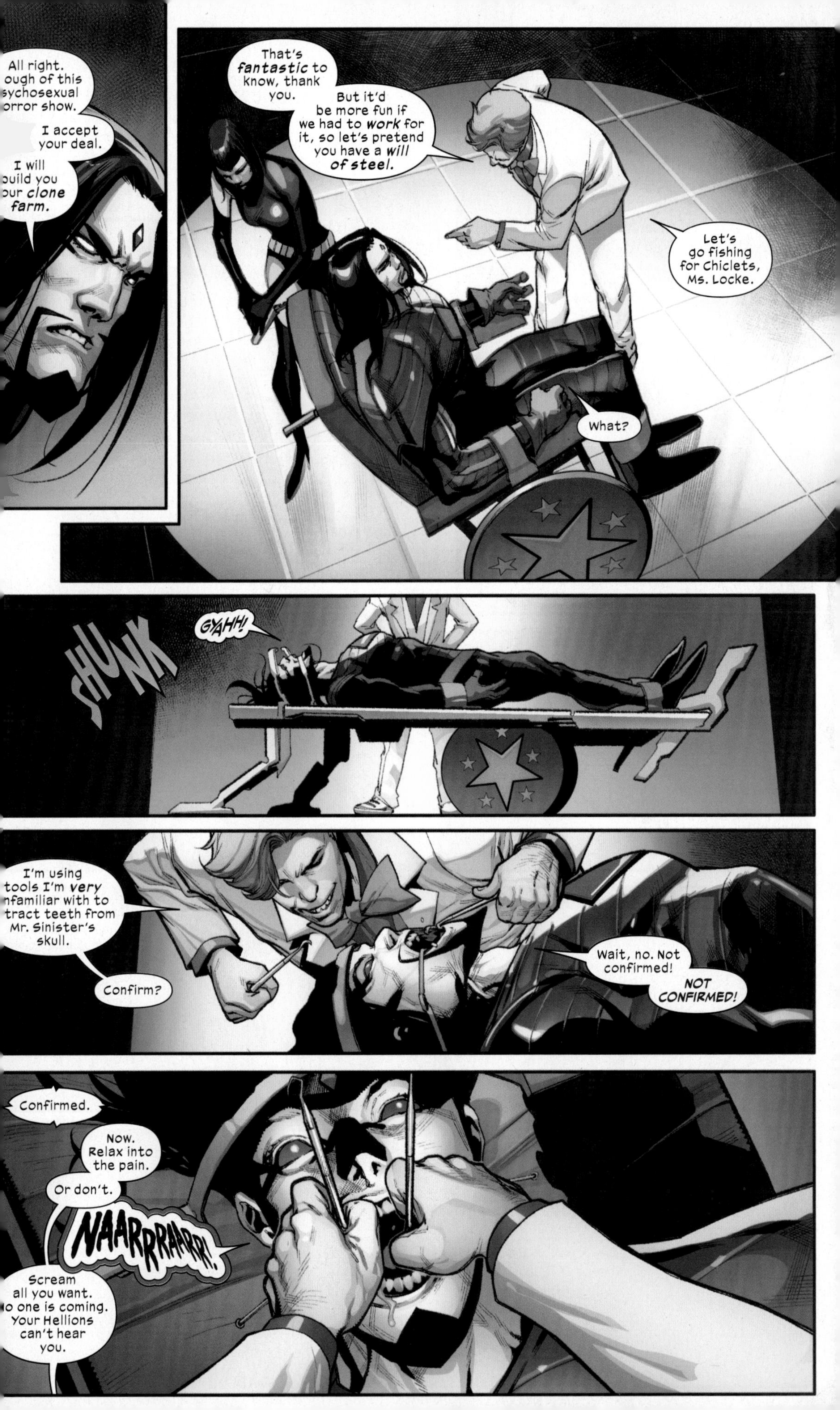

All right.
ough of this
sychosexual
orror show.
I accept
your deal.
I will
uild you
our clone
farm.
That's
fantastic to
know, thank
you.
But it'd
be more fun if
we had to work for
it, so let's pretend
you have a will
of steel.
Let's
go fishing
for Chiclets,
Ms. Locke.
What?
SHUNK
GYAHH!
I'm using
tools I'm very
nfamiliar with to
tract teeth from
Mr. Sinister's
skull.
Confirm?
Wait, no. Not
confirmed!
NOT
CONFIRMED!
Confirmed.
Now.
Relax into
the pain.
Or don't.
NAARRRAARR!
Scream
all you want.
o one is coming.
Your Hellions
can't hear
you.

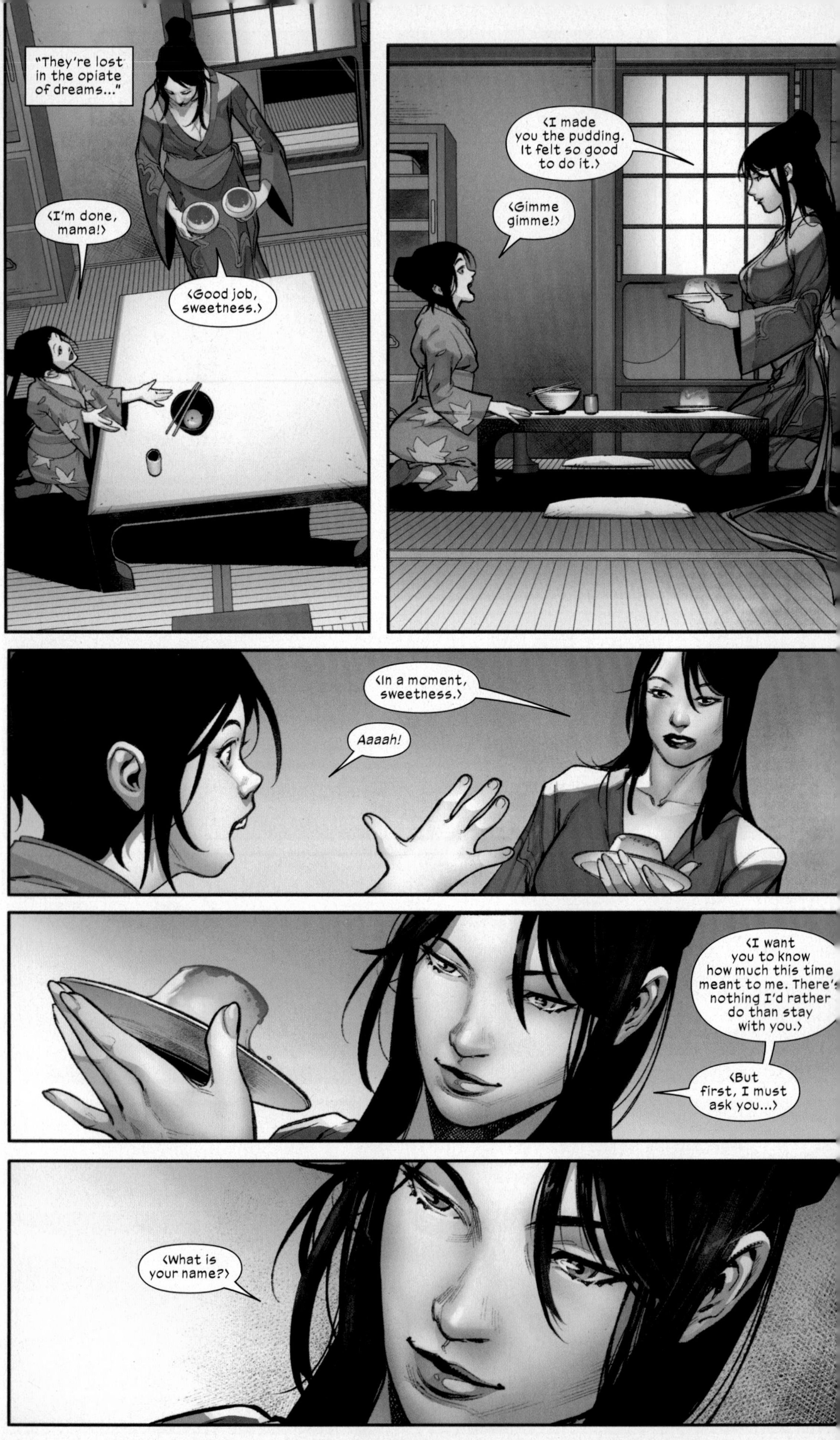
"They're lost in the opiate of dreams..."
‹I'm done, mama!›
‹Good job, sweetness.›
‹I made you the pudding. It felt so good to do it.›
‹Gimme gimme!›
‹In a moment, sweetness.›
Aaaah!
‹I want you to know how much this time meant to me. There's nothing I'd rather do than stay with you.›
‹But first, I must ask you...›
‹What is your name?›

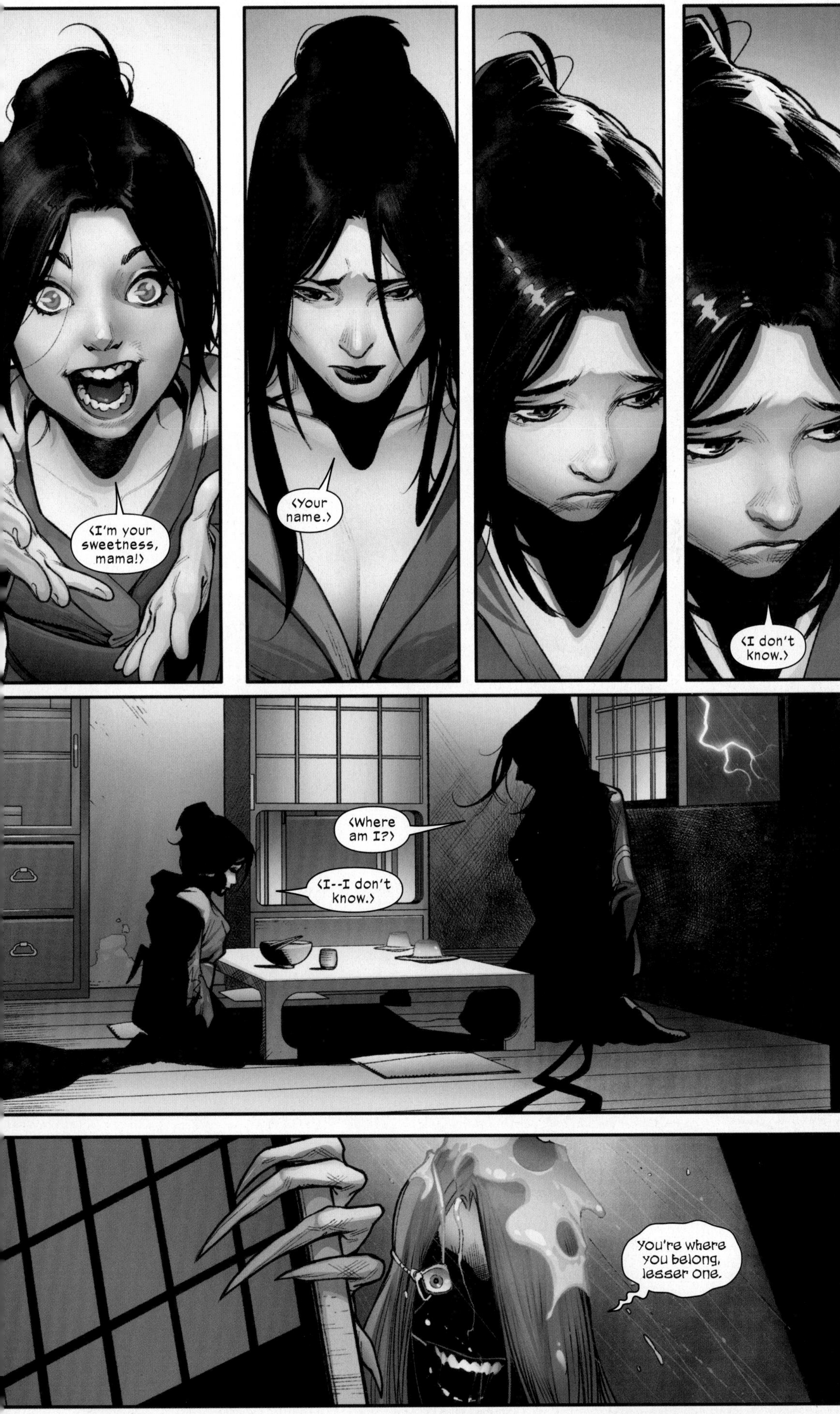
‹I'm your sweetness, mama!›
‹Your name.›
‹I don't know.›
‹Where am I?›
‹I--I don't know.›
You're where you belong, lesser one.

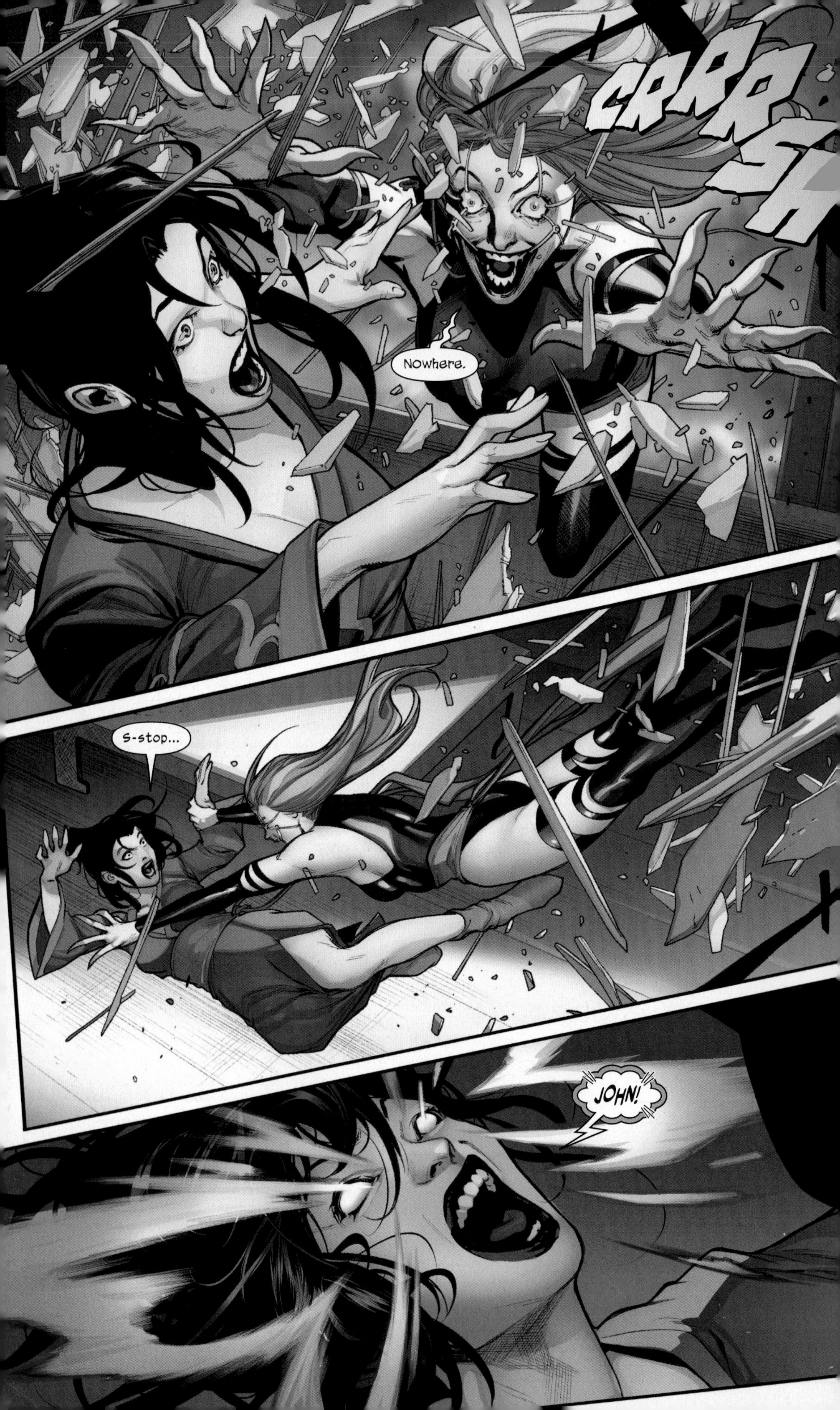
CRRASH
Nowhere.
S-stop...
JOHN!

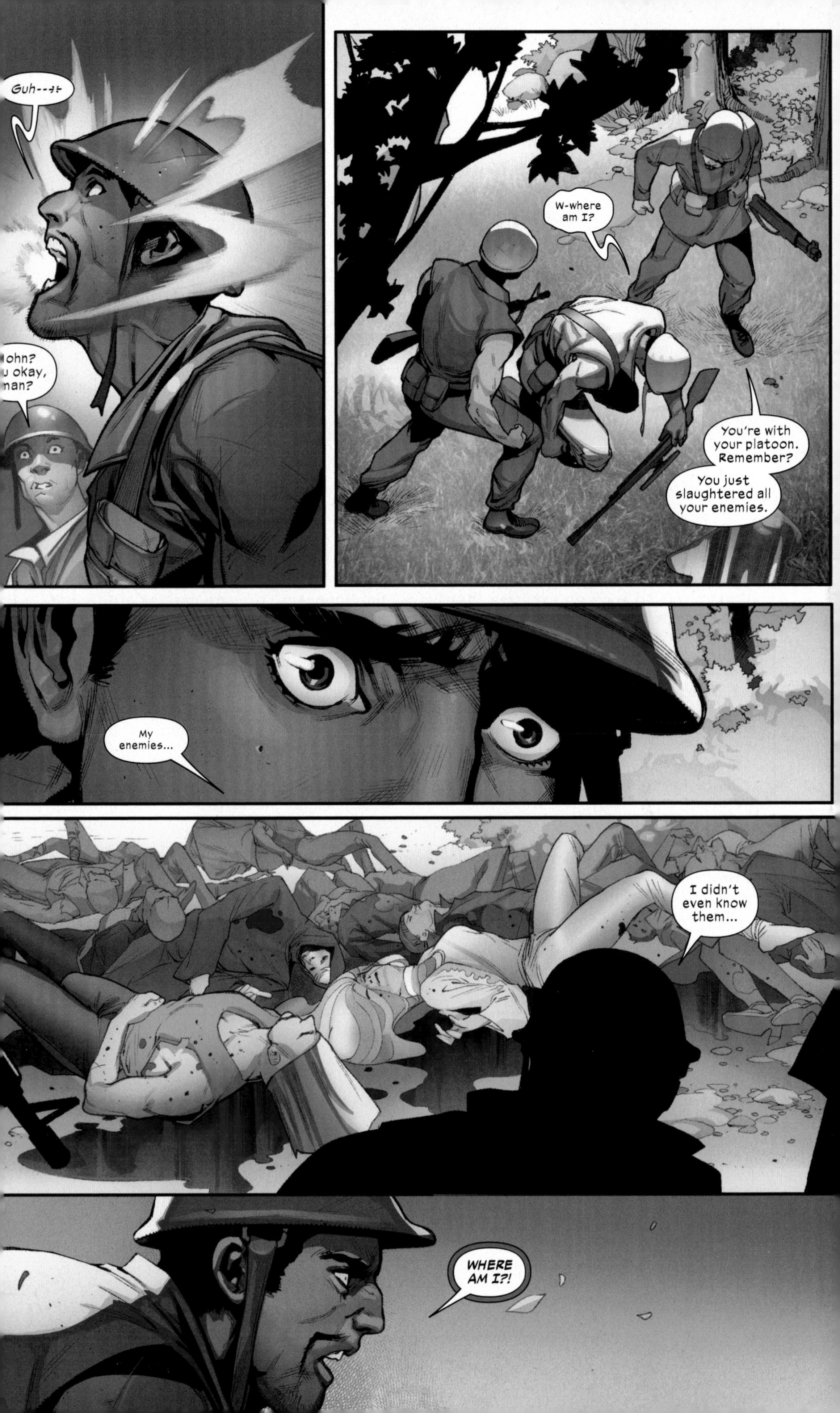
Guh--‼
ohn? u okay, nan?
W-where am I?
You're with your platoon. Remember?
You just slaughtered all your enemies.
My enemies...
I didn't even know them...
WHERE AM I?!

MURDERWORLD
INTERNAL CORRESPONDENCE

From: Arcade

To: All Murderworld Employees

Subject: Some reminders

As you're no doubt aware, we have guests at Murderworld. This is what we train for, people. As such, I offer a few reminders to help keep our ship afloat in this sea of blood.

1. While no employee should ever look me directly in the eye, some of you have taken this to such an extreme that I'm feeling **ignored**. I am the master of life and death, not a **friendly ghost**. May I suggest a cocked head, tilted downward like a submissive dog, acknowledging my presence while staying eye-contact compliant? This will keep me happy and you safe from Loyalty Protocols.

2. There is **no** congregating at any guest's Murder Deck. Yes, one of them is dressed as an egg. Now that we've gotten that out of the way, perhaps we can all get back to work before -- say it with me -- I have to activate Loyalty Protocols.

3. When I say, "I'm so furious I'm going to scissor-kick you in the throat," this is an invitation to stay perfectly still while I scissor-kick you in the throat. This is not an invitation to flinch or dodge said scissor-kick and put me at great physical risk. I had to L.P. someone for this last week, so putting it out there.

4. The hostages making up the leverage bank of your Loyalty Account are non-negotiable. The particular loved ones in said bank were put there for a reason. If you could swap them out with someone less loved for whatever reason, the entire foundation of Loyalty Protocols would be destroyed. **Let me put it this way:**

Continued on page 2 (of 13-page memo)

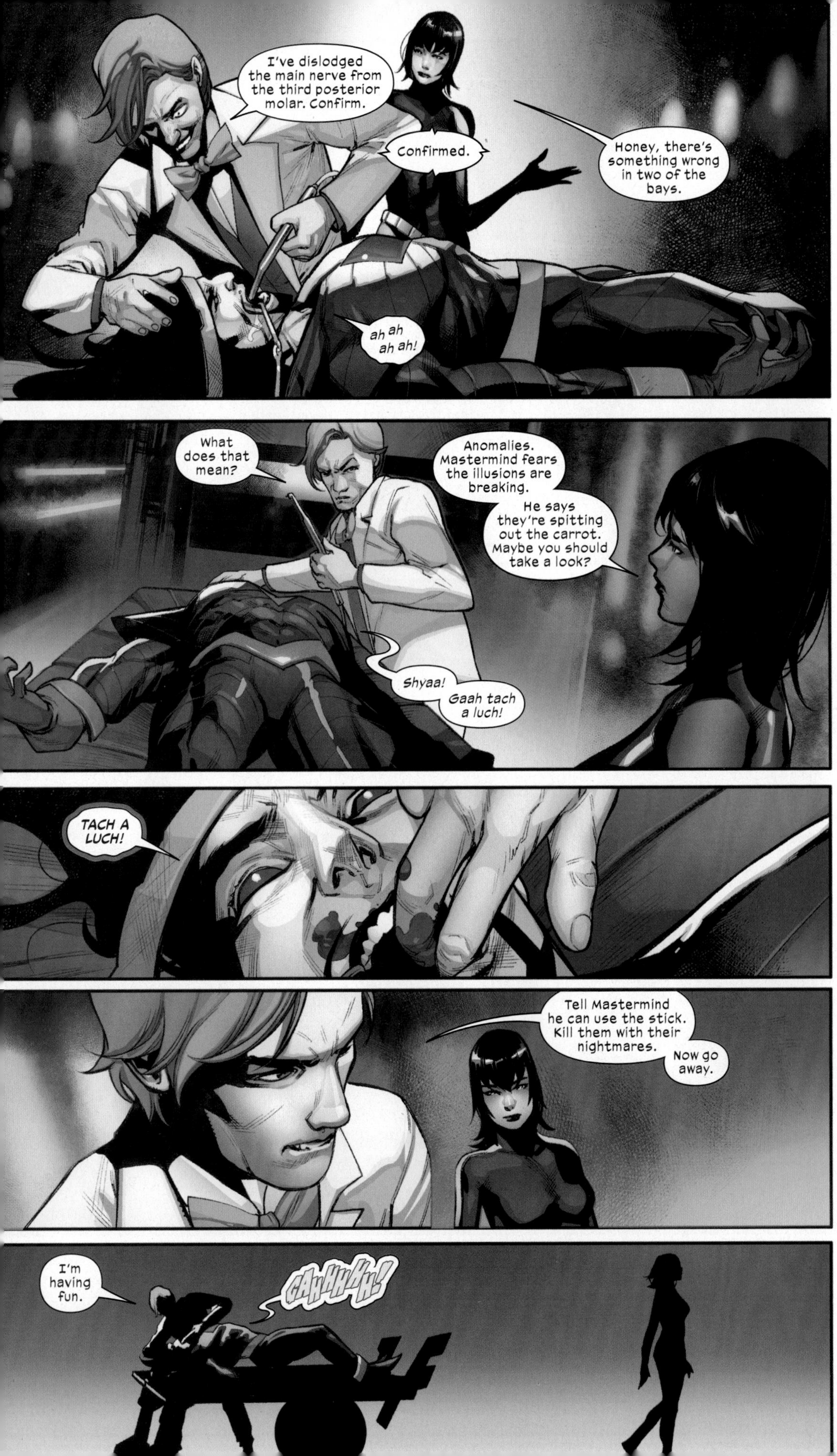

I've dislodged the main nerve from the third posterior molar. Confirm.
Confirmed.
Honey, there's something wrong in two of the bays.
ah ah ah ah!
What does that mean?
Anomalies. Mastermind fears the illusions are breaking.
He says they're spitting out the carrot. Maybe you should take a look?
Shyaa!
Gaah tach a luch!
TACH A LUCH!
Tell Mastermind he can use the stick. Kill them with their nightmares.
Now go away.
I'm having fun.
GAHHHHH!

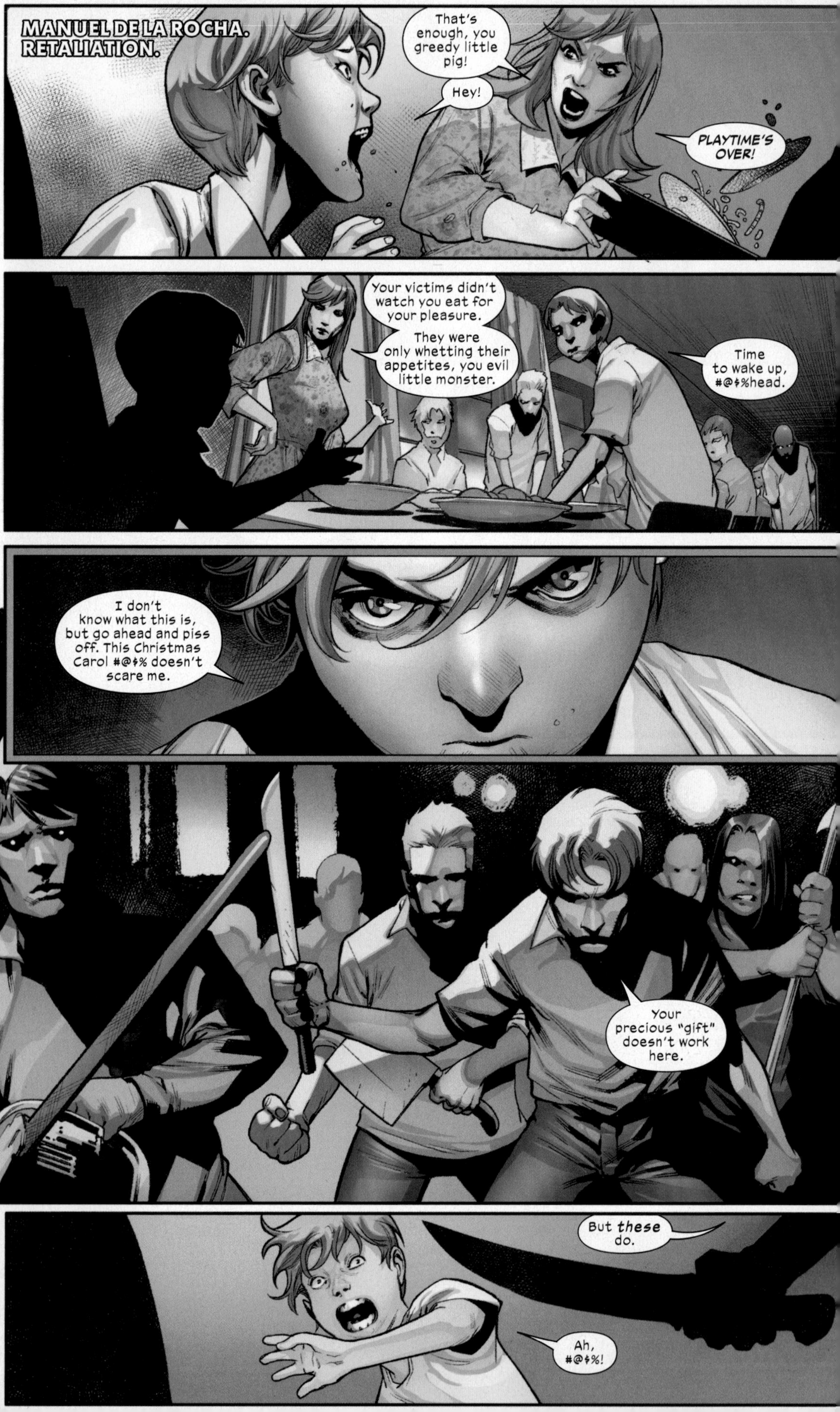
MANUEL DE LA ROCHA. RETALIATION.
That's enough, you greedy little pig!
Hey!
PLAYTIME'S OVER!
Your victims didn't watch you eat for your pleasure.
They were only whetting their appetites, you evil little monster.
Time to wake up, #@$%head.
I don't know what this is, but go ahead and piss off. This Christmas Carol #@$% doesn't scare me.
Your precious "gift" doesn't work here.
But *these* do.
Ah, #@$%!

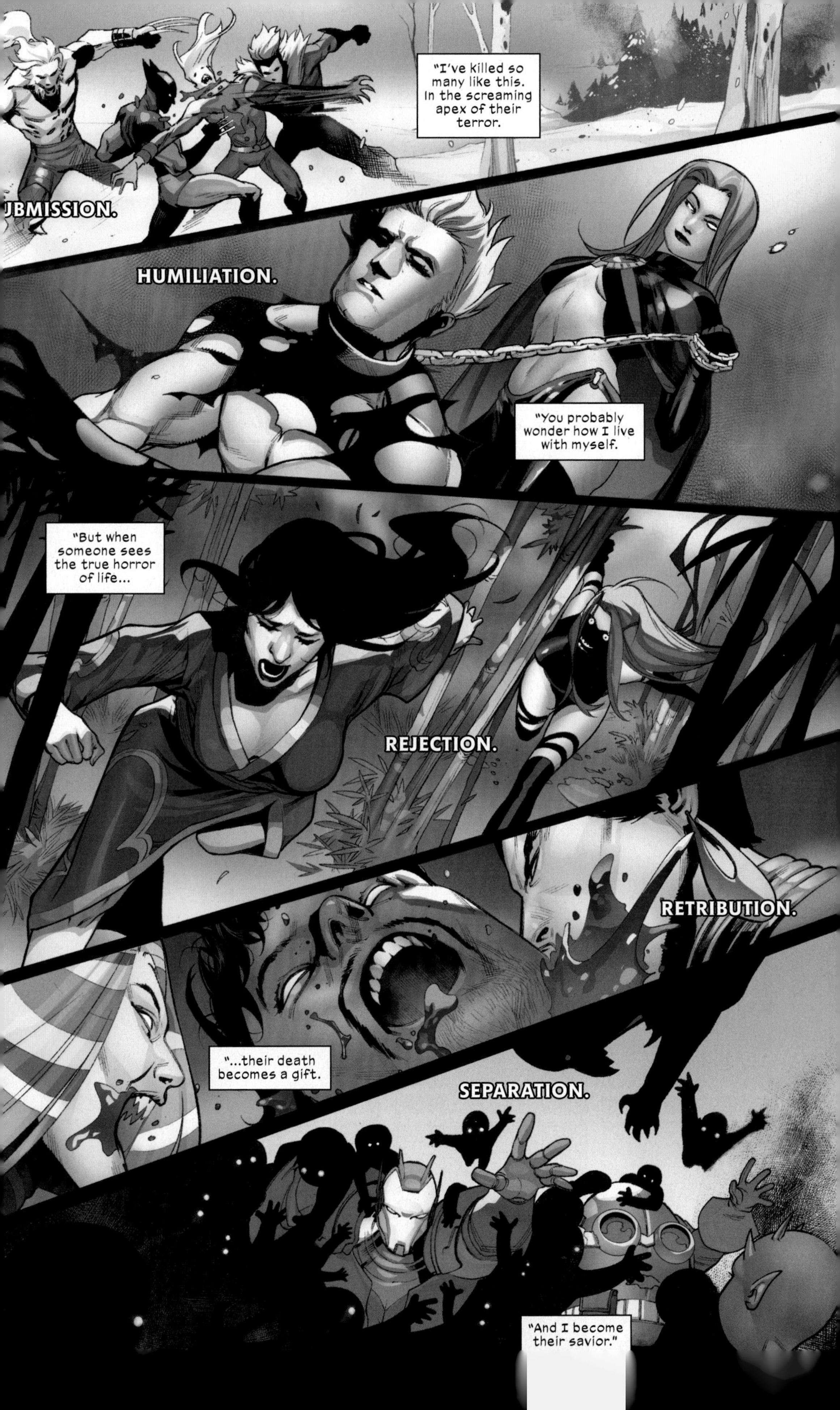
"I've killed so many like this. In the screaming apex of their terror.
UBMISSION.
HUMILIATION.
"You probably wonder how I live with myself.
"But when someone sees the true horror of life...
REJECTION.
RETRIBUTION.
"...their death becomes a gift.
SEPARATION.
"And I become their savior."

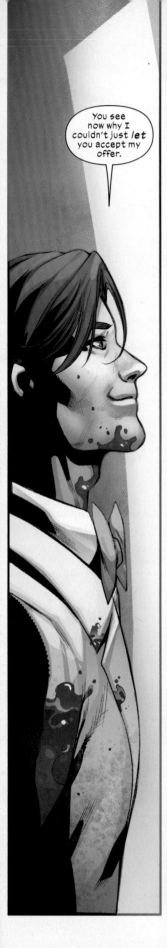

You see now why I couldn't just *let* you accept my offer.

I had to make you *desperate* to earn your release.

Enthusiastic to provide your help.

Do you understand?

Yessh.

Try again.

Confirmed. *CONFIRMED!*

Very good! Now that we're partners...

Let's play.

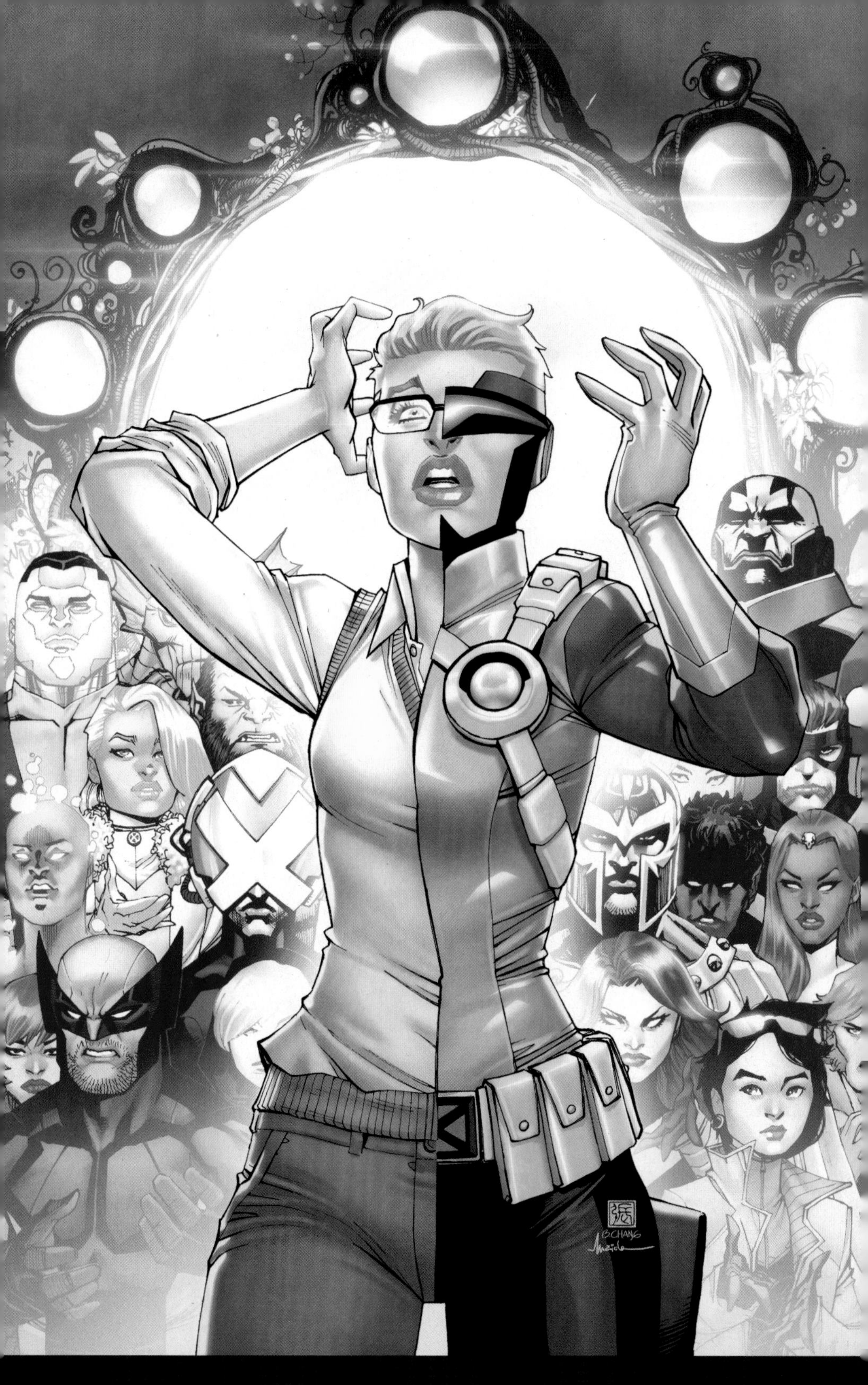

Children of the Atom #3 Variant by Bernard Chang & Marcelo Maiolo

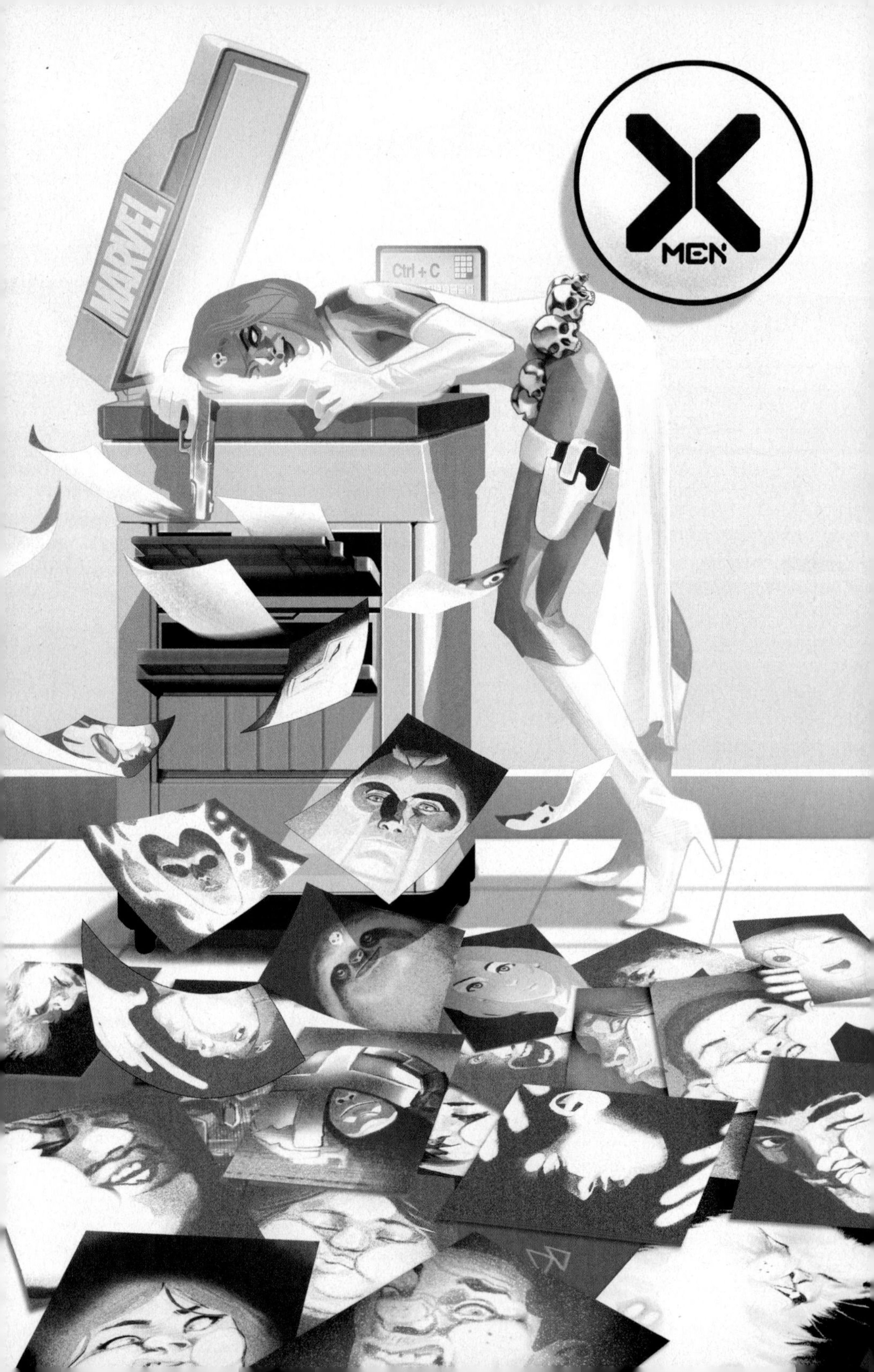
MARVEL
Ctrl + C
X MEN

[reign_of_x]

[kra_]
[koa_]